POLIS AND PSYCHE

STUDIA GRAECA ET LATINA
GOTHOBURGENSIA
XXX

POLIS AND PSYCHE

A MOTIF IN PLATO'S REPUBLIC

by

TORSTEN J. ANDERSSON

ACTA UNIVERSITATIS GOTHOBURGENSIS

Distribution:

ALMQVIST & WIKSELL

STOCKHOLM

———

ELANDERS BOKTRYCKERI AKTIEBOLAG
GÖTEBORG 1971

Till Ingrid

ACKNOWLEDGEMENTS

I thank Professor Henrik Sandblad most heartily for his stimulating criticism, generous encouragement, and invaluable aid of every kind during the years of my investigations. I am also greatly indebted to his Department of the History of Ideas and of Science at the University of Gothenburg. Drafts of my thesis have been discussed in Professor Sandblad's seminars, and I have found there a group of friends with a real interest in Plato's philosophy, of whom I would particularly like to thank Fil. lic. Dick Haglund and Fil. kand. Erland Sellberg.

Professor Cajus Fabricius has read the entire thesis in manuscript and has liberally contributed with criticism and advice for which I express my sincere gratitude. I am also much obliged to the editors of Studia Graeca et Latina Gothoburgensia, i.e. Professor Fabricius and Professor Erik Wistrand, for permission to publish my study in this series.

For inspiration and enlightment in the matters of scientific method I am indebted to Professor Håkan Törnebohm, the Institute for the Theory of Science at the University of Gothenburg.

Thanks are also due to the University Library of Gothenburg and the Royal Library in Stockholm for greatly facilitating my studies.

I also express my gratitude to Mr. Philip Lorraine, who has checked and greatly improved my English in style and clarity.

To my wife, who has assisted me in proof-reading and has patiently kept our family running while I have been engaged with Plato, I owe a special debt of gratitude.

Djursholm in September 1971

Torsten J. Andersson

LIST OF ABBREVIATIONS

Periodicals

AJPh	American Journal of Philology.
AJS	American Journal of Sociology.
CJ	Classical Journal.
CPh	Classical Philology.
CQ	Classical Quarterly.
JHI	Journal of the History of Ideas.
JHM	Journal of the History of Medicine and allied Sciences.
JHPh	Journal of the History of Philosophy.
JPh	Journal of Philosophy.
PAS	Proceedings of the Aristotelian Society.
PhR	Philosophical Review.
Ph&PhenR	Philosophy and Phenomenological Research.
Phron	Phronesis. A Journal of Ancient Philosophy.
RM	Review of Metaphysics.
SO	Symbolae Osloenses.

Other Works

CAH	*Cambridge Ancient History.*
HGP	*A History of Greek Philosophy* by W. K. C. Guthrie.
IESS	International Encyclopedia of the Social Sciences.
JC	Jowett-Campbell, *Plato's Republic.*
LJS	Liddell-Scott-Jones. *Greek English Lexicon.*
OCD	*Oxford Classical Dictionary.*
OSE	The Open Society and its Enemies by K. R. Popper.
RE	*Realencyclopädie der classischen Altertumswissenschaft,* ed. Wissowa, Kroll *et al.*

CONTENTS

PART SIX

EPILOGUE

PART SEVEN

A SUMMARY

PART EIGHT

TABLES

PART ONE

THE POLIS—PSYCHE MOTIF

CHAPTER I
SUBJECT, AIMS, METHOD

1. Synopsis.

To approach man by way of his society is a method of old standing in Western thought. In Plato and Aristotle this technique is fully established. In the following study, which is restricted to the *Republic*, we shall observe as a motif how *polis* (society) illustrates and explains *psyche* (personality).

Before I commence to explain the terms involved in this project, let us first see in brief how this reasoning is manifested. Already in *Bk I* Thrasymachus refers to the convenience of studying man in a political context, 338d7–339a4, 343b1–344c8. And when Socrates in *Bk II* is requested to investigate *dikaiosyne* (justice) and *adikia* (injustice) in *psyche*, he systematically introduces *polis* as an illustrative instrument for this purpose, 368c7–369a3. We are told that society and man are as two identical texts (*grammata*), the one written in letters larger than the other. The larger letters (*polis*) should be read first, making it easier to spell out the meaning of the smaller ones (*psyche*). Proceeding with the investigation, Socrates builds up a just city in thought, 369b5–412b7, which is completed and used for illustrative purposes in *Bks III* 412b8–*IV* 444a9. Its guiding qualities consist of three fundamental classes (by interpreters sometimes called orders, *Stände*, sometimes castes), which are combined with four principal virtues. By painstaking analyses, a replica of this pattern is found in the *psyche* of the righteous man. This structural similarity of society and man is commonly referred to in literature on the *Republic* as the analogy between *polis* and *psyche*. In *Bks V–VII* this double-text reading is abandoned, but is adopted again in *Bks VIII–IX*, where the analogy extends to cover also four notable types of disordered societies and their corresponding personalities. In addition to its strictly illustrative function, *polis* also frequently appears all through the *Republic*, as a term for the social and cultural environment, which forms and shapes man's character. Thus, both systematically and extensively, *polis* and *psyche* are related in a significant way.

It is common knowledge that *polis* and *psyche* are important topics in the *Republic*. Each of them leads to central doctrines in Plato's philosophy. Together they constitute a complex permitting different treatments. In our study they are primarily components of a motif, *polis* explains *psyche*. Though this kind of relationship is important, it is not to be regarded as the master key which opens up every lock; in the *Republic* many important subjects are discussed—politics, ethics, education and epistemology—each of which may demand an approach of its own. Taking up the study of the *polis-psyche* motif, we have chosen one distinct way of handling the dialogue. Following the line of thought which runs from *polis* to *psyche*, we will also notice an anti-motif, which is subsidiary to the motif and brings out and balances it; i.e. the reasoning directed from *psyche* to *polis*.

In face of the vast amount of literature on Plato and the *Republic*, one may well ask what prospects exist for a new study. The more a book has been subjected to scholarly study, the less are the chances of making discoveries. And to present new findings is the principal reason for writing a new book.

Appraising our possibilities in this respect, it is useful to distinguish between studies which are topic-directed and those that are motif-directed. If a subject is chosen as a topic for study, there are various extrinsic ways open to the explorer. These can be philological, biographical, cultural and social. But this way of justifying a new study is less obvious if one is to pursue a motif, as it is more distinctive in the pattern-achievement than in the fact-hunter's accomplishment of finding new or disregarded facts. The motif must help us to observe and collect kindred, but sometimes disconnected ideas, and to unite and shape them into a coherent line of reasoning without violating the general structure of the argument. Thus it remains to see to what use our motif can be put. As far as I know, this kind of approach has never been attempted before.

In exploring a motif, questions of a peculiar kind appear. On what empirical evidence is the motif founded? What is the aim of the motif? What job can it do? Are there more motifs to observe, and, if so, how are they related to each other? What relationship is there between motif and subject-matter? In this introduction, we are bound to discuss a number of such questions.

Plato's undertaking to describe the structure of personality by means of the structure of the society is, in modern terminology, the approach of the social psychologist.[1]) In this respect the *Republic* appears surprisingly modern. This sociological approach to the interpretation of man can particularly be studied in *Bks VIII–IX*, which are often overshadowed in literature by the contents of the middle books. Special attention is therefore given to these less observed parts of the dialogue. To match the social thought expressed there, the peculiar conditions of classical Greece must be borne in mind. This may excuse a cautious insertion of historical notes into the study.

The aims of our study are then (a) to pursue systematically the *polis-psyche* motif in the *Republic*, and (b) to notice at the same time the social psychological thought expressed there. By (a) we are invited to follow an ancient method of research as it is actually carried out in the *Republic*. In this respect we are exploring *polis-psyche* as a textual motif. By (b) a historical perspective is offered on the scientific significance of interpreting man in relation to his society. From this aspect, *polis-psyche* emerges as a motif of ideas.

2. Textual foundations

The interpretation of a text must begin with a careful reading of that text. There must be some basically accepted starting point for different readers. Some observations on the textual foundations of the motif are therefore called for. In commencing our investigation, attention is drawn to the words *polis* and *psyche*, which are the keywords of the motif. These can easily be located and counted. This registration is

Table A. Distribution of keywords

Keywords	I	II	III	IV	V	VI	VII	VIII	IX	X	I–X
πόλις	16	46	40	95	58	37	33	59	29	14	427
ψυχή	10	14	30	25	4	20	34	14	28	46	225

[1]) Cf. C. S. Hall & G. Lindzey, *Theories of Personality*, New York 1959, pp. 114 ff., and L. J. Bischof, *Interpreting Personality Theories*, London and Tokyo 1964, p. 230. See also p. 41 below, n. 1.

accounted for in *TABLE 1*, pp. 235–243. *Table A* is a survey of how the keywords are distributed in *Bks I–X* of the *Republic*.

Studying these figures, it should first be observed that *polis* and *psyche* are not the only words which support the motif. *Polis* and *psyche* have been recorded because they are the most manifest and frequent text-elements, being easily recognizable and highly expressive of the key-meaning of the two components. Towards the end of *Bk V* the term *politeia* begins to occur in a highly significant way, referring to the social, cultural and political structure of the model *polis*. And in *Bks VIII–IX* the general term *politeia* is often alternated with its special variants *timokratia, oligarchia, demokratia* and *tyrannis*. Even *psyche* is often exchanged in the text; ἀνήρ, ἄνθρωπος, ἰδιώτης, and ἐν ἑνὶ are examples of such substitutions.

Secondly it, should be noted that *polis* and *psyche* do not always operate as components of the motif; they occur especially in *Bks V–VII* with other and wider implications. In *TABLE 1* I have, however, registered all *polis-* and *psyche-* occurrencies irrespective of whether they are strictly motif-bearers or not. — Thirdly, the recording of the keywords should not be taken as a statistical procedure for inferring conclusions from frequences of words. Instead we may take it as a case of surveying; *TABLE 1* shows how the keywords are distributed and where one can find them.

So far, we have only rendered an account of isolated keywords. As, however, a clearly expressed and continued reasoning is to be explored, we next expect to find a number of *explicit utterances* placing *polis* and *psyche* (and their equivalents) in a significant relationship to each other. To satisfy the motif they must be of the type "π clarifies ψ", or "π facilitates the study of ψ", or, conclusively, "we have seen x in π, we now also see x in ψ".

The explicit utterances are registered in *TABLE 2*, pp. 244–252.

The most important of the explicit utterances is found in *Bk II*, the passage 368e2–369a3, which, as already mentioned, introduces *polis* and *psyche* by means of the simile of the two identical texts, cf. *TABLE 2*, nr. 7, p. 245. One may well think that there is here a useful key for the intrinsic study of the *Republic*. To this fundamental passage there are, in strategic places, a number of reformulations serving to uphold and develop the double-text method. — *TABLES 1* and *2* indicate together a line of approach and seem to guide us through extensive parts of the *Republic*.

3. Explicit utterances and the motif

The kernel meaning, which is based on all the explicit utterances, expresses the illustrative function of *polis*, namely that *polis* helps to explain the nature of *psyche*. The motif says: for the sake of clarity study *polis* first, and proceed then for comparison to *psyche*. This is the

Table B. Modes of the illustrative motif

Modes of the illustrative motif	Location of explicit utterances in the text	
Preparatory views	Bk I	338d7–339a4, 344a3–b1, 351d4–6, 351e9–352a8.
	Bk II	364e3–365a3, 366a6–b2.
	Bk IV	444b1–8, 445c9–d1, 449a1–5.
	Bk VIII	544a2–8, 544d6–e2.
Fundamental method	Bk II	368e2–369a3.
	Bk IV	434d6–e4, 443b7–c2.
	Bk V	472c4–d2, cf. b3–5
	Bk VIII	543c8–d1, 544e4–5.
	Bk IX	577c1–3.
Directive mode	Bk II	371e9–12.
	Bk IV	427c6–d7, 431b4–7.
	Bk VIII	545b3–6, 545c8–9, 550c1–2, 555b3–6, 562a4–5, 564a3–4, 566d5–6.
	Bk IX	577c5, 580d3–5.
Executive mode	Bk IV	435b9–c2, 440e10–441a3.
	Bk VIII	548d6, 553a1–4, 557a9–b2, 558c8–9,
	Bk IX	571a1–3, 578b1–5.
Conclusive mode	Bk IV	441c4–7, 441c9–d6, 441d8–e2, 442d2–3, 442d7–9, 444a4–6.
	Bk VII	541b2–3.
	Bk VIII	549b9–10, 553e2–3, 554a2–8, 554a10–b1, 554b2–3, 555a8–b2, 559e4–e7. 561e3–7, 562a1–2.
	Bk IX	575a1–3, 576c6–8, 576c10–11, 577d1–5, 577d10–e3, 577e5–578a2, 578a4–5, 579e2–6, 590e1–591a3.
	Bk X	605b5–c4.
Other relevant expressions	Bk IV	442e4–443a1.
	Bk VI	497c7–d2.

kernel meaning of the motif, of wich we find three modes. (1) is *directive* and says: look at *polis* first, then at *psyche*; (2) is *executive* and says: *polis* is inspected, now turn to *psyche*; and (3) is *conclusive* and asserts: comparing *polis* and *psyche*, we conclude that. . .

Table B is a survey, based on *TABLE 2*, showing the main modes and appearances of the motif.

Having thus seen how the *polis-illustrates-psyche motif* is manifested in the *Republic*, we can read the explicit utterances as more or less complete variants of the double text method. This method is first clearly expressed in *Bk II* 368e2–369a3. To mark its importance for the continued investigation Socrates returns to it in *Bks IV* and in *Bks VIII* and *IX*. Actually one finds preparatory views of it in *Bks I–II*. But the actual employment of the motif is accessible by means of a study of how its directive, executive and conclusive modes operate. As can be seen from the above table these modes dominate *Bks IV* and *VIII–IX*.—We may maintain that the illustrative motif is based on a clearly expressed and recurrent idea, indicating a systematic movement of thought. By reason of position, repetition, scope and significance I call this line of thought a *motif*.[1])

Later on we shall further develop the reasoning running from *polis* towards *psyche*. Now it seems, however, expedient to define the meaning of *polis* and *psyche* in their capacity as components of the motif.

Polis refers in this respect to the *community* or *body of citizens*,[2]) classed in different functions. Starting to build up his model society Socrates qualifies the term *polis* with the stipulation of co-operation, the settlement of enough people in the joint undertaking of satisfying our many needs, 369c1–4. And in the continued analogies (*Bks VIII–*

---

[1]) I am in this study employing the term *motif* pragmatically for my aims. I do not think, however, that my usage of the term deviates singularly from common practice.—In art, music, literature the term motif often means a distinctive feature manifesting itself in the composition. So in music a motif is a recurrent melodic phrase or a passage, and in literature it may be some particular idea running through the text; sometimes, for instance in art, it is spoken of as a controlling or guiding idea. Cf. *The Shorter Oxford English Dictionary*, rev. and ed. by C. T. Onions. And for further information: J. T. Shipley, *Dictionary of World Literary Terms*, London 1955; E. Frenzel, *Stoff-, Motiv- und Symbolforschung*, Stuttgart 1963, 26 ff.; W. Krogmann, *Reallexikon der Deutschen Literaturgeschichte*, Berlin 1965; and W. Kayser, *Das Sprachliche Kunstwerk*, Bern 1965, pp. 59 ff. (and later eds).

[2]) *LJS, s.v. πολις.*

IX), where the diseased societies are exposed, this feature of co-operation is changed into competition and disintegration. With such a stress on social structure, the term *polis* tends in the continued investigation to be fused with *politeia*, taken in its wide, social, and political meaning.[1] This shift of terms from *polis* to *politeia* (which is not radically carried out) can be studied from *Bk IV* 445c9 and onwards.

Psyche is, like *polis*, an ambiguous term in Greek literature. *Personality*[2]) may, however, indicate its meaning as a component of the motif, i.e. one's own self as it is constituted by the way one is composed of reason, emotions and appetites. Like *polis*, *psyche* thus has some sort of constitution, being composed of parts which are functionally or disfunctionally ordered. Plato frequently speaks metaphorically of the *politeia* of the inner man, cf. p. 109 below.

Plato is concerned in the *Republic* with five types of societies and five types of men. *Polis* and *psyche* retain their structural meaning all through these types. Both *polis* and *psyche* consist of parts which can change places, and grow or decline in force. This plasticity of *polis* and *psyche* is a necessary requirement for their roles as components of the motif.

4. The polis-psyche complex of thought

Having extracted *polis* as an illustrative device, we must now see how it stands within the wider complex of the *polis-psyche* thought.

The first question we must ask ourselves is how can *polis* illustrate *psyche?* Socrates only touches upon it in his presentation of the double-text method; *polis* is larger than the individual, therefore it is easier to study *dikaiosyne* there, 368e5–369a3. Later, however, Socrates argues in support of his method. An exhaustive answer to our question is offered if we reverse the order of the keywords: instead of the *polis-psyche* direction one gets the *psyche-polis* orientation. A number of important

---

[1]) About the nature of the *polis*, cf. V. Ehrenberg, *The Greek State*, 2 nd. ed., London 1969, pp. 88 ff.

[2]) Cf. U.v. Wilamowitz-Moellendorff, *Platon*, Berlin 1919, vol. I, p. 337.—O. Gigon writes: "Verhältnismässig spät berücksichtigt das griech. Denken die Erfahrung, dass das Handeln von verschiedenen, ja entgegengesetzten Antrieben beherrscht sein kann. Die Psyche wird zum Ort innerer Konflikte mehrerer S.n-Teile. Die bes. durch Platon (rep.) begründete pluralistische Psychologie unterscheidet eine Hierarchie von Teilen: Vernunft (Phronesis), Mut (Thymos), Begehren (Epithymia)." *S.v. Psyche, Lexikon der alten Welt*, Zürich und Stuttgart, 1965.

discourses can be reduced in fact to the dictum *man makes polis*. Let us examine the elements substantiating this view.

Polis consists of persons, 369b5–c4; the more unified the citizens, the better the city, 462c10–d7, 464b1–3; the nature of a *polis* varies with its kind of citizens, 544d6–e2; for this variability there are ethnological arguments, 435e1–436a3. It is, however, the small number of gifted and able citizens who determine the nature of the society for good or bad—of mediocrity nothing great can be expected, 495a10–b6. To create and uphold the model *polis*, men of the best possible type must be produced, 456e6–7; therefore the philosopher-kings should rule, 499a11–c2. The importance of the élite is obvious in many ways, as is illustrated for instance in the definition of *sophia*, 428e7–429a3. And already at 417a5–6 the small class of guardians is mentioned as the saviours of the *polis*. The discussion in the middle books about the education and function of the philosopher-kings is of course of paramount importance. By means of their statesmanship these superior personalities mould the *polis*. This thought is varied in *Bks VIII–IX*: different kinds of bad rulers produce different kinds of bad societies. Change in any society originates at the top of the power-pyramid.—Referring to such elements of thought we thus perceive a new motif, saying that *man makes polis*. Its basic proposition is pronounced in *Bk V*, 473c11-e2. The passage says that unless the philosophers become kings, or *vice versa*, the rulers become philosophers, the cities will never have rest from their troubles; philosophy and politics must meet in the same persons. Thus our criteria for a motif (position, repetition, scope and significance) hold also for this second line of thought. In the review of the text the *man-makes-polis* motif will be further observed.

We have asked for an explanation of how *polis* can illustrate man. As a first step we were led to consider the importance of the élite. But as, according to the *Republic*, no citizen is uninfluenced by the general social and cultural conditions of his society, we must also consider how the *polis* acts upon the individual. *Polis* ultimately consists of individuals, but *sociologically* it is composed of classes, which, as the case may be, are related to each other in co-operation or competition. Roughly speaking, the individual contributes to the well-being of the model *polis* only as a competent member of one of its three classes.[1]) *Polis*

---

[1]) Cf. J. P. Maguire, *The Individual and the Class in Plato's Republic, CJ*, vol. 60 1964–65, pp. 145 ff.

moulds man by means of social institutions such as class-system, family, educational system and property etc. In the *Republic* there is a wealth of sociological thought describing how the socio-cultural conditions determine the characters of the citizens. Thus we may also extract a third and very powerful motif, namely *polis makes man*, cf. p. 118 below.

The second and the third motifs, *man makes polis* and *polis makes man*, compete formally with each other. They are, however, complementary instruments for analyzing the extremely complicated question of how man and society are related to one another. They represent two ways of looking at the *polis-psyche* complex. Together the second and the third motifs also explain how *polis* can illustrate man.

In considering the various ways in which *polis* and *psyche* are related in the *Republic*, we may finally ask, if there is not also a fourth motif— namely, *man illustrates polis*. At first this seems far-fetched. But we may well take the five types of men as *representative personalities*, highly expressive of the ethos found in their respective societies.—This aspect is described in *chapter XVI*.

5. Motif and anti-motif

The four motifs of the *polis-psyche* complex of thought can be arranged in the form of a quadrangle.

Graph A. CONSTRUCTION OF MOTIF AND ANTI-MOTIF

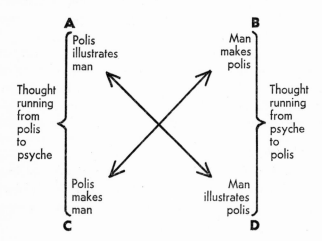

The quadrangle shows how these motifs are related to each other. As, however, four motifs are difficult to handle, I have reduced them to two. A and C are therefore thrown together into one motif, saying that *Polis illustrates and moulds man*. I refer below to this conjunction as the *polis-psyche motif*, or often as simply the *motif*. In this new constructed motif, our first one, traced in *TABLE 2*, continues to play a leading role.

As against the *polis-psyche* motif, B and D may be conjoined to an anti-motif expressing the idea that *men make up, determine and represent polis*. This line of thought I call the *psyche-polis motif*, or often simply *the anti-motif*.

Our prime concern is with the *polis-psyche* motif. It is closely tied up with the double-text method, which is fundamental for the systematic investigation carried out throughout *Bks II–IV* and *VIII–IX*. As it is a basic idea in sociology and social psychology that man is both illustrated and formed by the society wherein he lives, we are also able to see the *polis-psyche motif* as a *motif of ideas*, cf. p. 40 below.

The discourses on education are prominent. W. Jaeger, writing on *paideia* as a motif of ideas in Greek culture, gives a lengthy account of its importance in the *Republic*.[1]) There are two large sections about education to observe, *Bks II* 376c7–*III* 412b7 and *VII* 521c1–541b5. The former deals with the primary education of the guardians, the latter deals with higher education, aiming ultimately at *dialektike*, i.e. the philosophic method. But even outside these sections one finds numerous references to the importance of *paideia*; an impressive metaphor (424d1–2) compares education in *mousike* to a citadel.—There is an important connection between the *paideia*-discourses and our motifs. Men of the best kind are needed to create a good city. But as they are not to be found ready-made, they must be developed by a careful process of education. By education *polis* moulds man. The stress is on education for leadership. The leaders in their turn are to shape and preserve the *polis*; here we see the features of the anti-motif.

6. Motif and analogy

The model version of the *polis-psyche analogy* is established in *Bk IV*. From a functional point of view the model *polis* is divided into three

---

[1]) W. Jaeger, *Paideia: the Ideals of Greek Culture*, I–III, transl. by G. Highet, New York 1943—1945, vol. II, pp. 198 ff.

fundamental classes, in German literature aptly called *Lehr-*, *Wehr-und Nährstand*. These classes form a hierarchy. In order to uphold the organic form of unity there are also four ethical constituents, *sophia*, *andreia*, *sophrosyne* and *dikaiosyne*. This socio-cultural pattern, which is discovered in *polis*, constitutes the larger letters. Guided by the larger text, and by means of empirical considerations and self-analysis, the corresponding pattern is found in the soul. *Polis* and *psyche* thus are both considered as functional agents; both are endowed with tripartite structure, and in both the cardinal virtues are distributed in the same way. Whether one thinks of society or man, this is the right constitution, *politeia*. But the right constitution is in both cases easily changed. And this brings us over to four typical forms of derangements in *Bks VIII–IX*. The original analogy of *Bk IV* is in this way extended to illustrate also in timocracy, oligarchy, democracy and tyranny the basic resemblance between *polis* and *psyche*.

Speaking about the analogy between the model *polis* and the righteous man, the term *established analogy* will be used. The four other analogies treated in *Bks VIII–IX* are called the *extended analogies*, and speaking of all five, the term *general analogy* is applied. The basic resemblance between *polis* and *psyche* in the general analogy does not lie in a large number of characteristics common for both of them, but in the ingenious use that is made of these characteristics.

The *polis-psyche* analogy and the *polis-psyche* motif are of course closely allied. In the analogy some properties are selected and composed for comparison. In the motif, *polis-psyche* operate as an interpretative instrument in order to help the reader to see as much as possible of the *polis*-background and the social thought which permeate the *Republic* and explain how *polis* can illustrate man. A well-established motif may prove to be an expedient device for the intrinsic study of the *Republic*. In stimulating our sociological imagination some knowledge of small group and community sociology is no doubt advantageous; I refer particularly to the concept of *Gemeinschaft* as it was developed for research by F. Tönnies and others.[1]) In this connection I have found R. A.

---

[1]) The canonical exposition of the terms *Gemeinschaft* and *Gesellschaft* by F. Tönnies embodies a distinction "which in one form or another can be traced back to Plato and Aristotle", writes W. G. Runciman, *Social Science and Political Theory*, 2 nd. ed. Cambridge 1969, pp. 151–152.

Nisbet's inquiry of the unit-ideas of sociology helpful.[1]) But we must at the same time avoid the temptation of reading into the *Republic* "doctrines that did not become explicit until later".[2])

7. Motif and theme

What is the subject-matter or the theme of the *Republic*, and how is the motif related to it?

The title indicates a work on politics. And this may be said.[3]) But already in ancient times it was found that the title was inadequate to the declared or formal subject, and the *Republic* was therefore given a second title, περὶ δικαίου .[4]) But even so it seems inadequately titled. By a study of *Bk I* (see *Graph D*, p. 62) and the entire structure of the dialogue, we are inclined to observe also the opposite term, *adikia*, injustice. That *adikia* rivals *dikaiosyne* in importance is confirmed in *Bk II*, where they are both set up as the expressed objects of investigation, 358b4–7, 367b2–5, cf. 376c8–d3; this is confirmed again in *Bk V*, 472b3–5,

Reflecting on the meaning of *dikaiosyne* and *adikia*, it is essential to see that these terms point out structural features of *agents*, whether it is a society or an individual. The extended analogy between *polis* and *psyche* rests on this fact.[5]) *Dikaiosyne* and *adikia* have then to do with how the society and the personality are ordered, and what kind of con-

---

[1]) *The Sociological Tradition*, New York, 1966.

[2]) Cf. R. Robinson, *Plato's Earlier Dialectic*, 2nd. ed. Oxford 1953, pp. 3 ff.

[3]) The title presents hardly, writes Grote, "a clear idea either of its proclaimed purpose or of its total contents. The larger portion of the treatise is doubtless employed in expounding the generation of a commonwealth generally... Nevertheless the avowed purpose of the treatise is, not to depict the ideal of a commonwealth, but to solve the questions, What is Justice? What is Injustice?..." G. Grote, *Plato and the Other Companions of Sokrates*, 3 vols. London 1865, vol. III, pp. 122–123. — The title is misleading, thinks E. A. Havelock. Only about a third of *Bks II–X* deals directly with political theory, which occupies *Bk II* 368e–374e, *Bks III–IV* 412b–434a, *Bk V* 449a–473b, and *Bks VIII–IX* 543a–576b, together about 81 Stephanus pages out of 239. *Preface to Plato*, Oxford 1963, p. 18, n 37.

[4]) The sub-title, probably a later addition, is found in *Par. A* and other MSS, comments Campbell, vol. III, p. 1.

[5]) See Chapter II, p. 61 ff. — It may be mentioned that there is a French translation by La Pillonnière, printed in London 1726, bearing the sub-title *du juste, et de l'injustice*.

stitution they have. The term for this is πολιτεία. In presenting the keywords for inspection, we have observed the tendency of the terms *polis* and *politeia* to converge towards the same meaning. And this convergence is extended to the field of personality; we may speak of the inner city of man and its constitution. It is of interest in this connection to note that the title *ΠΟΛΙΤΕΙΑ* is found in some MSS in the plural form *ΠΟΛΙΤΕΙΑΙ*.[1])—We may take *Politeia* as short for five types of constitutions, one righteous and four unrighteous, each of them found in *polis* as well as in *psyche*.—*Psyche* is therefore involved in the subject-matter as an object for examination, while *polis* is employed in the investigation as a methodical device; and the motif is instrumental to our study of how this method is carried through.

8. Motif and structure

The term *structure* is used in many ways.[2]) With this term I mean simply how the total argument of the *Republic* is broadly organized.

It has often been noted that the traditional division of the dialogue into ten books does not correctly indicate the main stages of the argument. In its own way, however, the traditional division has been convenient in helping the reader to get through the long dialogue. Another pragmatic division is that used in the Stephanus edition 1578.[3]) Its pages (with sub-divisions from A to E) became the accepted reference system in all scholarly dealings with Plato. Before turning to the structural views, let us measure the length of the Greek text by the Stephanus standard.

In this admirable edition the text is produced in even lines, irrespective

---

[1]) Campbell, vol. III, p. 1, and Burnet, note on the title *ΠΟΛΙΤΕΙΑ*.

[2]) A reported general definition is "the natural relation of the constituent parts of a whole determining its peculiar character". Cf. *The Shorter Oxford English Dict.*, Oxford 1964.—In fact the structure of the *Republic* is often discussed in terms of natural parts, or natural division or *Gliederung*.—A special definition is "sum of the relationships of the parts of a literary whole to one another", *Encyclopedia of Poetry and Poetics*, ed. by A. Preminger, N. J. 1965. The term *structure* has been used in various fields and with various meanings. For an account of its application to literary research I refer to I. Jonsson, *Idéer och teorier om ordens konst. Från Platon till strukturalismen.* Lund, 1971, pp. 204 ff.

[3]) *Platonis Opera quae Extant Omnia.* Ex. nova Ioannis Serrani interpretatione, ... Henr. Stephani de quorundam locorum interpretatione iudicum. etc. T. 1–3. Parisiis 1578. T.2.

as to whether it is a case of short questions and answers (as in 349a–e) or a monologue (as in 365a–e). This form of printing, which may be tiresome for the reader, is convenient for our purpose of text measurement; in the cases where there are exceptions from the standard length of the lines (=7 cm) they have been adjusted to the equivalent of standard lines. Here is a summary of our measurements.

Table C. A quantitativ aspect of the Republic

Bks	Standard lines of the Steph.ed.	%
I	1 346	10.5
II	1 250	9.8
III	1 450	11.4
IV	1 268	9.9
V	1 456	11.4
VI	1 277	10.0
VII	1 243	9.7
VIII	1 241	9.7
IX	1 002	7.8
X	1 257	9.8
Total	12 790	100.0

The longest are *Bks III* and *V*, each covering 11.4 per cent of the total text, *Bk IX* is the shortest, covering only 7.8 per cent.

L. Campbell begins his essay *On the Structure of Plato's Republic* by saying that it divides naturally into five sections, "which are marked off with elaborate forms of transition by Plato himself".[1] These *natural parts*, as they are often called, are Bks I, II–IV, V–VII, VIII–IX and X. To some scholars this judgement has seemed true,[2] but others have been less convinced. Jowett, Nettleship and Bosanquet reject the judge-

---

[1] *Plato's Republic*, ed. with notes and essays by B. Jowett and L. Campbell, Oxford 1894, I–III, vol. II, *Essays*, p. 1.

[2] So Wilamowitz: "Unverkennbar ist, dass 1 und 10 einander entsprechen, 2–4 und 8–9 ebenso", vol. II, p. 180.

The same *Gliederung des Gesprächs* into five *Hauptteilen* is found in Apelts translation, though with the slight divergence that 327a–331c (the conversation with Cephalus) is marked off as *Einleitung*, pp. xx–xxiii. And in the translation of Chambry there is a *plan schématique du dialogue* established by A. Diès where *les grandes divisions* are the same as those of Campbell's.

ment that *Bk I* falls congruently in with the first natural part. Instead they put the dividing line at pag. 368, where Socrates begins his investigation after the speeches of Glaucon and Adeimantus, and which covers almost the first half of *Bk II*. Later scholars have made new divisions, causing the traditional division into ten books to appear less rational; well-known is Cornford's dictum, which says that the traditional division is "an accidental expedient of ancient book-production" having little to do with the structure of the argument.[1])

In taking up the subject of structure, we must look for some suitable ground of division. The parts must help us to read and understand the *Republic*, to find if possible its inner balance, paying due regard to the transitions made by Plato himself. Using our motif for this task, it seems sound to begin at that section of the text which most clearly states what Socrates is requested to do and how he sets about doing it, i.e. 357a1–369b4 *Bk II*. Subject and method are here systematically presented.[2]) The double text method is introduced here, and the long discussion is set in motion. From this point of departure we may be able to mark out the main stages of Socrates' investigation. To check the plausibility of our divisions, I have given for comparison the opinions of some well-known scholars. For the sake of brevity they are presented in the form of a table. see pp. 30–31, *Table D*.

There is a considerable agreement on how the *Republic* is composed in its major parts. Considering its length and complication it is, however, not surprising that there are differing opinions on detail. The division which emanates from the projection of the motif has not yielded any extreme results. Its distinction lies in the second part, emphasizing the program of the investigation announced in *Bk II.*—In *Table E*, p. 32, I give some figures resulting from our divisions.

A few observations are required. Take first *part 3* and *part 6*, in which the *polis-psyche* motif prevails. They include together about 5,650 lines out of a total of 12.790, the equivalent of about 45 per cent of the total text. Here one also finds the highest frequency of key-words,

---

[1]) Cf. Preface to Cornford's translation of the *Rep.*, p. iii.

[2]) It is in this connection of some interest to observe that when A. Krohn builds up his conception of the *Republic* as an unsystematic work he abstracts from this fundamental methodology. Instead he adopts as a key-proposition that the wind of the conversation must be followed (394d8–9); Plato "lässt sich von dem *pneuma* seines Geistes tragen", *Der Platonische Staat*, Halle 1876, pp. 3–4, 57, 209.

Table D. A comparative view of structure

1	2	3
Traditional division into ten books.	Main parts according to this study.	Reported divisions and conclusions
Bk I Steph. 327a1– 354c3. Contains 1346 lines in Steph. ed.	*Part 1* =the whole of *Bk I*.	**A.** *Internal features. Aporetic* end as in the early dialogues; in *Bk II* 357a1–2 *Bk I* is called a προοίμιον; stylometric argument, cf Lutoslawski pp. 319 ff. **B.** *Additional views.* Functions as an introduction (Adam, Cornford, Diès, Shorey, Friedländer, Crombie.) **C.** *Contrary views.* Jowett, Bosanquet, Nettleship extend the introductory part to 367e. Lately H.D.P. Lee has followed this practice. *From the aspect of the motif, Bk I* makes an instructive introduction, cf Chapter II, pp. 64 ff.
Bk II 357a1– 383c7. 1 250 lines.	*Part 2* =357a1 –369b4. 562 lines.	**A.** See (A) above.—Lutoslawski, 322 ff. **B.** Cornford and many others include the whole of *Bk II* with *III* and *IV* in their second main part. **C.** H. Leisegang (*RE*, 2451) makes 358b–368c (the speeches of Glaucon and Adeimantus) a second part in his *sieben Abschnitte.* *From the aspect of the motif* the second main part should, I think, embrace the section 357a1 to 369b4. Thus it centres around the subject-matter *and* the method.
	Part 3 =369b5 to end of *Bk IV*. 3 406 lines.	A–C. See above. *From the aspect of the motif* 369b5 is the starting point for the actual application of the double-text method. Socrates begins to construct the model *polis.*
Bk III 386a1– 417b9. 1 450 lines.		**A.** No explicit directions about division. B–C. None of the above-mentioned authors set off *Bk III* as a main part on its own. *From the aspect of the motif* the whole of *Bk III* is included in the third main part.
Bk IV 419a1– 445e4. 1 268 lines.		**A.** No explicit directions about division. **B.** The above-mentioned authors include the whole of *Bk IV* in the same main part. **C.** Cornford deviates by transporting the last page of *IV* to an appendix=445b5–471c. *From the aspect of the motif* alternative (B) is preferred. The whole of *Bk IV* belongs to the third main part.

1	2	3
Bk V 449a1– 480a13 1 456 lines.	*Part 4* =449a1 –471c3. 1 037 lines.	A. After a conclusive reflection, 449a1–5, Socrates is interrupted and the discussion deviates from its planned course, cf. *Bk VII* 543c4–6. Stylometric argument Luto-slawski 323–324. B. Leisegang makes 449a–471c a main part; über das Wesen der Gemeinschaft (τίς ὁ τρόπος τῆς κοινωνίας, 449c8). C. Cornford's opinion, see (C) above. *From the aspect of the motif* 449a1–471c3 contains social questions not paralleled in the structure of *psyche*.
Bk VI 484a1– 511e5. 1 277 lines. *Bk VII* 514a1– 541b5 1 243 lines.	*Part 5* =471c4 to end of *Bk VII*. 2 939 lines.	A. At 471c4 the discussion takes a new course: is the model *polis* realizable? An internal sign is that this subject is called *the third wave*, the most formidable of them all, 472a3–4. B. Cornford and Leisegang make 471c4-end of *Bk VII* a main part. C. Lee makes a new division at 421c1. *From the aspect of the motif* alt. (B) seems most attractive. Thus the section 471c4, *Bk V*, to 541b5 *Bk VII* (die Herrschaft der Philosophen und ihre Bildung) makes the fifth main part.
Bk VIII 543a1– 569c9. 1 241 lines. *Bk IX* 571a1– 592b6. 1 002 lines.	*Part 6* =543a1 to end of *Bk IX*. 2 243 lines.	A. At 543c4–6 Plato indicates explicitly that *Bks V–VII* constitute a digression. B–C. All the above-mentioned authors make a main part of *Bks VIII* and *IX*. *From the aspect of the motif* alternative (B–C) is strongly supported.
Bk X 595a1– 621d3. 1 257 lines.	*Part 7* =the whole of *Bk X*.	A. At 595a1–3 it is retrospectively said that the *polis* was founded on right principles. C. Cornford has divided *Bk X* in two parts: 595a1–608b10 and 608c1– end of the book. *From the aspect of the motif* there are, it seems, not sufficient reasons for such a division.

Table E. Structure and frequency of keywords

1	2	3	4	5	6
Structural parts	Number of lines in Steph. ed.	Number of *polis*-words	Number of *psyche*-words	Number of keywords (col. 3+4)	Number of keywords per 1 000 lines.
Part 1	1 346	16	10	26	19
2	562	7	5	12	21
3	3 406	174	64	238	70
4	1 037	48	4	52	50
5	2 939	80	54	134	46
6	2 243	88	42	130	58
7	1 257	14	46	60	48
Total 1–7	12 790	427	225	652	51

counted per 1,000 lines, cf. column 6. Concerning *part 6* (=*Bks VIII–IX*) it is important to know that the frequency of our key-words is unable to represent the prevalence of the motif fairly. That is because new words like *politeia, timokratia, oligarchia* etc. frequently replace the word *polis*, cf. p. 18 above. There is, furthermore, a difference between the key-words when they operate strictly as components of the motif (as in *parts 3* and *6*), and when they do not (as in *parts 4, 5 and 7*).

9. *Structural aspects.* (a) *parts 3 and 6*
In the following discussion of how the structural parts are related to each other this graph may be useful.

Graph B. STRUCTURAL PARTS OF THE REPUBLIC

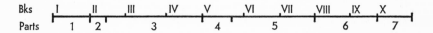

Part 3 and *part 6* are no doubt intimately bound up by the methodological directions of *part 2*[1]); that this connection is blurred by the intervening discussions in *parts 4 and 5* is another matter. Let us then

---

[1]) See for instance R. L. Nettleship, *Lectures on the Republic of Plato*, 2 nd. ed. London 1961, p. 162.

with some reason assume that *part 3* and *part 6* belong to one and the same thought experiment. But instead of looking for corroborative features from *part 3* in the reasoning of *part 6*, we may read the parts in the reversed order, searching for traits of *Bks VIII–IX* in *Bks II–IV*.

The reason for such a reading is that *adikia* (which is systematically exposed in *part 6*) has previously, in *Bks I and II*, been subjected to analysis in terms of disintegration.

Socrates' criticism of the teaching of Thrasymachus in *Bk I* implies that the limitless aspiration for gratifications (*pleonexia*) makes men unable to act together, cf. 349b1–350c11.[1]) *Adikia* breaks up the unity of the society. It even dissolves the unity of the inner man himself. Wherever *adikia* is found, it is disintegrative. The analysis of *adikia* in *Bk I* offers an indirect approach to *dikaiosyne*.

Further on in *Bk II*, 372e2–373e7, attention is again drawn towards the notion of *adikia*. Socrates is developing the model *polis*. Then he passes over to the exposition of the swollen *polis* and the genesis of *adikia*. The consumption of the citizens has passed the limit of necessity, ὑπερβάντες τὸν τῶν ἀναγκαίων ὅρον, 373d10. They live in luxury. To satisfy their expanding demands, the *polis* drifts into aggressive wars. And with the origin of war the roots of all sorts of evil are found. That the notion of this ὑπερβαίνειν (overreach) is akin to the πλεονεξία of *Bk I* seems obvious.—Add to this that Socrates was requested to explain both *dikaiosyne* and *adikia*. That Plato had planned to investigate *dikaiosyne* and *adikia* as a pair of opposites is furthermore evident from 444b1 in the end of *Bk IV*.[2])

Plato might then just as well, it seems, have put *part 6* before *part 3*. Already at the opening of the investigation the reader would then have been acquainted with Plato's profound knowledge of society and man, his theory of social dynamics, his acute psychological analyses, and his abhorrence for social divisions. These features motivate together the excessive insistence on social and personal unity which dominates the reasoning about the model *polis*. Had Plato put his survey of the existing societies in the beginning of his investigation, he would further have saved himself from the speculative task of describing how an ideally perfect city collapses, which is an undertaking lying outside the field of descriptive sociology.

---

[1]) In 349b1–350c11 the expressions πλέον ἔχειν and πλεονεκτεῖν occur frequently.

[2]) 444b ff. Οὐκοῦν στάσιν τινὰ αὖ τριῶν ὄντων τούτων δεῖ κτλ.

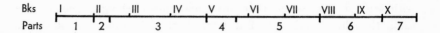

When this is said, we must see that there is an inner resistance against allowing *part 3* and *part 6* to change places. There are at least three arguments for the traditional order between these parts: the beginning of *Bk VIII* is explicitly attached to the end of *Bk IV*; there are certain features of symmetry in the architecture of the two parts; and when Socrates describes the degenerating cities he starts from the condition of the ideal *polis*.[1] — The order between *part 3* and *part 6* is fixed. These cannot change places like railway carriages and travel in both directions. *Bks II–IV* and *VIII–IX* then belong to one and the same thought experiment, *carried out in its own rational way*. Reading *part 3* in the light of *part 6* one finds, however, an impressive arsenal of empirical arguments also in the former, (cf. p. 107 below). It is not simply that one part is loaded with all the empir ical and the other with all the speculative arguments.[2]

(b). Parts 4 and 5

It has often been noted that these two parts are digressive; K. Praechter speaks in this connection about "auffallende Eigentümlichkeiten der Disposition".[3]

Let us take *part 4, Bk V* 449a1–471c3. The keywords are also found here, cf. *TABLE 1*. But as *polis* is not here used in the strictly illustrative way its frequency points only very superficially to the interconnection of *part 4* with *parts 3 and 6*. What is said about family, men and

---

[1] "Plato hat möglicherweise eine Entstehung der Verfassungsformen aus dem Idealstaat zuerst nicht angenommen. Der Wortlaut am Schluss des IV. Buches besagt wenigstens davon Nichts. Nach diesem gedachte er nur die Hauptformen der politischen Organisation zu zeichnen, und es stand ihm frei, für den Ursprung derselben ein beliebiges Prius zu postuliren." Krohn, p. 208.

[2] Cf., however, R. S. Brumbaugh, who thinks that the early main parts of the *Republic* "could hardly be more anti-empirical", while the second one "could hardly encompass more detailed data and observation"; *Bks VIII–IX* "could not have more empirical detail per line cited for confirmation if the most taciturn modern sociologist had composed them". *A New Interpretation of Plato's Republic*, *JPh*, vol. LXIV 1967, pp. 666 ff.

[3] *Grundriss der Geschichte der Philosophie*, vol. I Berlin 1926, p. 270.

women, child-rearing etc. does not call forth further parallels with *psyche*; at least no such analogies are explicitly mentioned. *Part 4* then falls outside the domain of the *polis-psyche* analogy. This is indicated also by *Table E*, cf. p. 32 above, where *psyche* occurs only four times while *polis* has 48 appearances. *Polis* is discussed *qua polis*. This is a digressive feature.

On the other hand, however, it is the model *polis* of *part 3* which is discussed all the time. And this is of course a unifying link. The additions of *part 4* also serve to strengthen the *polis*, and make it more convincing as a model. Returning to *part 4* from the study of *part 6*, which is centred around the dangers of social change, the need of these additional reinforcements stand out more clearly. Reading, for instance about the bad effects of private property and private family in timocracy, the supporting reasons for the upper class communism in the model *polis* are demonstrated. From *part 4* there are thus links to both *part 3* and *part 6*.

Part 5 (471c4 in *Bk V* to the end of *Bk VII*) is quite rich in keywords; of *polis* there are 80 occurrences, of *psyche* 54. The interruption at 471c4–e5, however, marks a deviation from the main route. Socrates then makes a distinction between constructing a model *polis* and investigating its realizability, 472c4–d2. If you invent a *polis* for illustrative purposes you are not bound also to discuss how the model can be turned into a reality. Another digressive feature is that the double text method has been abandoned, and the method of dialectics is introduced.

We have proposed that there is a link to the motif from the antimotif. And these discussions about *polis-psyche* and *psyche-polis*, held in the light of education, politics and epistemology, constitute a unifying bond. With this in mind, the keywords gain in significance, indicating a broader view of the *polis-psyche* complex than is professed in *part 2*.

If *parts 4 and 5* are read as one long line of reasoning, integrative signs are found at both ends of it, cf. *TABLE 2*, nrs 26 and 29. They remind the reader of what has been achieved by means of the double-text method. Another important sign of integration is found in *Bk IV* 435c9–d5. At a crucial point in the development of the double-text method, Socrates suddenly mentions the existence of a safer way, a better method. It is the μακροτέρα καὶ πλείων ὁδὸς recurring as the μακροτέρα περίοδος in *Bk VI*, 504b2, c9; that these expressions corre-

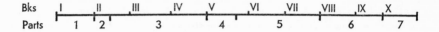

Bks	I	II	III	IV	V	VI	VII	VIII	IX	X
Parts	1	2	3		4	5		6		7

spond is evident from 504b1–7.[1]) Another pair of reciprocal expressions is the communistic formula ὅτι μάλιστα κοινὰ τὰ φίλων ποιεῖσθαι of *Bk IV*, 424a1–2, and its reccurrence in *Bk V*, ὅτι κοινὰ τὰ φίλων ἔσται, 449c5, cf. 453c10–d3. A connection is here established between the short formula in *Bk IV* and the lengthy exposition of *Bk V*. There are thus bonds between *part 3* and *parts 4* and *5*. Admitting the digression of the middle books Plato tried to bridge this gulf.

What then is the relation between *parts 4 and 5* to *part 6?* In the beginning of *Bk VIII* one finds two connecting links. One link (543c7–544b10) connects with the very beginning of *Bk V* 449a1–5, and is of a formal kind. The other (543a1–c3) indicates vaguely what has earlier been said about the socio-political conditions of the model *polis*. But there seems to be no direct references in *part 6* to *Bks |V–VII*. Part 6 is, we have maintained, wholly characterized by its intimate relationship with *part 3*.

On pages 33–34 *part 3* was read in the light of *part 6*. Let us this time employ *part 6* on the middle books.[2])

In *part 6* the evil effects of *stasis* both in society and personality are exhibited in an overwhelming way. Its economic, social and cultural causes are demonstrated, and the lack of competent leadership is revealed. Society is a victim of competing classes. Even the families are divided. A series of special studies describes how the disorganized personality is generated.

Bearing this in mind, we turn to *part 4*. In 462a2–d5, we find the counterpart to the discourse on digression. There is no greater harm than disunion and dissent, no greater good than co-operation and unity;

---

[1]) "It is in itself highly probable", writes Adam, "that the most important passages referring forward or backward to one another throughout the dialogue were either written together, or at all events revised by Plato side by side". vol. I, pp. 244–245.

[2]) A general precondition for this sort of tentative reading is that one is not operating with casually chosen parts, but with systematic divisions, which have earlier been discussed and found functionally important for the movement of the total argument.

society should be *one*, in the sense that an individual is a psycho-somatic whole, cf. pp. 125–126 below. Around this nucleus is based the whole of *part 4*, with its radical provisions for unity. It appears as if the forceful review of the changing and degenerating societies in *part 6* has motivated the extra reinforcements of the model *polis* which are found in *part 4*.

From *part 4*, there is but a short step to the question of realization (*part 5*). Capable rulers and adequate knowledge are needed to build a good city.—Two vivid pictures of contemporary conditions are also to be observed in *part 5:* (a) the simile of the ship, its captain and crew, 488a7–489a2; and (b) the explication of how potentially good characters are spoiled by the bad social and cultural environment in which they grow up, 490e3–497a5, cf. pp. 137–139 above. In these two sections Plato foreshadows what is said in *part 6*, or, if we practise reversed reading, he supplements more information about democracy in *part 5* to what is found in *part 6*.

(c) Parts 1, 2 and 7

That *Bk I* is introductory and constitutes *part 1*, we have already assumed; cf. *TABLE 2*, preparatory views, nrs 1–4. *Part 2* marks out, we have said, what Socrates is requested to do and introduces the double-text method; subject and method are in this section systematically presented. *Part 2* contains the fundamental argument for our divisions.

Before leaving the topic of structure we must add some notes on *Bk X*, our *part 7*. This part falls into two sub-divisions, (a) 595a1–608b10 and (b) 608c1–621d3. The former is an addition to the discourse on the principles of literary education carried on in *Bks II and III*, the latter section is a return to the professed subject of *dikaiosyne, adikia* and *psyche*. It is rounded off with the myth of Er, forming the grand finale of the dialogue.

It is easy to point out the digressive features of the *Republic*, but it takes some constructive effort to establish it as a unity. According to Adam the digression is only formal.[1]) For Campbell, the unity of the *Republic* is not syllogistic like that of a treatise; it is partly the unity of

---

[1]) In reality Bks V–VII fulfil "the hopes held out in sundry parts of III and IV"... (414a, 416b, 423e, 435d, 439e, 442c), and "complete the picture of the perfect city and the perfect man by giving us Plato's third or crowning effort—the philosophic City and the Philosopher-King", vol. I, p. 274.

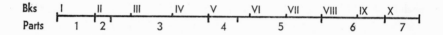

Bks	I	II	III	IV	V	VI	VII	VIII	IX	X
Parts	1	2	3		4		5		6	7

a philosophic movement, partly the unity of a piece of art.[1]—By a study of the *polis–psyche* analogy we are disposed to see the break in method manifested in *parts 4 and 5*. Pursuing the motif and the anti-motif, we see, however, unifying bonds. Reading forwards and backwards we have seen the interdependence of the structural parts.

We may then think of the keywords not only as motif–supporting elements but also as a thread of Ariadne leading through the more or less labyrinthine text of the *Republic*.[2]

10. Reading and reviewing

There is a prevailing attitude, it seems, that in approaching the *Republic* one must be equipped with a super-view, provided by a reading of everything Plato ever wrote; dealing, for instance with the meaning of *diakosyne* in the *Republic* one must first know what Plato says on

---

[1] Vol. II, pp. 9–10.—The obvious solution to the break constituted by Bks V–VII "belongs to Plato's concealment of his art, like the palinode of the Phaedrus, the hiccough of Aristophanes in the Symposium...", p. 4.

[2] The digression constituted by *Bks V–VII* has been the subject of heated disputes. In 1876 A. Krohn published *Der Platonische Staat*, which provoked discussion. Supported by earlier investigations (esp. K. Fr. Hermann, *Geschichte und System d. plat. Philos.*, 1839), Krohn proposed that *Bks I–IV* and *VIII–IX* were written before BC 391, and that Plato afterwards had re-edited the work, inserting *V–VII*. Other notable works to the same opinion were E. Pfleiderer, *Zur Lösung der Platonischen Frage*, 1888, and W. Windelband, *Platon*, 1900. E. Rohde, *Psyche I–II* 1910, was a representative of this camp of opinion; Krohn and Pfleiderer had proved the matter, II, pp. 265–267. See also *CJ*, vol. II, pp. 4 ff.

Th. Gomperz, *Griechische Denker I–III*, opposed vigorously this "Umwälzungstheorie"; the practice to introduce a subject, then abandon it in order to return to it, is according to Gomperz a technique intimately bound up with Plato's art, vol. II pp. 360–361.—A. E. Taylor, it may be mentioned, made a firm stand against "the fanciful modern speculations" about an earlier edition, *Plato*, Meridian books, New York 1957, p. 264. An intermediary position is taken by Jowett. "Whether this imperfection of structure arises from an enlargement of the plan; or from the imperfect reconcilement in the writer's own mind of the struggling elements of thought..." cannot be decided. Intr. to the *Rep.*, 5.—Lately G. Ryle, *Plato's Progress*, Cambridge 1966, has revived the theory of two different editions of the *Rep.* pp. 244–250.

this subject in all his other works.[1]) As an alternative to this practice, the *Republic* can very well be studied as a book on its own. It provides extensive reading, treats of many topics, is rich in arguments and belongs to the mature work of a master-writer. By piecemeal reading it offers, within its own textual space, a rich field for persistent activities.

But the *Republic* can of course be read in many ways. Thus we must accept a number of rival, more or less over-stressed and topic-directed interpretations.[2]) This gives on the other hand birth to the quest for integrated and principled reading.[3]) In this respect the method of the *polis-psyche* motif appears to be a possible way of approach.

The keywords and the explicit utterances give only a fragmentary picture of the *Republic*. A broader view is therefore needed. That is acquired by my reviews of the text, contained in the chapters II–XV. These reviews aim to make my reading known and controllable to others. The chapters are projections resulting from the pursuit of the *polis-psyche* motif, which is constructed of material from the *Republic* itself. An advantage is that we can offer for inspection not only the results of our reading, but also (in contrast to the more or less intuitive ways of reading) the interpretative instrument itself, cf. *TABLES 1 and 2*.

A review is not a translation. Pursuing the motif, some portions of the text strike us as more interesting than others. It is necessary, of

---

[1]) Cf. C. W. R. Larson, *The Platonic Synonyms, ΔΙΚΑΙΟΣΥΝΗ* and *ΣΩΦΡΟΣΥΝΗ*. *AJPh.* 72 1951 pp. 395–414.

[2]) The Stephanus edition contains 12,790 text-lines, each measuring 7 cm, making together a textual distance of about 890 meters. In arriving to the end of such a reading-tour you find that owing to your own dispositions and Plato's alluring way of exposition you are unevenly effected by the text; some parts strike you as more interesting than others. The *Republic*, writes E. Barker, seems to fall into a number of treatises, each occupied with its separate subject: metaphysics, moral philosophy, education, political science, and philosophy of history cf. *Greek Political Theory, Plato and his Predecessors*, London 1951, p. 145; you could add as well psychology and literary criticism. By the attitude of impressionistic reading one is disposed to group the dialogue around one or the other of one's favorite topics.

[3]) "Even though 'reading' be used broadly enough to include critical understanding and sensibility, the art of reading is an ideal for a purely personal cultivation. As such it is highly desirable, and also serves as a basis of a widely spread literary culture. It cannot, however, replace the conception of 'literary scholarship, conceived of as a super-personal tradition." R. Wellek and A. Warren, *Theory of Literature*, London 1955, p. 8.

course, that full account is taken of the textual bases of the motif. On the other hand, it is also desirable that something of the general content of the dialogue should be represented. We must see the relation of the *polis-psyche* argument to other forms of reasoning.

We cannot expect that our method makes us resistant to biassed interpretation. To envisage the seriousness of this question we need only remember the political and cultural issues inherent in the *Republic*. There are also a number of pictures, images and metaphors which inspire ideological association; cf. the use of analogical expressions such as the shepherd, the dog and the sheep.[1]) Also there is the inverted employment of the *polis-psyche* analogy by which the *psycho-somatic* unity of a person illustrates the organic quality of the *polis*.[2]) As a social scientist Plato uses *polis* to elucidate *psyche*, while as an ideologist he uses *psyche* to persuade us about his *polis*. This traffic between *polis* and *psyche* in both directions is also practised by Plato's readers, and explains, no doubt, some of the resultant disagreements. In our case some comfort can be had, however, from the fact that Plato's political thought is secondary here to *the scientific idea of explaining personality by means of social and cultural structure.*

11. Motif of ideas

We have suggested that *polis-psyche* as a motif of ideas is to be based upon the social psychological thought expressed in the *Republic*. What justification is there for applying the term social psychology?

---

[1]) Cf. 343b1–c1, 345b7–e3, 375a2–376b6, 404a9–b2, 422d4–7, 440c7–d3, 451c4–e7, 459a1–460c7 and 466c6–d4.—Referring to such passages, and by a frequent employment of the term *human cattle*, Popper performs part of his criticism of Plato's political ideas. *The Open Society and its Enemies*, vol. I, *The Spell of Plato*, London 2 nd. ed. 1952, p. 46, and n. 32 (2), p. 226.

[2]) Barker writes, that in constructing the *polis* to illustrate the nature of the soul, Plato to some extent makes a *petitio principii*: he builds a state to illustrate man; but he presupposes a knowledge of man in building it, p. 163. This observation recurs more stressed in E. Topitsch, *Sozialphilosophie zwischen Ideologie und Wissenschaft*, Neuwied 1961. "So legt Platon sein geistesaristokratisches Staatsideal dem Aufbau des 'Seelenstaates' zugrunde und fordert sodann, dass die richtige Staatsverfassung der richtigen Verfassung der Seele entsprechen soll. Hier werden also die vorausgesetzten politischen Grundsätze nicht in den Kosmos projiziert, sondern gewissermassen in die Seele introjiziert und dann mit der Autorität von 'Wahrheiten über das Wesen des Menschen' wieder in den Bereich der Politik rückübertragen", p. 36.

Briefly it may be said, that in the entire field of research on human relations, social psychology is basically concerned with how the individual is in various ways influenced by other individuals[1].)

What is distinctly Plato's contribution?

For the sake of convenience, I have chosen three angles of approach. (1) The small group aspect; (2) the public life aspect; and (3) the cultural aspect.

(1) The importance of the small groups, notably the family, in the formation of the personality is *systematically* observed in *Bks VIII–IX*. Writing on timocracy, oligarchy, democracy and tyranny, Plato observes in each case how the corresponding personalities are formed within the closer relationships of family and friends; cf. 549c2–550b7, 553a6–553e3, 559d7–562a3, and 572b10–573c10. Worthy of note is the account of how the opposing elements in society act upon the family and split it up, and how this division in the family is—to use a modern term—internalized in the personality of the young man who grows up in that family.[2])

(2) Man is also strongly influenced by the activities of the larger groups, assemblages, masses and the way of life of the people around him. A good example of this type of influence is given in *Bk VI*, 492b5–c8. Plato describes "the many" who crowd the Assembly, the law courts, the theatre, the camp or any other large group. They shout and clap till the rocks and the whole place ring with their applause and clamour. How is a man, exclaims Socrates, to safequard his self-possession in such a situation? What sort of private education can hold out against

---

[1]) "Social psychology deals with those elements in the ideas, emotions, attitudes and habits of individuals which derive from, and relate to, the fact that man lives in social-cultural relations with his fellows". K. Young, *Encyclopaedia Britannica*, 1956. ". . . an attempt to understand and explain how the thought, feeling, and behavior of individuals are influenced by the actual, imagined, or implied presence of other human beings". G. W. Allport, *Handbook of Social Psychology*, ed by G. Lindzey. 1954, vol. I, p. 5.

[2]) There is, among others, also a social-psychological reason for studying small groups, writes T. M. Mills. "Because social pressures and pressures from the individual meet in the small group, it is a convenient context in which to observe and to experiment on the interplay among these pressures." And, Mills goes on, small groups are essentially microcosms of larger societies, presenting in miniature "societal features, such as division of labor, a code of ethics, a government, media of exchange, prestige rankings, ideologies, myths, and religious practices". *The Sociology of Small Groups*, New Jersey 1967, pp. 2–3.

such a torrent of opinions? What can save him from being swept away downhill to the popular standard of right and wrong?

(3) The aspect of culture. In chapters X–XIII I have reviewed the socio-cultural changes discussed in *Bks VIII–IX*. We must now draw attention to the cultural reform work of *Bks II–III*, which contain an unsparing criticism of the contemporary cultural conditions. The human soul is a tender thing nourished not only on literature and music, but also on the products of every other kind of creative art and handicraft, 401a1–a8. Cultural achievements must therefore be supervised so that the guardians may not "grow up among representations of moral deformity, as in some foul pasture where, day after day, feeding on every poisonous weed they would, little by little, gather insensibly a mass of corruption in their very souls".[1] They should instead live from childhood as in a healthy land (ὥσπερ ἐν ὑγιεινῷ τόπῳ) constantly surrounded by noble examples of every kind, 401c4–d3. And in *Bk VI* 492d9–e6 we read that no individual can match the force of public opinion; see also 491d1–492b3, 365a4–c6, 595a1–608b10.

It is evident that Plato's social thought is mixed up in the complex of his political and ethical speculations. This ideological frame has tended to overshadow his social analyses. While the *Republic* is much observed in the history of political thought, it is rather the reverse in the realm of social science.[2] — Today, of course, the gulf existing between

---

[1] 401b8–c3, here in Cornford's translation.

[2] Sociologists and social psychologists pay little attention as a rule to the times before Comte and Spencer. Cf. A. Menzel, *Griechische Soziologie*, in Akademie der Wissenschaften in Wien, Sitzungsberichte 216, Wien und Leipzig 1936, pp. 3 ff. Of note is the anti-historical attitude of A. W. Small, American pioneer of sociology as a branch of science, and leader of the Chicago school. Safeguarding scientific sociology from being mixed up with speculative social thought, Small advanced the view "that the chief significance of Plato for sociology is as a brilliant example of what sociology is not"; and, he adds, "if *method* is the chief test of sciences, then sociology and *The Republic* are as far apart as mechanics from magic", *AJS*, vol. XXX 1924/25, pp. 513–533, 683–702. In contrast we may refer to another sociologist, R. M. MacIver, who wrote, that the *Republic*, the greatest achievement of Hellenic thought, "was the first and greatest of sociological treatises". The *Republic* is a work on the theme of community. Plato saw, MacIver continues, that all the different factors (such as ethics, economics, politics, family life, education, philosophy, art, literature) are bound together within the unity of one common life. *Community. A Sociological Study*, London 1936, pp. 54–55. Other reactions against the anti-historical attitude are the works of E. S. Bogardus, *The Development of*

classical scholarship and the social sciences is easily explained. The student of the social sciences knows more about the Trobrianders, Nuer, and Hopi than about the Athenians, writes A. W. Gouldner, who has tried to bridge this gap.[1])

The *Republic* is about *dikaiosyne* and *adikia*, which are ethical terms. The prescriptive purpose of the dialogue is not compatible with the descriptive ideals of modern social science, and this should be observed. From the perspective of social psychology the richness of the *Republic* is explained by its dominating aspect that man is a social being and must be understood and described in relation to his society.[2]) We are given a social interpretation of man. From a modern point of view this interpretation deserves attention. Within the branches of social psychology and personality research an increased use of a social frame of reference is noted. The rapidly growing amount of literature on the subject of social structure and personality is an indication of this development. Observing *polis-psyche* as a *motif of ideas*, we are not in the first place asking what man is, but how he is formed and how he can be studied.

"It was a turning point in Greek culture and Greek thought", writes E. Cassirer, "when Plato interpreted the maxim 'Know thyself' in an entirely new sense. This interpretation introduced a problem which was not only alien to pre-Socratic thought but also went far beyond the limits of the Socratic method. In order to obey the demand of the Delphic god, in order to fulfil the religious duty of self-examination and self-knowledge, Socrates had approached the individual man. Plato

---

Social Thought, New York 1940, and H. Becker and H. E. Barnes, *Social Thought from Lore to Science*, New York. 1961 A more penetrating view of Plato's "greatness as a sociologist" is, however, given by K. R. Popper in his *The Open Society and its Enemies*, first ed. 1945.—That, however, the tradition instigated by Small still is alive, can be seen from more recent works such as H. Maus, *Geschichte der Soziologie*, pp. 1–120, in *Handbuch der Soziologie*, vol. I, Stuttgart 1955, and J. Madge, *The Origins of Scientific Sociology*, London 1963.

[1]) *Enter Plato. Classical Greece and the Origins of Social Theory*, London 1967, p. 4.

[2]) "Unter allen sozialpsychologischen Untersuchungen, die uns die antiken Schriftsteller überliefert haben, dürfte doch wohl jene die bedeutendste sein, welche Platon in den Büchern VIII und IX seiner 'Politeia' angestellt hat, . . . Dabei soll durchaus nicht verschwiegen werden, dass unser Philosoph vielfach konstruktiv vorgeht, dass ihm die Wirklichkeit, die sehr beschränkte Wirklichkeit der griechischen Staatenwelt, nur die Folie abgibt für ethisch-politische Postulate. Aber es bleibt noch immer eine ansehnliche Fülle von Beobachtungen übrig, die zur deskriptiven Soziologie gerechnet werden können". A. Menzel, p. 42.

recognized the limitations of the Socratic way of inquiry. In order to solve the problem, he declared, we must project it upon a larger plan. The phenomena we encounter in our individual experience are so various, so complicated and contradictory that we can scarcely disentangle them. Man is to be studied not in his individual life but in his political and social life."[1])

12. Survey of scholarship.

To avoid being tossed about between the various kinds of interpretations and opinions found in the vast literature on Plato and the *Republic* it is necessary to establish some genuine relationship with the dialogue itself. For better or for worse, the method of reading the *Republic* with the assistance of the *polis-psyche* motif is the outcome of my personal engagement with that text.

My understanding of what Plato says in the *Republic* is based on (a) an extended comparison between a number of translations (see the bibliography), *and* (b) a parallel reading of the Greek text, Burnet's edition.

It should be noted that I am not a philologist. The study which I have undertaken is a philosophical interpretation of Plato's thought as it is steered by the motif.

The short survey of previous research concerning the *polis-psyche* relationship which follows is, needless to say, incomplete. The *polis-psyche* complex of thought figures more or less in different kinds of works ranging from comprehensive expositions to highly specialized papers on some segment of the text or aspect of Plato's thinking. We are thus bound to find that Plato's views on society and man are commented upon from many points of view. This makes it extremely difficult to ascertain the results of earlier research on the *polis-psyche* complex.

(a) Comprehensive expositions

Surveys of this kind have an initial decision to make. Should Plato be discussed topic by topic, or dialogue by dialogue? The drawback with the former is that it divides up *polis* and *psyche* into separate branches

---

[1]) E. Cassirer, *An Essay on Man. An Introduction to a Philosophy of Human Culture*, New Haven 1945, p. 63.

of knowledge.[1]) However, the relationship between society and man is not ignored in works of this wide scope. L. Robin says that the comparison between the classes of the society and the parts of the soul commands the whole dialogue.[2]) And G. Grote, T. Gomperz, P. Friedländer and P. Shorey, to mention only a few authors of comprehensive works, all observe the analogy between the structure of the society and the structure of the soul. In Ueberweg-Praechter one finds an instructive table showing the similarity between *Stände/Tugenden* and *Seelenteile/Tugenden*.[3]) And in *RE*, to mention also an encyclopedia, the relationship between *polis* and *psyche* is noticed.[4])

(b) Commentaries and companions

In a comment on 368e–369a J. Adam says that Plato here "lays down the method to be pursued in the rest of the treatise, except in books

---

[1]) Plato's philosophy is "recalcitrant to topical classification", writes H. Cherniss. *Lustrum. Internationale Forschungsberichte aus dem Bereich des Klassischen Altertums.* 1959/4, 1960/5, Göttingen 1960–1961.—A good example of topical division is found in E. Zeller's *Die Philosophie der Griechen*, 2:1. Hildesheim, 1963. A number of myths and doctrines about man taken from the entire *Corpus Platonicum* is there reviewed. The speculative side of the topic dominates: man and the universe, man and eternity, the soul and anamnesis, metempsychosis and pure reason etc. Divorced from this treatment, we get, on the other side, an abstract of Plato's political and philosophical teaching about the state; *Bks VIII–IX* are

not reviewed. By such a topical treatment the passage to Plato's sociological reasoning on the borderland between society and man is blocked.—That this disposition to isolate *psyche* from *polis* is still dominant can be gathered from Cherniss' pragmatic classification in *Lustrum*; under the subject of *psychology* you find the following subdivisions: (a) the soul's constitution and immortality; (b) soul as epistemological subject; (c) soul as autokinetic cause; and (d) soul as desire and daemon.

[2]) *La Pensée Grecque et les Origines de l'Esprit Scientifique*, Paris 1963, p. 231.

[3]) K. Praechter, *Die Philosophie des Altertums*, Ueberweg, vol. I, Berlin 1926, p. 275. See also the arrangement by E. Voegelin, based on Praechter, in *Order and History*, vol. III, *Plato and Aristotle*, 1957, p. 109.

[4]) *S.v. Plato*, by H. Leisegang, who writes: "Die nun folgenden Erörterungen über das *Werden und Wesen der Polis* sind nur eine Hilfskonstruktion zur Lösung des gestellten ethischen Problems. Es handelt sich also weder um eine Utopie, eine, 'Behandlung von Staatsproblemen in dichterischer Form' . . ., noch um einen für die Verwirklichung bestimmten Verfassungsentwurf . . . Das zeigt schon die Überleitung 368D." *RE*, 2455.

V–VII, which are professedly a 'digression', and X, which is of the nature of an epilogue. At each successive stage in the exposition of his subject, Plato reminds us more or less explicitly of the method which he here proposes to follow."[1])

In addition to Adam's indispensable work there is the monumental Jowett-Campbell, *Plato's Republic*, vols. I–III, Oxford 1894, and the commentaries supplied by O. Apelt, F. M. Cornford and P. Shorey to their translations of the *Republic*.

Another kind of running commentary is B. Bosanquet, *A Companion to Plato's Republic*, London 1895.[2]) *Bks VIII–IX* are according to Bosanquet related to the end of *Bk IV* by the method of negative verification. R. L. Nettleship's *Lectures on the Republic of Plato* appeared in 1897.[3]) The reasoning of the dialogue is here pursued from beginning to end. The postulate upon which the *polis-psyche* method rests, writes Nettleship, "is that all the institutions of society, class organization, law, religion, art, and so on, are ultimately products of the human soul, an inner principle of life which works itself out" in the outward shapes of the society. Actually, he says, the correspondence between *polis* and *psyche* is not an analogy; Plato's position is "that the life of the state is the life of the men composing it, as manifested in a way comparatively easy to observe".[4]) — *Scholia Platonica* bears witness to the fact that recognition of the correspondence between *polis* and *psyche* is of a long standing.[5])

(c) *Monographs on the Republic*

During the last quarter of the nineteenth century the so called *Platonische Frage* was a matter for heated debate. The discussion took on the line, it seems, that Plato might well have inserted complementary arguments in some later edition, but that he was, on the other hand, a

---

[1]) *The Republic of Plato*, vols. I–II, 2 nd. ed. with an introduction by D. A. Rees, Cambridge 1963; first ed. 1902.

[2]) It was inspired by the appearance of W. Leaf's *Companion to the Iliad*, and is adapted to Davies and Vaughan's translation, first published 1852.

[3]) First published in *Philosophical Lectures and Remains*, vol. II.

[4]) Nettleship, pp. 67–68.

[5]) Cf. notes to 435b, 440e. *Philological Monographs* published by the American Philological Association Nr. VIII 1938 ed. by W. C. Greene.

great deal more systematic than was maintained by A. Krohn and his school of opinion.[1]

Nettleship, we saw, disapproved of the term analogy.[2] This term has survived, however, to denote the similarity between city and soul in the *Republic*. N. R. Murphy devotes a chapter of his book to this topic. It is an illustrative analogy.[3] The comparison of the city with a person does not mean that the parts of the soul are 'personified'. Nor does it imply, if one reverses the relationship, that the citizens lose their personality and, absorbed by their social functions, are 'depersonified'. The fact that states and persons are comparable in some respects provides no basis for extending the comparison to other respects in which it is clear to everyone that states and persons differ. "There is then a resemblance between soul and city in these respects that in each there is (a) a ruling element in which its wisdom is located; (b) an element of force, energy, and spirit, which provides the ingredient of courage, . . .; (c) a πλῆθος of 'first-order' activities which provides the means and material conditions of its life and enriches it with pleasures."[4] To assert more similarities is not warranted by the structure of the analogy, concludes Murphy.

I. M. Crombie, *An Examination of Plato's Doctrines*, vols I–II, London 1962–1963, belongs to the comprehensive works which discuss Plato's doctrines topic by topic. The first volume is, however, devoted to *Plato on Man and Society* and contains a lengthy review of the *Republic*. A just city "means one which preserves the proper relationships between its citizens, rather than one which acts justly towards other cities. It will emerge later that right behaviour towards others depends on

---

[1] "Die Zeiten", writes M. Pohlenz summing up the discussion, "wo die Erklärer von Platos Staat ihre Aufgabe darin sahen, überall Unstimmigkeiten und Widersprüche aufzuzeigen und daraufhin das Werk in möglichst viele Stücke zu zerreissen, die ebenso viele Stadien platonischer Entwicklung darstellen sollten, dürfen wir heute als überwunden betrachten. Campbell, Gomperz, Räder, Ritter u.a. haben gezeigt, dass die meisten Anstösse, die man genommen hatte, durch bewusste künstlerische Absicht zu erklären sind." *Aus Platos Werdezeit*, Berlin 1913, p. 207.

[2] Also H. W. B. Joseph, *Essays in Ancient & Modern Philosophy*, Oxford 1935, has thought the term analogy less suitable, p. 82.—Perhaps both Nettleship and Joseph were thinking of analogy not as an expository device, or as a model, but as primarily a vehicle of deriving conclusions.

[3] *The Interpretation of Plato's Republic*, Oxford 1951, p. 89.

[4] Murphy, pp. 69–70.

right internal relationships (442–3), and this will be applied to the individual as well as to the city. Essentially the just man is the man with a certain internal adjustment, from which adjustment just behaviour flows."[1])

R. C. Cross and A. D. Woozley also touch upon the *polis-psyche* comparison in their book on the *Republic*. Socrates does not use it to make analogical conclusions. "His procedure is far bolder and less self-critical. . . he takes it as unquestioned that justice in a city is the same as justice in a man, and therefore there is nothing doubtful about examining the large-scale model straightaway.[2]") As an introduction to the procedure this is unsatisfactory, but it becomes less surprising as the *Republic* proceeds; Plato "was well aware both of the presupposition, and of the need to argue for it. Furthermore, he does later argue for it (435e), when he maintains that the individual man must have the same characteristics as the city, for otherwise the city itself could not possess them. . ."[3])—Cross and Woozley bestow, like Murphy and Crombie, slight interest upon *Bks VIII–IX*, the extended analogies.

(d) Special aspects of the Republic

The threefold partition of the soul is according to W. Lutoslawski introduced "in order to show the parallelism between the three classes in a state. . . and the parts of an individual soul. This analogy between the individual and the state, which can boast of such a long history after it had been invented by Plato, is not the idea of a young Socratic pupil, but of the Master of the Academy, and is a consequence of the theory of ideas."[4]—That the middle books throw new light upon the *polis-psyche* analogy is maintained by H. J. Krämer.[5]) K. Gaiser has stressed the place

---

[1]) Crombie, vol. I, p. 89.

[2]) *Plato's Republic. A Philosophical Commentary*. London 1964, p. 76.

[3]) Cross and Woozley, p. 77.

[4]) *The Origin and Growth of Plato's Logic*, London 1905, p. 281.

[5]) *Arete bei Platon und Aristoteles*, Heidelberg 1959. Krämer writes: "Die knappe Vergegenwärtigung der Strukturelemente des politischen Organismus hat gezeigt, dass dieser Staat mit seiner Gliederung nach einzelnen ἀρεταί und seinem Drang zur Einheit in der Vielheit dem Gefüge des inneren Menschen unmittelbar zur Seite tritt. Die Bezeichnung auch des Staates als κόσμος (506, 540) hat sich bei genauerer Betrachtung im einzelnen als sinnvoll erwiesen. Dass das transzendente παράδειγμα für Individuum und Staat zusammenfällt (500D ff., 592B, vorbereitend 435A f.), stimmt mit der Strukturverwandtschaft beider überein. Der κόσμος-τάξις-Seinslehre ist damit ein neuer Bereich endgültig erschlossen." pp. 115–116.

of the analogy *kosmos-polis-man* in Plato's systematic theory of history.[1])

P. Grenet has provided an inventory of Plato's analogies. One purpose of analogy is to serve as a vehicle for going beyond the limits of our actual experiences. The method of the two texts is, however, used to explicate objects which are difficult to apprehend, "même s'ils sont donnés dans notre expérience".[2])

R. Robinson has also examined Plato's use of analogies. He finds them frequently employed but little discussed in the middle dialogues to which the *Republic* belongs. Robinson observes three analogical complexes in the *Republic*, among them the great one between the city and the man. This analogy is itself presented by means of another analogy: big letters/small letters. The passage of the two texts *suggests* the analogy between city and man; the term analogy is not used. "The passage regards analogy as a method of discovery and not also as a method of proof or argument."[3]) Robinson notes, furthermore, that the city is not an actual city but one constructed in thought. Plato, thinks Robinson, ought to have selected actual cities that were commonly reputed to be just. "No doubt he might beg the question in deciding which actual cities were just; but he begs it far more definitively in constructing his own."[4])

G.E.R. Lloyd draws attention to the passage 434e–435a, where the need is expressed for testing in the individual what is found in the city.[5])

From analogy it is but a short step to the topic of Plato's metaphors. An instrument for access to this rich field of study is provided by P. Louis, *Les Métaphores de Platon*, Rennes 1945. To this may be added C. J. Classen, *Sprachliche Deutung als Triebkraft Platonischen und Sokratischen Philosophierens*, München 1959, especially the third chapter, *Erweiterung von Metaphern für die Seele zu Gleichnissen und ihr Einfluss auf Platons Psychologie*.

---

[1]) K. Gaiser, *Platons Ungeschriebene Lehre*, Stuttgart 1963, cf. pp. 260 ff.

[2]) *Les Origines de L'Analogie Philosophique dans les Dialogues de Platon*, Paris 1948, p. 53.

[3]) *Plato's Earlier Dialectic*, 2 nd. ed., Oxford 1953, pp. 211. ff.

[4]) Robinson, pp. 211–212.

[5]) *Polarity and Analogy. Two Types of Argumentation in Early Greek Thought*. Cambridge 1966, p. 397. Cf. also H. J. Krämer, who writes: "Der Arete-Begriff von 500c kennzeichnet nicht nur das normative Gebilde des 4. Buches als κόσμος und τάξις, sondern auch das entartete im 8. und 9. entsprechend als ἀκοσμία und ἀταξία," p. 116.

50

Polis and *psyche* are the two components of our motif. Each of them can be studied as a topic, and there is copious literature on both. Background-information about the nature and life of the Greek *polis* is obtainable from many sources. Particularly may be mentioned. V. Ehrenberg, *The Greek State.* E. Barker,[1]) A. Verdross-Drossberg,[2]) T. A. Sinclair,[3]) and H. Ryffel[4]) throw light on Plato's political theory from the general aspect of ancient political thought. Ideological criticism is supplied by many authors.[5]) As, however, the *polis-psyche* motif is conducive to Plato's social psychological method I have refrained from taking up the topic of politics.

Graph C. CENTRAL POSITION OF TRIPARTITE PSYCHE

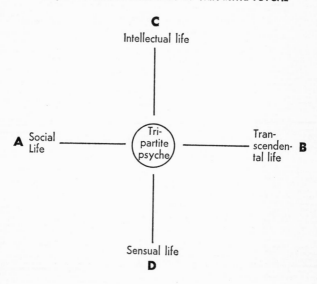

[1]) *Greek Political Theory*, London (many editions).

[2]) *Grundlinien der antiken Rechts- und Staatsphilosophie*, Wien 1946.

[3]) *A History of Greek Political Thought*, London 1961.

[4]) *ΜΕΤΑΒΟΛΗ ΠΟΛΙΤΕΙΩΝ Der Wandel der Staatsverfassungen*, Bern 1949.

[5]) Exponents of different kinds of ideological criticism are K. R. Popper, A. D. Winspear (*The Genesis of Plato's Thought*, New York 1956), and E. A. Havelock (*The Liberal Temper in Greek Politics*, London 1957). For a defence there is R. B. Levinson (*In Defense of Plato*, Harvard, Cambridge, 1953). Se further R. Bambrough, *Plato's Modern Friends and Enemies*, in *Plato, Popper and Politics*, ed. by R. Bambrough, Cambridge, 1967

The soul is subject to inspection in the *Republic*. Piloted by the analogy we come to the topic of the tripartite *psyche*. The central importance of *psyche* is illustrated by *Graph C*.

In the *Republic* the *A-aspect* dominates *Bks II–V, VIII–IX* 576b10; the *B-aspect* is stressed in *Bk X* 608c1–621d3; the *C-aspect* is conspicuous from *Bk V* 471c4 to the end of *VII*; and the *D-aspect* is discussed from *IX* 576b to the end of that book.—We are primarily engaged in the *A-aspect*, which is concerned with how—within the framework of social life—the three parts of the soul collaborate or conflict with each other and thus constitute different patterns of personality.

How is man influenced by other men? This is a topic belonging to the A-aspect. Education is one mode of influencing people. To a large extent the *Republic* is a book concerned with human character-building, writes W. Jaeger. To Plato "all education is spiritually a function of the community, whether it is 'free' or officially directed by the state. . . It is actually the influence of the state and society that educates men and makes them into whatever society wants. Public meetings, law-courts, the theatres, the army, and all other assemblies where an excited crowd applauds or boos the speeches of an orator—these are the places where men of every age are moulded."[1] Jaeger notes the reciprocity of man and society[2]; the spirit of a constitution "has been created and given

---

[1] *Paideia*, vol. II, p. 269.

[2] *Paideia*, II, p. 323.—These two ways of influence (from *polis* to *psyche*, and from *psyche* to *polis*) are in our study acknowledged by means of the motif and the anti-motif. Which form of influence is prior to the other in the *Republic*? This is a much-discussed question. K. Praechter writes: "Dass (die Annahme von Seelenteilen) aus der Dreiteilung der Staatsgemeinde hergeleitet ist und nicht umgekehrt diese aus ihr, steht schon durch den Vorgang der politisch-ökonomischen Trichotomie des Hippodamos . . . ausser Zweifel . . .", p. 274. A similar opinion is given by E. Topitsch, who thinks that Plato has offered a sociomorph interpretation of the soul. "Dass es sich bei der dort entwickelten Lehre von den drei Seelenteilen nicht um eine originale psychologische Theorie handelt, sondern um eine ziemlich künstliche Übertragung eines vorausgesetzten sozialen Schemas auf das Seelenleben . . . ist bereits vor geraumer Zeit erkannt worden"; already E. Pfleiderer thought so, writes Topitsch, *Vom Ursprung und Ende der Metaphysik*, Wien 1958, pp. 124 ff.—The opposite view has of course not been without defenders. Lately A. Graeser has maintained the priority of the psychical structure. It is true that *polis* is employed; "Doch entspricht dieser Duktus nur der schriftstellerischen Absicht (369c8), den Grundgedanken zunächst im grossen, also am Beispiel einer Polis zu exemplifizieren. Die Struktur erhält somit grössere Transparenz: Das

its special character by the type of men who have made the state that suits them. This does not exclude the fact that the type of the community, once it takes form, usually stamps the individuals living under it with its own mark." In this way "the perfect man can be shaped only within the perfect state; and vice versa, to construct such a state, we must discover how to make such men".[1])

J. Wild[2]), N. Almberg[3]), R. W. Hall)[4], and H. D. Rankin[5]) have all written books more or less concerned with the topic of man and society. Almberg explains Plato's differential psychology and the psychology of types; in doing so he has found the works of W. Stern (*Die Differentielle Psychologie*) and E. Spranger (*Lebensformen*) helpful.—For more sociologically oriented treatments of the *Republic* I refer to the books by Popper, Menzel and Gouldner above mentioned.

It is commonly agreed, I think, that the *Republic* reaches its summit with *Bks VI–VII*.[6]) The contrast between the dialectic thought of these books and the less exalted thinking of *Bks II–IV, VIII–IX* is glaring. *Bks VI–VII* are often taken as the touchstone by which the whole of the *Republic* should be judged; Plato's scientific method is that of dialectics. In his investigation of Plato's myths, P. Frutiger implies that most of the thinking in II–IV and VIII–IX should be regarded as mythical.[7])

---

kleinere und logisch frühere wird sich aus dem Analogen heraus interpretieren lassen." *Probleme der platonischen Seelenteilungslehre*, München 1969, p. 13, n. 1; published in *Zetemata*, Heft 47. See also Adam, vol. I, p, 227.

[1]) *Paideia*, vol. II, p. 259.

[2]) *Plato's Theory of Man*, Cambridge Mass. 1946.

[3]) *Till Platons Differentiella Psykologi*, Lund 1946. Lunds Universitets Årsskrift N. F. Avd. 1, Bd 43, Nr 1.

[4]) *Plato and the Individual*, The Hague 1963.

[5]) *Plato and the Individual*, London 1969.

[6]) See for instance H. Gauss, *Philosophischer Handkommentar zu den Dialogen Platos*, vol. II:2, Bern 1958, p. 119. See also O. Utermöhlen, *Die Bedeutung der Ideenlehre für die platonische Politeia*, Heidelberg 1967, p. 9.

[7]) Taking the term myth in a very broad sense "nous appelons donc mythique—outre les récits nettement légendaires, mais à l'exclusion des allégories—tout ce que le philosophe expose, soit d'une façon symbolique, soit en marge de la 'science' véritable et sans l'aide de la dialectique, c'est-à-dire comme une probabilité, non comme une certitude". *Les Mythes de Platon*, Paris 1930, p. 37.—Thus Frutiger singles out as mythical the foundational work of the model *polis*, *Bk II* 369b–374d; the reasoning about the tripartite soul, *Bk IV* 434e–441c; and the comparison between the decomposed cities and their corresponding personalities, *Bks VIII–IX* 545c–576b.

(e) Papers on particular sections or subjects of the Republic

Consulting the bibliographical literature one finds that the continued discussion on the meaning and interpretation of various passages of the *Republic* has been conducted in journals of different kinds.[1]) M. B. Foster and J. D. Mabbott started in the *Mind* 1937 a discussion on the question of justice, class and individual in the *Republic*.[2]) R. Demos and R. S. Bluck continued the debate in the *Classical Quarterly* 1957– 1959.[3]) F. A. Wilford, R. W. Hall, J. B. Skemp and R. Hoerber next contributed to the discussion, the forum being the *Phronesis* 1959–1961.[4]) In 1963 D. Sachs published an article in the *Philosophical Review* about a fallacy in the *Republic*, which was answered by R. Demos in the same periodical 1964.[5]) Again, in 1965–1969 the question of mistake, and the topic of justice in individual and state have been debated; C. Kirwan, R. G. Mulgan and J. B. Skemp in the *Phronesis*.[6]) Among other articles which are more or less concerned with the *polis-psyche* relationship can be mentioned J. P. Maguire in the *Classical Journal* 1964/65, and J. Schiller in the *Journal of the History of Ideas* 1968.[7]) Further G. F. Hourani and G. B. Kerferd have discussed Thrasymachus' defi-

---

—A discussion on of Frutiger's approach is found in P-M. Schuhl, *Études sur la Fabulation Platonicienne*, Paris 1947, pp. 27 ff.

[1]) The bibliographies by *Engelmann-Preuss, Klussmann, Lambrino* and *Marouzeau* cover the period 1700–1924. The content of the articles are indicated in two ways: (a) by reference to portions of the text according to the Stephanus apparatus; and (b) by defining the topic. (a) enumerates of about 125 particular passages from the *Republic*. Correlating these passages with the explicit utterances of our *TABLE 2*, one does not get the impression that the *polis-psyche* method has attracted much attention.—The above-mentioned systematic bibliographies are continued annually in *L' Année Philologique*.

[2]) Foster, *A Mistake of Plato's in the Republic*; Mabbott, *Is Plato's Republic Utilitarian?*

[3]) Demos, *Paradoxes in Plato's Doctrine of the Ideal State;* Bluck, *Plato's 'Ideal' State*.

[4]) Wilford, *The Status of Reason in Plato's Psychology;* Hall, *Justice and the Individual in the Republic;* Skemp, *Comment on Communal and Individual Justice in the Republic;* Hoerber, *More on Justice in the Republic*.

[5]) Sachs, *A Fallacy in Plato's Republic;* Demos, *A Fallacy in Plato's Republic?*

[6]) Kirwan, *Glaucon's Challenge;* Mulgan, *Individual and Collective Virtues in the Republic;* Skemp, *Individual and Civic Virtue in the Republic*.

[7]) Schiller, *Just Men and Just Acts in Plato's Republic;* Maguire, *The Individual and the Class in Plato's Republic*.

nition of justice in the *Phronesis* 1962 and 1964 .[1]) Needless to say, these discussions have been of great value for my study. For a list of the literary tools employed I refer to the bibliography in the end of the book.

13 Prospects of a new study

Though the *polis-psyche* complex of thought has attracted much attention, there has not been as yet a systematic examination of how *polis* functions in relation to *psyche* in the total argumentation of the *Republic*. Accurate observations and valuable comments abound in previous treatments. There is also a growing tendency in the last two decades to observe more of the interplay between the three components—individual, class and society—in the reasoning of the dialogue. But as these observations often emanate from different approaches, and often yield contradictory results, they do not constitute a satisfactory line of approach for a systematic study of the subject we have chosen. We have therefore had to acquire an operative basis for our undertaking, and to construct a motif which is instrumental to our purpose.

Perhaps this study can contribute somewhat to the technique of intrinsic text-interpretation. One can also cherish a hope that the establishment of the *polis-psyche* motif may add a little towards more cumulative research on the subject of man and society in Plato's thinking, or even in ancient thought generally. In this way the construction of the *polis-psyche* motif might be of interest also in its capacity as a motif of ideas in the Western tradition of social thought.

Having surveyed the literary resources, let us also throw a glance on those conceptual instruments which were devised for our special purpose.

First we may mention the concepts of *keyword* and *explicit utterance*. The former serves as an indicator, the latter as a motif-bearer.

Secondly there are the concepts of *motif* and *anti-motif*. Together they direct our attention and provide connections between kindred but detached discourses, focussing our observation all the time on the *polis-psyche* relationship. To bring out clearer the systematic use which

---

[1]) Hourani, *Thrasymachus' Definition of Justice in Plato's Republic;* Kerferd, *Thrasymachus and Justice: a Reply;* Kerferd had earlier published an article on this subject in *Durham University Journal*, n.s. IX, 1947/48.

Plato makes of *polis*, we employ three *modes* of the motif. They are characterized as *directive, executive* and *conclusive*.

Thirdly, in examining further the systematic character of the *Republic*, we have made a distinction between three kinds of the *polis-psyche* analogy: the *established analogy* concerned with the nature of *dikaiosyne* in society and man; the *extended analogies* covering the four main forms of *adikia* existing in society and man; and the *general analogy* which embraces both the mentioned types of analogies, and offers a wider perspective on Plato's social philosophy such as we find it in the *Republic*.

Fourthly, it should be noted that our undertaking to *review* the *Republic* supplements our engagement with keywords, explicit utterances, and analogy in serving to lay open to the reader our interpretation of the text, so that he can check our treatment of the *Republic* and see for himself the contextual bearing.

Finally, in the face of all that has been written on the *Republic*, one may well ask if there is any particular observation in this study that has not been previously propounded at some time or other. To cope with this kind of healthy scepticism I take refuge in a quotation:

One does not expect novel cards when playing so traditional a game; it is the hand which matters.[1])

---

[1]) I. A. Richards, *Principles of Literary Criticism*, London 1960, p. 1.

PART TWO

THE REQUEST AND THE APPROACH

CHAPTER II
PROOIMION
(Bk I:327a1–354c3)

1. Conversation with Cephalus

328c5-331d9. *Polis* (city) and *tropos* (character) are mentioned already in the introductory conversation with Cephalus. The fame of a citizen may be related to the greatness of his city, but man's happiness is dependent on the nature of his character, 329d–330a; if we are well-ordered and good-tempered (κόσμιοι καὶ εὔκολοι) the burden of age is quite tolerable. Wealth makes life easier, but its importance must not be exaggerated. Its chief merit is that it helps one to avoid dishonest living. The feeling of righteousness, instrumental to peace of mind, turns out to be a more enduring pleasure than those of the flesh.—In a few words, this is the sentiment of old Cephalus.

Dike and *adikia* are another important pair of concepts to observe.[1] They represent the rival forces of right and wrong. At 331c2 the key-term *dikaiosyne* appears for the first time in the *Republic*. It is, from now on (varied with τὸ δίκαιον), to occur often.

2. Discussion with Polemarchus

331e1-336a10. What is *dikaiosyne*? The task of defining it is handed over to Polemarchus from his father.[2] The young man refers to a saying by Simonides, that doing right is to give each man his due, i.e. what is appropriate to him.[3] Defending the proposition he takes it to mean

---

[1] 330d8–e1, "the first casual allusion to the subject of the *Republic*". Adam, vol. I, p. 9.

[2] What was Plato's object in first introducing Cephalus as a great lover of discourse (328c5–d6), and then rapidly eliminating him? The question is discussed by J. T. Kakridis, *The Part of Cephalus in Plato's Republic*, Eranos, vol. XLVI 1948, pp. 35 ff.

[3] 331e3–4, . . . τὸ τὰ ὀφειλόμενα ἑκάστῳ ἀποδιδόναι δίκαιόν ἐστι.

that friends should be helped and enemies harmed,[1]) which seems to have been the conventional opinion.[2])—This argument is, however, not to be pursued here.[3]) Let us only observe that the context is the individual's way of life in his relation to friends and enemies. To analyse *dikaiosyne* within the framework of friends and enemies only, seems a little strange to the modern reader; such a dichotomy excludes the greater part of the population, i.e. all those whom I do not know personally, and, being neither my friends nor my enemies, are nevertheless entitled to fair treatment. To the ancient man, living in his small-sized *polis*, the reference to personal relations was probably more inclusive than we tend to think.[4]) Besides, the term 'friends' can of course mean different things, in politics for example, it may be interpreted as helping one's own class and harming other classes.[5])

The short conversation with Polemarchus ends with some conclusions about the contrary effects of *dikaiosyne* and *adikia*. They differ as heat does from cold. Doing harm cannot be the business of the just man, but of his opposite, the unjust man, 335d3–12. The conclusions are provisional, but there is an underlying belief that *dikaiosyne* is something active and useful, belonging properly to the human sphere (ἀνθρωπεία ἀρετή, 335c4). The opinion that it is right to help one's friends and harm one's enemies does not, Socrates suspects, emanate from some really wise man, but from some rich and self-asserting man of the despotic type, 336a1–7. Our attention soon is directed to this kind of man.

3. Encounter with Thrasymachus

336b1-347e7. With the entry of Thrasymachus into the discussion, the perspective changes from the sphere of private behaviour to that of political. Another mark of difference is that the notion of *adikia* increases in importance. It is of interest to see how these changes occur.

The contribution of Thrasymachus is that right is in the interest of the stronger.[6]) As the term 'stronger' is ambiguous, Socrates asks him to clarify what he means.[7]) Thrasymachus then refers to the different political constitutions: tyrannies, democracies and aristocracies, 338d7–8.

---

[1]) 332d5–6, ... ἡ τοῖς φίλοις τε καὶ ἐχθροῖς ὠφελίας τε καὶ βλάβας ἀποδιδοῦσα.

[2]) Commonplace in Greek morality. Nettleship p. 17.

[3]) The main steps of the argument is recorded by Krämer, pp. 44–46.

[4]) Cf. Apelt, note to 332, pp. 432–433.

[5]) Cf. A. W. H. Adkins, *Merit and Responsibility*, Oxford 1960, p. 223.

[6]) 338c1–2, τὸ δίκαιον οὐκ ἄλλο τι ἢ τὸ τοῦ κρείττονος συμφέρον.

[7]) 338d5–6, ἀλλὰ σαφέστερον εἰπὲ τί λέγεις.

In each state (338d10), he says, the power is in the hands of the rulers, and each ruling body uses the power to further its own interests.[1] In this respect, rulers everywhere do the same thing. And that 'might is right' holds true not only in politics but also in private life, as, for example, in business. In politics, however, the truth and force of the proposition is best studied. The easiest way to this knowledge is to observe the operations of the successful tyrant.[2]

With this turn in the dialogue *polis* is introduced as a relevant and facilitating object for the study of *dikaiosyne*. But is 'ruling' in the interest of the rulers?

Socrates thinks that ruling aims at the advantage of the ruled. To Thrasymachus this is sheer nonsense. Bringing up the analogy between shepherd/sheep and ruler/ruled he asks if one really can mean that sheep are tended for the benefit of the sheep themselves; the genuine ruler always thinks of what advantage he can get out of his human sheep, 343b1–c1.

There is a Thrasymachian programme for the study of power (343d1–344b1): observe the operations of the rulers; notice the positive relations between policy and prosperity; watch to whose advantage the laws work; see the adaptations of the ruled to the interest of the rulers; and focus your attention especially on the tyrant.

This reference to tyranny, as an illustrative example, foreshadows what is later to come; the challenge to study despotism is dealt with in *Bks VIII–IX*, and the technique to compare extremes gets the status subsequently of a calculated method. The lines indicated by Thrasymachus sound empirical enough, but he seems to have overstrained the evidence. There may also be other motives for political activity, says Socrates. Good men may be forced into politics by fear of being ruled by men worse than themselves, 347b5–e6. The good do not go to politics to enrich themselves. But to Thrasymachus conventional *dikaiosyne* functions in another man's interest, 343c3–4. To promote one's own interest, one must practise *adikia*. Thus it happens that the analysis of injustice attracts much interest.—*Graph* D below shows the frequency of the *dike-* and the *adikia*-words in *Bk I*.

Traditionally the *Republic* is reported to be about *dikaiosyne*. But the high frequency of *adikia* words heightens our attention to the role played by *adikia* in connection with the analysis of *dikaiosyne*. As a matter of fact, the *polis-psyche* motif is expanded by a continued discus-

---

[1] Cf. *TABLE 2*, nr 1, p. 244 below.
[2] *TABLE 2*, nr. 2.

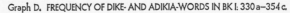

Number of
occurrences

Graph D. FREQUENCY OF DIKE- AND ADIKIA-WORDS IN BK I: 330 a–354 c.

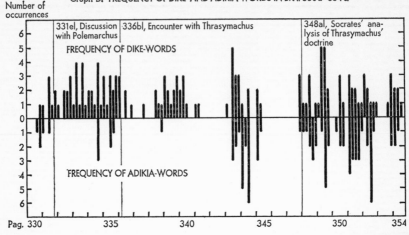

Pag. 330   335   340   345   350   354

sion about this polarity.[1]) The examination of *adikia* in the section 348a1–352d6 can be considered as an indirect approach towards *dikaiosyne*.[2]) Let us therefore recount this part of the dialogue.

4. Socrates' preliminary view

348a1-354a11. Thrasymachus has been commending a creative sort of *adikia* resultant in power and wealth.[3]) In defence of his thesis, he resorts to the notion of a grand and complete injustice.[4]) The unjust man is stronger, freer, and more commanding than the just one.[5]) Wisdom and forethought now take sides with *adikia*, and their opposites go with *dikaiosyne*, 348e2–3. It is a question of advanced *adikia*, not

---

[1]) Friedländer with good reasons calls this polarity a basic conflict, *Plato* vol. III, London 1969, pp. 70–71.

[2]) There is here an indication of a view dominating the whole of the rest of the *Rep.* Nettleship, p. 41. So also Adam, vol. I, p. 56. And Bosanquet, thinking of the *dikaiosyne-adikia* relation, says that "the corroborative value of negative instances is plainly present to Plato's mind in this discussion . . . ", p. 61.

[3]) 344a1, . . . τὸν μεγάλα δυνάμενον πλεονεκτεῖν; cf. 348d5–6, . . . οἷοί τε ἀδικεῖν, πόλεις τε καὶ ἔθνη δυνάμενοι ἀνθρώπων ὑφ' ἑαυτοὺς ποιεῖσθαι.

[4]) 344a4, τὴν τελεωτάτην ἀδικίαν; 344c2 τὴν ὅλην ἀδικίαν; 348b9 τὴν τελέαν ἀδικίαν. —Thucydides, writing of the great inter-state war, gives many examples of the might-is-right principle. "His reports supply the necessary background to an outburst like that of Thrasymachus in the *Republic*, and throw light on the current interpretation of such conceptions as human nature, law, justice, advantage or interest, necessity, and their mutual relations." Guthrie, *HGP*, vol. III, p. 85.

[5]) 344c4–6, οὕτως, ὦ Σώκρατες, καὶ ἰσχυρότερον καὶ ἐλευθεριώτερον καὶ δεσποτικώτερον ἀδικία δικαιοσύνης ἐστὶν . . .

happy-go-lucky thefts or robberies. This is the Thrasymachian super-man theory in politics.

Attacking the notion of *complete adikia* (349c ff) Socrates starts from the point of view that the unjust man has an unrestricted desire, invariably subjecting him to a competition for dominance. Wherever he is (being with just or unjust men) he always claims more than is his due. So *adikia* generates discord. Without *dikaiosyne* to promote co-operation, any body of men is disabled, whether the agent is a *polis*, an army, or a band of robbers. *Adikia* and *dikaiosyne* invariably produce opposite results; the one has to do with conflict, hate and war, the other with harmony and friendship, 351d4–6. Wherever two men, citizens or slaves, are bent on unjust action they will become enemies, 351d8–e4. Then Socrates jumps to the conclusion that this principle applies also to the single individual;[1] in man himself (ἐν ἑνὶ) *adikia* has the same invariable effect: πρῶτον μὲν ἀδύνατον αὐτὸν πράττειν ποιήσει στασιάζοντα καὶ οὐχ ὁμονοοῦντα αὐτὸν ἑαυτῷ, ἔπειτα ἐχθρὸν καὶ ἑαυτῷ καὶ τοῖς δικαίοις,[2] 352a6–8. Thus *adikia* breaks up the inner man so that he loses the unity of his personality.—The section 351e9–352a8 should be observed because here we meet for the first time in the *Republic* the notion of the disorganized self.[3] The heart of the matter is *pleonexia*, the blind and limitless desire for gratification, which fires the machinery of anti-social dynamics in both society and man. The weakness of *adikia*, we may conjecture, is that it does not supply confidence and a reason for long-term co-operation. *Adikia* belongs to the sphere of competition and self-interest. Thus, we may hold, it is a *contradictio in adjecto* to speak of complete *adikia*, cf. 352c3–8. Because it is disfunctional it has no place in the ordered activities of a social whole.[4] If there is any degree of concord in social relations it must be

---

[1] It has been observed by various authors that this assumption of the similarity between societies or groups of men and the inner state of the individual stands unsupported, as Plato does not here discuss the inner structure of man. Cf. E. L. Harrison, *A red herring in Plato's Republic*, Eranos, 60/1962, pp. 122 ff.

[2] About the development of the word *homonoia* towards an individualistic concept, meaning to be in harmony with oneself, cf. R. Höistad, *Cynic Hero and Cynic King*, Uppsala 1948, pp. 107–110. See also Guthrie, *HGP*, vol. III, pp. 149–150.

[3] Cf. *TABLE 2*, nr. 4.

[4] "Hier gipfelt die Gedankenfolge (351e–352a): die ἀδικία behält ihre eigentümliche Wirkkraft ... Sie lockert die Kohäsion, löst zentrifugale Bewegungen aus: στάσις, μάχη, μῖσος, ἔχϑρα, διαφορά, setzt so das Gebilde — sei es Staat, sei es Individuum — zu sich selbst in Widerspruch und hemmt es in der natürlichen Entfaltung seiner Kräfte ..." Krämer, p. 52.

due to the power of *dikaiosyne*, which in this way becomes another name for social cohesion. At 353d3–e8 there is an important assertion about *psyche:* the special function of the soul of man is to rule his life, an undertaking that should be done with the help of *dikaiosyne*.[1]) Finally Socrates relates *dikaiosyne* to *eudaimonia*, and *adikia* to the opposite, 353e10–354a9.

5. *Conclusions and observations*

We have met a number of preliminary attempts to say what *dikaiosyne* is. Most important for the following investigation is the discussion with Thrasymachus.[2]) In the course of this dispute the terms *dikaiosyne* and *adikia* come to predicate agents instead of acts.[3]) Also the two components of our motif, *polis* and *psyche*, are foreshadowed; as for the occurrence of these terms (and other words of similar meaning) I refer to *TABLE 1*, p. 235 ff.

As a proem to the manifest establishment of the *polis-psyche* motif in *Bk II*, the predication "unjust state" (πόλις ἄδικος, 351b1), analogous to "unjust person", should be noticed. To speak about a just or an unjust state, as we do in ordinary language about a just or an unjust person, is in the *Republic* not merely a matter of linguistic habit. Socrates indicates that any agent in the human field exemplifies, in its behaviour, either the ground-pattern of order or disorder. A just *polis* denotes a state where the social forces make for unity. Analogously, the same balance of powers is found in the just person.

Bk I is important for the understanding of the *polis-psyche* motif. *Dikaiosyne* and *adikia* are introduced as a preliminary to the double

---

[1]) Joseph has noted that this "is the first emergence in the *Republic* of the notion that there is a constitution in the soul of any man comparable to what may exist in any community of men, so that justice and injustice are the same in a man and in a community, and according to the degree in which either prevails in them different and corresponding types of man and community arise". *Essays in Ancient and Modern Philosophy*, Oxford 1935, p. 38.

[2]) As for the question, What is the ethical standpoint of Thrasymachus? see Guthrie *HGP*, vol. III, pp. 91 ff, and the literature there mentioned.

[3]) Murphy emphasizes the distinction between (a) the justice of the agent (city or man), which is the virtuous condition in that agent, and (b) the justice of its acts, referring to the rightness of the acts themselves, p. 71.

text examination begun later.[1]) The discourse on *adikia* is especially valuable. While *dikaiosyne* is completely re-argued in *Bks II–IV*, *adikia* is not fully treated until *Bks VIII–IX*.—This Platonic view about the antithesis between the destructive force of *adikia* and the co-ordinating power of *dikaiosyne* has no doubt deep roots in the Greek *logos-dike-kosmos* speculation.[2]) But in the *Republic* the context is not the philosophy of nature but the philosophy of society and man.

Bk I contains material both for the motif and the anti-motif. The Thrasymachian reference to politics as facilitating the study of *dikaiosyne* and *adikia* belongs to the former. On the other side, the thought that *psyche* has the function of directing man's life, belongs to the latter: society is conceived as made up of men (souls). However, *Bk I* should not be pressed too hard. We had better accept Plato's own verdict 357a1–2 and take it simply as a proem. In all fairness we may then also read it as an introduction to the study of the *polis-psyche* motif.[3]) Both *polis* and *psyche* occur as important items, but are not yet established as components of the motif. As can be gathered, however, from *TABLE 2*, nrs 1–4, we are not left without preparatory views.

---

[1]) "Die Stelle (352c) beschliesst eine Reihe von Grundmotiven der platonischen Philosophie in sich, die hier zum ersten Male auftreten. Vor allem die Parallelisierung von Staat und Individuum zum Zwecke der Veranschaulichung der *Gerechtigkeit* und ihrer *immanenten* Wirkungsweise, das Bild von der 'Grossen Schrift' in 'Politeia II' also, gewinnt hier schon Erscheinung." Krämer, p. 53.

[2]) The *Gorgias*, 507e6–508a4. φασὶ δ' οἱ σοφοί, ὦ Καλλίκλεις, καὶ οὐρανὸν καὶ γῆν καὶ θεοὺς καὶ ἀνθρώπους τὴν κοινωνίαν συνέχειν καὶ φιλίαν καὶ κοσμιότητα καὶ σωφροσύνην καὶ δικαιότητα, καὶ τὸ ὅλον τοῦτο διὰ ταῦτα κόσμον καλοῦσιν, ὦ ἑταῖρε, οὐκ ἀκοσμίαν οὐδὲ ἀκολασίαν.—Cf. E. Cassirer, *Logos, Dike, Kosmos in der Entwicklung der Griechischen Philosophie*, Göteborgs Högskolas Årsskrift 1941:6, Göteborg 1941.

[3]) It seems quite settled that *Bk I* actually functions as an introduction and was intended as such. Whether it was originally planned as a first part, or possibly composed earlier as a dialogue of its own, and was later revised by Plato in order to suit the *Republic* is another question. The latter standpoint prevails, I think, in modern literature. Reconsidering the topic Friedländer has arrived at the same result. In vol. III he raises the question of how the so called *Thrasymachus* was built into the *Republic*, pp. 66 ff. Friedländer thinks that the passage 345b–348c is the special addition in this integration. The passage forebodes what is said in the middle books about the philosopher-kings and the motive for their reign. —As, however, the preconceptions one finds in *Bk I* are relative to what one considers especially important in the later books, it seems rather arbitrary to decide on this or that section as the special product of Plato's editorial revision.

CHAPTER III
THE REQUEST
(Bk II:357a1–367e5)

1. Classification of goodness

357a1-358e2. What is Socrates requested to do? And how is he asked to do it? To these demands, articulated by Glaucon and Adeimantus, we must now turn.

Glaucon speaks first. He wants to know where Socrates really stands. If there are three kinds of good a), b) and c), into which of them is *dikaiosyne* to be placed? The classes are: a) those rather harmless pleasures which are welcome for their own sake; b) those things (such as wisdom, sight and health) which are good both for their own sake and for their consequences; and c) those which are painful in themselves but pursued for their consequences only, 357b4–d2. Socrates singles out the second class as the highest, and places *dikaiosyne* there, 358a1–3.

Such a choice does not agree with the opinion of most people. They place *dikaiosyne* among the painful things, pursued only for their pleasant results, 358a4–9. The Socratic position is thus made clear both in relation to the classification of different kinds of goodness and in relation to the general opinion. The answer given may seem a bit oracular, for Socrates has not yet argued his standpoint. On the other hand we can take the proposition as the expression of a conviction which should be declared beforehand: firstly it should be made clear that the subject to be discussed is not a trivial one, and secondly the proposition must be reasonably distinct in order to make an attack possible, which is just what Glaucon and Adeimantus are intent upon doing.

Glaucon wants to know what *dikaiosyne* and *adikia* are each by themselves, what power each of them has in the human soul, all motives of profit being left out of account.[1]) *Psyche* is to be explored, *polis* is not mentioned. Thus the formal subject-matter is clearly introduced.[2]) It also stipulates how Socrates should answer the request.[3]) *Dikaiosyne* should be argued against the contrary case of *adikia*. On this method the Thrasymachian views are to be forcefully and systematically restated. Socrates approves of the plan 358e1–2, and Glaucon, acting as the devil's advocate, delivers his model speech. Here follow a few notes on its content and structure.

2. Glaucon's speech on adikia

358e3–362c8. People generally think that *adikia* is good for the agent and evil for the victim. As, however, it is generally impossible to practise *adikia* without suffering the disadvantages which outweigh its pleasures, people have agreed to avoid both, and establish *dikaiosyne* as a compromise. This is the reported origin of justice. *Adikia* is natural 358e3, 359c5, and *dikaiosyne* is conventional, 359a2–4. That *adikia* is natural indicates that man is disposed to use his powers (intellectual and physical) for the things he wants, whereas the much-praised *dikaiosyne* signifies no more than what men (prompted by their individual weakness) can agree to make it represent.

But Glaucon has more to add. *Dikaiosyne* is practised against men's will; they adhere to it only because they are unable to act freely. To illustrate his argument, the story of the ring of Gyges is told, 359c6–360d7; the ring gave its owner the faculty of becoming invisible when needed. If there were two such rings, one for the just and one for the unjust man, the one would act as the other. Both would pursue their own interests, and from their behaviour no difference between them would be detected. Having the ring no man could be expected to have such an adamantine character as to remain with *dikaiosyne*, 360b4–5;

---

[1]) 358b4–7. ἐπιθυμῶ γὰρ ἀκοῦσαι, τί τ᾽ ἔστιν ἑκάτερον καὶ τίνα ἔχει δύναμιν αὐτὸ καθ᾽ αὑτὸ ἐνὸν ἐν τῇ ψυχῇ, τοὺς δὲ μισθοὺς καὶ τὰ γιγνόμενα ἀπ᾽ αὐτῶν ἐᾶσαι χαίρειν.
Cf. 358d1–2. See also p. 221 below, where the request is divided-up in its sub-demands.

[2]) The *Republic*, by its name devoted to problems of the state, is here surprisingly announced as an examination of *dikaiosyne* and *adikia* in the *psyche*. Cf. Apelt. Introd. p. v, and Havelock, *Preface to Plato*. pp. 3 ff.

[3]) 358d3–6. διὸ κατατείνας ἐρῶ τὸν ἄδικον βίον ἐπαινῶν, εἰπὼν δὲ ἐνδείξομαί σοι ὃν τρόπον αὖ βούλομαι καὶ σοῦ ἀκούειν ἀδικίαν μὲν ψέγοντος, δικαιοσύνην δὲ ἐπαινοῦντος.

this thought-experiment gives strong evidence (μέγα τεκμήριον, 360c5) of the inferiority of *dikaiosyne*.[1])

Another step to be noted in Glaucon's argument is the introduction of the *method of the extreme types*, 360e1–361d6. The just and the unjust man should be put side by side as radically opposed extremes, the former considered under unfavourable, the latter under favourable circumstances. The unjust man must be imagined as perfect in his line, being completely unrighteous, but appearing most respectable and just, adorned with the glamour of success. The radically opposite kind of man must be stripped of everything except justice, being equipped instead with misfortune and evil reputation.—The next passage (361d7–362c8) contains the conclusion that the unjust man has chosen the better way of life.

What is, from our point of view, most significant in Glaucon's speech?

The request is dressed in the form of an imaginary experiment (359b6–c1) with two extreme types of character. After the master of injustice has been described 360e6–361b5, the just man is then put up as a contrast.[2]) His picture is drawn in the opposite way to that of the unjust.[3]) Their lives are driven, each in its line, into their extremes.[4]) Socrates characterization of the method is apt; the two types are like a pair of statues, polished up as for an exhibition, 361d4–6.—The types have hardly, as far as I can see, any ontological status. It is of no consequence in this examination, as to whether such persons exist or not in this world. And, as it is definitely not a question of Forms in the special Platonic sense, it is also irrelevant whether such types exist in any other world, cf 472c4–d2.

The types are admittedly constructed ones, but they are not to be confused with constructs of the modern kind, which are invented in order to grasp the complexities of the empirical world.[5]) The latter may

---

[1]) Glaucon, playing the role of the *advocatus diaboli*, does not believe in the superiority of *adikia*, nor does Adeimantus, 361e1–362a3.

[2]) 361b5–8. τοῦτον δὲ τοιοῦτον θέντες τὸν δίκαιον αὖ παρ' αὐτὸν ἱστῶμεν τῷ λόγῳ ἄνδρα ἁπλοῦν καὶ γενναῖον, κατ' Αἰσχύλον οὐ δοκεῖν ἀλλ' εἶναι ἀγαθὸν ἐθέλοντα.

[3]) 361c3–4. γυμνωτέος δὴ πάντων πλὴν δικαιοσύνης καὶ ποιητέος ἐναντίως διακείμενος τῷ προτέρῳ·

[4]) 361d2. . . . ἵνα ἀμφότεροι εἰς τὸ ἔσχατον ἐληλυθότες, . . .

[5]) Cf. K. Mannheim, *Ideology and Utopia*, London 1960, p. 190.

well be constructed by exaggeration of some observable traits,[1]) (thus, being in a sense also extremes), but they do not necessarily go in pairs of opposites as those employed by Glaucon.

In his appeal to facts, Thrasymachus had called attention to the outstanding example of the tyrant. But when he was forced to retreat to the argument of the infallible master ruler, the existing tyrant with his would-be shortcomings became less of a lion.[2]) So the discussion deviated from social realities to conceptual things. Glaucon, who did not try to revive the empirical foundations for the Thrasymachian generalizations at 338e1–339a4, introduces instead his method of the extreme types. This is done, I think, in order to demonstrate that there are no theoretical or supposed super-natural checks against the free practice of *adikia*. It is absurd to think that *dikaiosyne* is anything more than the result of agreement between ordinary men in reciprocal positions. *Dikaiosyne* cannot then be a very great thing. If *adikia* agrees with nature, and is handled with skill, it may be stronger. From a rational point of view *adikia* deserves to get its *raison d'être* soberly examined.

Socrates is challenged to discuss the nature of pure justice as an opposite to the nature of pure injustice, 358b1–d6. Glaucon has brought us to the workshop of speculative philosophy, the method of the extreme types being one of the instruments for such experiments.

3. Adeimantus' speech on adikia

362e1-367e5. Adeimantus next scrutinizes the arguments with which *dikaiosyne* is generally upheld. Social prestige, useful connections, economic success, and every kind of reward is bestowed upon the just, who will prosper both on earth and in heaven, while the unjust man is plunged into the underworld, 362e1–363e4. There is also another variant of common opinion. *Dikaiosyne* is troublesome to practise, and the gods often allot misfortunes to good men. On the whole *adikia* pays better, for the gods may be bargained with; for such aims there are sacrifices and charms, 363e5–365a3. Weighing the two ways of life against each other the clever young man is bound to choose *adikia*, adopting the

---

[1]) Cf. N. S. Timasheff, *Sociological Theory*, New York 1955, p. 177.

[2]) In a sample of unjust men you may select one as typical, having the necessary properties in an exceptionally high degree. Nevertheless he is capable of making mistakes. Though radically unjust he is still no super-man.

art of seeming to be just, but really being unjust.[1]) There is an arsenal of weapons with which to fight justice: secret societies, the art of oral persuasion, and, of course, naked force, 365d2–366d6, cf. 492c4–d7.

As a matter of fact, argues Adeimantus, the whole contemporary culture is based on the calculus of profit, 366d7–366e5. If someone had really made clear to you that *dikaiosyne* is superior to *adikia*—and how each of them affects your character—everybody would be his own keeper, guarding himself against wrongdoing. But no one has made this demonstration, 366e5–367a4.

Thus Socrates is by Glaucon and Adeimantus requested to demonstrate by rational argument (1) that *dikaiosyne* is superior to *adikia*, 367b2–3; (2) that the one produces good and the other evil in the soul, 367b3–5; and (3) that the righteous man is happier (reputation excluded) than the opposite kind of man, 361d3, 367b5–e5. The remainder of the dialogue can be seen as an answer to this challenge.

4. Conclusions and observations

Diakaiosyne and *adikia* continue to hold the interest. The change of perspective that took place in *Bk I* is preserved and most emphatically expressed in the request. As the objects of the search are the just and the unjust characters, the question about the nature of the *psyche* becomes important.

We are also informed how the investigation should be conducted. There is a stipulation about the method of the extreme types, promising an extended employment of the polarity between *dikaiosyne* and *adikia*; this opposition is now systematized. Together with this insistence on typological demonstration goes a general predilection for rational argument and proof.[2]) The method of the extreme types is not called forth in order to class empirical phenomena, but to state beyond all appearances what *dikaiosyne* and *adikia* "each of them really is, and what effect each has, in itself, on the soul that harbours it, when all rewards and consequences are left out of account".[3]) When Socrates

---

[1]) There is, writes Guthrie, nothing heroic in this picture of *adikia*; it is "a rather sordid mixture of greed, envy, pettiness and fear". *HGP*, vol. III, p. 99.

[2]) 367b2–5, μὴ οὖν ἡμῖν μόνον ἐνδείξῃ τῷ λόγῳ ὅτι δικαιοσύνη ἀδικίας κρεῖττον, κτλ. and 367e1–5, μὴ οὖν ἡμῖν ἐνδείξῃ μόνον τῷ λόγῳ ὅτι δικαιοσύνη ἀδικίας κρεῖττον, κτλ.

[3]) 358b3–7 quoted at p. 67, n. 1.—Above in Cornford's transl.—In reading about this task, "we wonder", exclaimes H. A. Prichard, "how he ever came to think that he could execute it". *Moral Obligation*, Oxford 1949, p. 105.

takes over, he does not restrict the far-reaching demands involved in the request; this forebodes that we are in for a course in speculative philosophy.

As can be gathered from *TABLE 1* (pp. 235–236) the term *psyche* is mentioned five times, vaguely meaning that persons are conditioned by our ethical standard of behaviour. We are also given to understand that *psyche* has a force of some kind.[1]) It may be conjectured that by means of activity and sensitivity, an interplay of influences is possible between persons or souls.

Polis occurs three times: 362b2, 364e5 and 366b1. It is not yet expressly bound up with *psyche* as an illustrative device. Nevertheless its illustrative function is twice indicated in advance: not only individuals manipulate justice and choose smoother ways, but so evidently do the big cities, 364e3–365a3, 366a6–b2, cf. *TABLE 2*, nrs 5 and 6.

But *polis* is present in the speeches of Glaucon and Adeimantus in another and more fundamental manner. The cultural climate of the contemporary city is morally ruinous for the young man growing up there, cf. 365a4–c6. The predicament of the talented young man, living in a corrupt society, is mentioned here for the first time in the *Republic*. This predicament is manifest in *Bk III* 401b1–d3 and in *Bk VI* 494b5–495b6 and it is systematically repeated in *Bks VIII–IX* 549c2–550b7, 553a9–553d8, 558c11–559d2 and 572b10–573c10.

Friedländer has shown that from the speeches of Glaucon and Adeimantus, topical connections can be established with various parts of the *Republic*.[2]) In short: as a re-statement of the Thrasymachus' argument they point backwards to *Bk I*, and as systematic questions they point forwards to the long discussion called forth.

---

1) 366c2, δύναμις ὑπάρχει ψυχῆς. Cf. 353d3–4, 353d9.
2) *Plato*, vol. III, pp. 70–71, 73–79.

CHAPTER IV
THE DOUBLE TEXT METHOD
(Bk II:367e6–369b4)

1. Polis—an illustrative device

368c4–369b4. Socrates now takes over, and this marks a new start in the structure of the argument.

How are souls to be inspected? Socrates admits that it is no easy matter. Keen sight is required. Not being endowed with this precious gift, some method is needed which can compensate our shortcomings. The procedure could be as follows. Supposing one is short-sighted and has to read a text in small letters from some distance away. Someone then discovers that the same letters are set up in a larger scale in some other place. One could first of all read the larger letters and then proceed to the lesser ones, comparing them to see if they are the same.[1]

What relevance has this procedure on the question in debate, 368d8– e1? The answer is that *dikaiosyne* is spoken of as belonging to an individual as well as to a whole city; the adjective "just" can in both cases be predicated.[2] Further, and this is important, *polis* is larger than an individual.[3] Accordingly *dikaiosyne* may exist in greater proportions in the community, being easier to observe there than in the person.[4]

---

[1]) 368d1–7. ἐπειδὴ οὖν ἡμεῖς οὐ δεινοί, δοκῶ μοι, ἦν δ' ἐγώ, τοιαύτην ποιήσασθαι ζήτησιν αὐτοῦ, οἷανπερ ἂν εἰ προσέταξέ τις γράμματα σμικρὰ πόρρωθεν ἀναγνῶναι μὴ πάνυ ὀξὺ βλέπουσιν, ἔπειτά τις ἐνενόησεν, ὅτι τὰ αὐτὰ γράμματα ἔστι που καὶ ἄλλοθι μείζω τε καὶ ἐν μείζονι, ἕρμαιον ἂν ἐφάνη οἶμαι ἐκεῖνα πρῶτον ἀναγνόντας οὕτως ἐπισκοπεῖν τὰ ἐλάττω, εἰ τὰ αὐτὰ ὄντα τυγχάνει.

[2]) 368e2 ff. Cf. *TABLE 2*, nr 7.

[3]) 368e5. Οὐκοῦν μεῖζον πόλις ἑνὸς ἀνδρός;

[4]) 368e7–8. Ἴσως τοίνυν πλείων ἂν δικαιοσύνη ἐν τῷ μείζονι ἐνείη καὶ ῥᾴων καταμαθεῖν. On this line a selection of translations may be of interest.—". . . larger proportions, easier to make out", Cornford; ". . . more abundant and more easily discernible", Jowett; ". . . the amount of justice in the larger entity is greater, and so easier to recognize", Lee; ". . . more justice in the larger object

Polis should therefore be studied first. After that you should return to the individual, trying to identify in the lesser structure what has been found in the larger.[1]) Finally, it is added that if, in rational argument (ϑεασαίμεϑα λόγῳ) one first took up the study of a community "coming into being" (γιγνομένη πόλις, 369a5), there would be opportunity to see also *dikaiosyne* and *adikia* in their early development.—Such is the plan for the investigation, a job which is expected to be troublesome, 369b2–3.

2. Parallel text-reading

The section 368d1–369a7, where Socrates describes his method and systematically introduces *polis* as a tool for the inspection of souls, is of central importance for the motif. First the method is characterized as a study of two parallel texts, and secondly we are told what is to be understood by this picture. Thrasymachus had already referred to political life as a suitable field of observation in an approach to the factual meaning of *dikaiosyne*. Now *polis* is introduced, not as a club to be swung wildly, but as a well-calculated instrument for the examination of characters. In this context the *polis-psyche* motif emerges as a method-directed line of thought. Confronting the subject-matter with the motif, we see that the former is about the nature of *dikaiosyne* and *adikia* manifested in the *psyche*, while the latter has to do with *how* this matter should be explored. *Polis* is there as an illustrative device.[2]) It is to its operation in that capacity that we must now turn.

The picture of the method as a comparison between two texts is suggestive. First, it gives you the impression that there is a sequence of one-one relations between the individual letters of the two texts. Let us call this vertical approach the *letter aspect*. It may be illustrated thus, see next page.

---

and more easy to apprehend", Shorey; "Vielleicht also findet sich die Gerechtigkeit in einem Grösseren auch in grösserem Masse vor und in leichter erkennbarer Gestalt", Apelt; ". . . une justice plus grande dans le cadre plus grand, et par là plus facile à déchiffrer", Chambry.

[1]) 369a1–3. ἔπειτα οὕτως ἐπισκεψώμεϑα καὶ ἐν ἑνὶ ἑκάστῳ τὴν τοῦ μείζονος ὁμοιότητα ἐν τῇ τοῦ ἐλάττονος ἰδέᾳ ἐπισκοποῦντες.

[2]) Cf. R. Demos, *A Note on Plato's Republic*, RM, vol. XII, No. 2, 1958, p. 300. Demos calls it an "instructional device"; "ein Mittel der Darstellung", Utermöhlen, p. 15.

$$Polis: \quad A \quad B \quad C \quad D \quad \ldots$$
$$\downarrow \quad \downarrow \quad \downarrow \quad \downarrow$$
$$Psyche: \quad a \quad b \quad c \quad d \quad \ldots$$

There are the corresponding letters A to a, and B to b etc. It follows that A should be identified before a and so on for each pair of letters. This stipulation of *the methodological priority of the larger letters* is of course of vital importance for the motif.

Secondly, the picture of the two texts suggests a horizontal approach. The set of larger letters forms a system of words and sentences, a written piece of information, which the smaller letters repeat. The *texts* are identical in meaning. If you read the larger text first it is easier to, decipher the micro-text. This we may call the *textual aspect*.

Of course both aspects must be applied in the actual text-interpretation. One must first try the easier version, then one must make sure that both versions contain the same information. Interpreting the texts, one may be bound to identify letter for letter in the vertical way. Thus a comparative spelling is instrumental in establishing the common meaning of the texts, see also 434d5–435a3. The picture of *polis* and *psyche* as two parallel texts is ingeniously contrived, but the simile should not be pressed too far. If one applies the letter-aspect too rigorously, one is invited to think that the society and the personality have a vast number of details corresponding to each other. One might become engaged in an unrestricted search for detailed similarities.[1] It would be wrong to think that the significance of the exploration simply grows with the number of analogies one can find; there is a word already by Theophrastus, that if one drives the comparison too far, one may lose the proper view.[2] At the outset it may be sound to balance the *letter-aspect* against the *textual aspect*. Anticipating what is to come, we should seize upon those elements which shape the pattern.

The image of the two texts does in one respect not fit in adequately with what Socrates is about to do: select certain characteristic traits of the social field (abstracting from a great number of others), and then pick out corresponding psychological traits to those first chosen. It is

---

[1] I think of the absurdities of the biological school of sociology, giving itself up to the discovery of various fanciful analogies. Cf. R. M. MacIver, *The Modern State*, London 1964, p. 449.

[2] Cited by O. Regenbogen, *Eine Forschungsmethode antiker Naturwissenschaft*, (in *Kleine Schriften* ed. by F. Dirlmeier) München, 1961, pp. 165–166.

as if in a given text we did not take into account all the words, but only read certain parts of the text.—To the moderns there is the concept of *isomorphism*, denoting the identity of structures based on some chosen set of pattern-forming elements.[1]) Even if this concept was not available to Plato, it may be used here to help characterize the type of relationship which seems to hold between *polis* and *psyche*.

If it is asserted that one structure could be used as an instrument for the study of another, one is bound to present some reasonable arguments for the method. Either you know somehow that this particular similarity exists, or you think that there is a universal law covering the both cases compared.[2]) The argument Socrates offers for the structural identity between *polis* and *psyche* is that we talk about *dikaiosyne* both in connection with an individual and a whole city, 368e2–3. As words are often used loosely, this is not much of a basis for a laborious examination. Plato, however, in due course explains how *polis* can illustrate *psyche*.

Having read *Bk I* as an introduction to the *polis-psyche* motif we are not altogether unprepared for the hypothesis that there are some structural affinities between our two components. It has been indicated that *dikaiosyne* and *adikia* are manifest in persons as well as in societies, see p. 64 above. There is also an extra-textual condition to notice. The idea of man as a microcosm was commonplace to the Greeks. The cosmos pattern belonged to the Greek property of settled ideas.[3]) The proposed method, even as it is presented, is not without support. And it seems the more respectable since it binds its practitioner to inspect not only the larger text (invoked as a matter of convenience), but also the smaller one in order to make sure that both versions are identical.

---

[1]) Cf. M. R. Cohen and E. Nagel, *The Nature of a Logical or Mathematical System* (in *Readings in the Philosophy of Science*), New York 1953, pp. 137 ff. See also R. Demos, *RM*, XII, p. 301.

[2]) "Analogy seems to be essentially an argument from a single case to a single case ... One case cannot really give us insight into another unless it gives us insight into the universal covering both; and yet analogy refuses to mention the universal." Robinson p. 207. Passing over to the great analogy between *polis* and *psyche* Robinson, however, thinks that the analogical manner in which the analogy is presented *suggests* a universal without saying what it is, p. 211.

[3]) Cf. *The Notion of 'Kosmos'* in Guthrie, *HGP* vol. I, pp. 206 ff.

What is to be asserted about *psyche* is not allowed to rest simply on *analogical conclusions*, but must be founded on comparative evidence.[1]

Let us confront this method of comparison with the analogical research-method of the ancient doctors.

O. Regenbogen has studied the method employed in three closely inter-connected books belonging to the Hippocratic writings: περὶ γονῆς, περὶ φύσιος παιδίου and περὶ νούσων IV. The subject of the two first books is the origin and development of the child until the time of birth. The fact that a child is dependent on its mother initiates a lengthy analogical reasoning; the embryo is related to the mother as the plant to the earth around it. An extensive account of the physiology of plants and related subjects is then given. The form of these comparisons is markedly stereotyped. The parallels, being more than only "rednerische Prunkstücke", represent a form of reasoning, important in the development of scientific thinking. The method rests on the following procedure: "ein Vorgang nicht anschaulicher Art wird einem zweiten anschaulichen verglichen, dergestalt, dass der erste durch den zweiten eine besondere Beleuchtung empfängt."[2] Through the method of analogy one is informed about processes inaccessible to sense perception.

This sort of analogical conclusion consists in projections from some *"anschaulicher Vorgang"* to some other *"nicht anschaulicher"*, whereas the double-text method allegedly depicts a procedure holding between two fields which can *somehow* be inspected, both of them.—From this point of view the Platonic method seems more advanced. On second thought one observes, that a great difference can be noted. The doctors spoke about organisms belonging to the realm of physical nature; they even made experiments from which they could proceed; initially they held themselves within the world of sense-perception. Plato's two components of comparison lack the distinctness of physical objects. The larger object, the illustrative medium, is not an actual city, but a constructed one. Gradually as the investigation proceeds *polis* takes the shape of an organic whole. That a given society is a whole, *like* a biological organism, is, however, not a fact but an idea.

---

[1] The analogy is used as a pointer to suggest a possible line of inquiry, says G. C. Field, and the "conclusions are arrived at on the basis of an examination of each side of the analogy on its own merits", *The Philosophy of Plato*, London 1949, p. 94.

[2] Regenbogen, p. 145.

4. Conclusions and observations

In *Bk I* Thrasymachus argued that the study of political behaviour could illuminate the real meaning of *dikaiosyne* and *adikia*. In this role, *polis* was mentioned a number of times. It is not surprising that Thrasymachus, as a sophist engaged in rhetorical and political education, was alive to this idea. As, however, *Bk I* is only quite loosely inter-connected with the following books, *polis* is not yet given a systematic place in the investigation. This happens first now in *Bk II*, where *polis* gains a strategical place in a strongly requested and carefully planned investigation spreading over a number of books. *Polis* is now linked up with *psyche* and acquires a highly *significant position* in its capacity as an illustrative mean. Thus also *polis* and *psyche* are established as components of our motif.

The relationship existing between the two components is likened to that of two identical texts. Towards the end of *Bk IV*, 434d2–435a4, Socrates explicitly returns to the double text method: what you have found by means of *polis* should not be accepted until you have seen it confirmed in *psyche*. This emphasis on the need of control is interesting, but must be seen, I think, in its methodical context, i. e. of rational speculation.

The section on method is short. And Socrates is not only brief but incomplete. Glaucon and Adeimantus had demanded that *dikaiosyne* and *adikia* should be confronted as radical opposites, cf. pp. 68 ff above. This stipulation is not mentioned here. It is, however, as we shall see, not forgotten.

Finally, if one sets out to illustrate the righteous soul by means of a constructed *polis*, the constructor must already know, at least roughly, what *dikaiosyne* is. In the light of this implication there is a notable difference between *Bk I* and *Bk II*, the former ending with Socrates saying that he does not know what τὸ δίκαιον is, 354c1–3.

PART THREE

THE DOUBLE TEXT STUDY (I)

CHAPTER V

A MODEL POLIS CONSTRUCTED IN THOUGHT

(Bk. II:369b5–III:412b7)

1. First polis

369b5-370c6. The *polis* to be studied is a rational construction,[1]
Ἴθι δή, ... τῷ λόγῳ ἐξ ἀρχῆς ποιῶμεν πόλιν, 369c9.

How, then, does a community come into existence? Looking at
it rationally the only apparent reason is that man is not self-sufficient.
As he cannot supply his many demands by himself, 369b5–7, men gather
together in one place in partnership for mutual benefit 369c1–3. Such a
settlement is called a *polis*.[2] The exchange of services is for the parti-
cipant's own good, 369c6–7.

This is the first principle on which the *polis* is founded. The community is called into being because it is useful.[3] No divinities are

---

[1] Drawing a distinction between the presentation of the method and its actual
application, I have divided the text here in order to mark the emergence of the
polis as an illustrative tool.—The start at 369b5 is also, we may note in passing,
an important event in the history of Western political and social thought. A vast
amount of comments, or rational reconsiderations, and of more or less utopian
thought springs from this well.

[2] 369c3–4. See *TABLE 1*.

[3] It is an economic community, declare Cross and Woozley, p. 79.—Plato's
emphasis on the economic background of the political life and his theory of the
primitive beginnings of society are examples of Plato's greatness as a sociologist,
writes K. Popper, *OSE* vol. I, p. 38. And Guthrie writes: "The mightier animals
prowl alone, relying on their individual strength and fierceness, but the weaker
pool their strength by going about in herds. In the *Republic*, on the other hand,
what brings men together is a purely human faculty that distinguishes them from
the beasts, namely diversity of function", *In the Beginning. Some Greek Views on
the Origins of Life and the Early State of Man*, London 1957, p. 100.

called in, no myths told.[1]) The argument offered is one of plausibility.
Man, because of what he is, needs *polis*, 369c10.

In its first stage the *polis* includes only four or five men; a farmer,
a builder, a weaver and one or two other men to provide themselves
with their elementary wants, 369d1–12. Production is from the beginning
organized through specialization and division of work, 369e2–370a6.
The reasons for this arrangement are as follows.

Nature has not made us all alike; talents are unevenly distributed.
We are not all fitted for the same sort of job.[2]) Work is better done if
it is undertaken by the specialist, talented and trained, who can do
the job at the right time, and not only when he feels inclined to do it,
370b7–c5. If production is undertaken ἐν κατὰ φύσιν καὶ ἐν καιρῷ the
amount of work is increased, the quality improved, and the process of
production facilitated, 370c3–5.

This, very small community is called the ἀναγκαιοτάτη πόλις, 369d11,
a name which indicates that the *polis* is dictated by natural conditions.
Its citizens are brought together by their needs, and the organization
of work agrees with nature. Division of labour is an important idea in
the history of economy and sociology.[3]) It is introduced in the *Republic*
in an economic context. The improvement of production and increase
of consumption is, as will later be observed, not the supreme goal.
Division of labour is also useful for acquiring social stability and order,
setting the citizens to work in their proper places.

2. Polis expanded

370c7-372d3. Thereupon the city is allowed to grow, and tool-

---

[1]) An absence of myths is the more conspicuous, as the myths connecting the
city-states with gods and heroes were numerous. Aristotle thought it awkward
that no nobler motive was mentioned in relation to the foundation of this "first
state", *Pol.* 1291a.—J. Stenzel has commented on Plato's straightforwardness.
It is surprising, he says, how Plato ("dieser als Utopist und Ideologe verschrieene
Philosoph") refrains from all supernatural foundations. *Wissenschaft und Staatsgesinnung bei Platon*, Kieler Univ.red. Kiel 1927. Reprinted in *Das Platonbild.
Zehn Beiträge zum Platonverständnis*, ed. by K. Gaiser. Hildesheim 1969, pp. 97 ff.

[2]) 370a7–b2. ἐννοῶ γὰρ καὶ αὐτὸς εἰπόντος σοῦ, ὅτι πρῶτον μὲν ἡμῶν φύεται ἕκαστος
οὐ πάνυ ὅμοιος ἑκάστῳ, ἀλλὰ διαφέρων τὴν φύσιν, ἄλλος ἐπ' ἄλλου ἔργου πράξει.—A. Krohn,
referring to more than a hundred quotations, tells us, "dass die *physis* der Central-
begriff des ursprünglichen Platonismus ist", pp. 8, 58.

[3]) Cf. G. Glotz, *Le Travail dans la Grèce Ancienne*, Paris 1920, p. 266.

makers, shepherds, merchants, sailors, shopkeepers, and some others are introduced. The volume of production is increased in order to make possible an exchange of goods with other states. In a first attempt Socrates looks at the *polis* as full-grown; the community is now much larger but organized on the same principles as before.

An attempt to spell out the larger text is undertaken. If the *polis* can be said to be fully grown, where are then *dikaiosyne* and *adikia* to be found?[1]—Adeimantus does not know, but he ventures that it may be a question of relationships, 372a1–2. The answer corresponds vaguely to the cues given. As, however, the question is taken up too early, the letters not yet being legible, the enquiry proceeds.

To make the larger text clearer, a picture is painted of the citizens way of life. We meet (372a5–d3) the literary motif of the simple life, ἁπλοῦς βίος.[2]) In summer the citizens work stripped and barefoot, in winter sufficiently shod and clothed. They bake their bread, drink their wine, enjoy their family life, praising the gods with garlands on their heads. For fear of poverty and war, they keep their families within the limits of their economy. They thus live peacefully and healthily, blessed with a long life.

This is idyllic. The scene is vividly visualized.[3]) You may with O. Apelt wonder at all this friendly spirit and the absence of any trouble whatsoever.[4]) Is this possibly an infusion of utopian dreams? Interpreters judge the scene very differently.[5])

The *polis* is built up in great blocks. Plato's interest is from the beginning focused on the three principal parts of the finally completed city. Economy of literary composition speaks for what has been called

---

[1]) 371e12–13. This is the first trial on the illustrative capacity of the *polis*. Adeimantus' answer (that it is ἐν χρείᾳ τινὶ τῇ πρὸς ἀλλήλους, 372a1–2), comments Campbell, has been prepared in the discussion with Polemarchus (333a–d), where justice is ἐν τῷ κοινωνεῖν, JC, vol. II, p. 3.

[2]) Cf. R. Vischer, *Das Einfache Leben*, Göttingen 1965, pp. 10–22, 48–56.

[3]) "Platon verwischt die nüchterne und steife Art der Disposition durch die Anschaulichkeit, mit der er das alltägliche Leben dieser Menschen ausmalt". Vischer, p. 50.

[4]) "Von Gewalttätigkeit, Willkür, Herrschgelüsten, Habgier, kurz von all den dunklen Mächten, die bei Gründung geschichtlicher Staaten in Frage kommen, ist hier überhaupt nicht die Rede." Note 31, p. 445.

[5]) Cross and Woozley, pp. 78 ff, notice no friendship but capitalistic self-interest guided by co-operation.

a mixed evolutionary and rational exposition.[1]) Giving us the genesis of his model city, he picks out those features which are essential for *polis* in its capacity of providing the larger text. Moreover, I think that the features of this "true and healthy city"[2]) are preserved in the finally completed *polis*, showing how the great majority of the people (i.e. the third of the three fundamental classes) is meant to live. Before long Plato is to concentrate his interest on the guardians. We have therefore reason to keep in mind what is here said about the life of the great majority of the people.

3. The swollen polis

372d4-373e8. If the idyllic scene is designed as a persuasive illustration, Glaucon is, at least, not moved by it. He sweeps it away brusquely, calling it a city for pigs (ὑῶν πόλιν, 372d4). He wants some higher standard of living: more comforts, better food (not only vegetables) and some luxuries, 372d4-e1. Socrates agrees to modernizing the *polis*, but points out that they will now depart from the healthy lines of development. Notwithstanding, the concept of simplicity is bound to reappear in various connections.[3])

In the next phase the "swollen state"—marked by over-consumption—is introduced, 372e ff. Choosing this roundabout way of exposition, the genesis in *polis* not only of *dikaiosyne*, but also of *adikia*, will be demonstrated, 372e3-6. So the community is increased and a multitude of new occupations is admitted in order to meet the new demands. The catalogue of new occupations is extensive, 373a1-373c7. Not only the material conditions are raised, but also the cultural. There are sculptors, painters, musicians, poets, playwrights, reciters, actors.

With the raised standard of living and the greater population, the basis of the economy must be improved. More land for cultivation is

---

[1]) Conceptual elements, implicitly conceived in the vision of the completed state, are explicitly fitted into the scene in an evolutionary time-order. Apelt. Einleitung p. xi.

[2]) 372e6. ἀληθινὴ πόλις; 372e7 ὥσπερ ὑγιής τις.

[3]) The word ἁπλοῦς is rather a loaded term. To the contemporaries it could mean unsophisticated simple-mindedness and foolishness. Plato sought to resurrect its older meaning: venerable and trustworthy simplicity. Cf. Vischer, pp. 13–15. See also A. O. Lovejoy and G. Boas, *Primitivism and Related Ideas in Antiquity*, 2nd. ed., New York 1965, pp. 155–156.

needed. The widening of the territory is done at the expense of a neigh-bouring state. The *polis* will be involved in war, 373d4–e3.

War arises out of unlimited acquisitiveness, 373e5–6. Directed towards unlimited consumption, the people has *trespassed the measure of necessity*.[1]) Suspending further judgements, Socrates merely concludes that with the origin of war we have also found the cause of most evil things, it may concern society or man.[2]) We observe that there is here a point of reference between the two components of the motif. And it would not be over-cautious to conclude it is within the frame-work of *adikia* that this reference is offered. What is said in this section (373d7–e7) about acquisitiveness without limit reminds us of *pleonexia*, the uncontrolled appetites, mentioned in *Bk I*, 349b1 ff. The section also points forward toward *Bks VIII–IX* and the analysis of *adikia* under-taken there.[3]) Finally the assertions about the swollen *polis* seems to include an impressive element of historic experience. Living as he did in the gloom that followed upon the Peloponnesian war, Plato's assumption that war is caused by aggrandizement, was written, we may presume, in large letters.[4])

Again we notice the well-calculated method of exposition. The *polis* is allowed to swell. As a matter of economic necessity this engenders war. The argument is realistic. With war comes the question of soldiering. An army is needed, and Socrates lets it march in, thus adding a constitu-ent element to the edifice.

The guardians (φύλακες, 374d8) are now mentioned for the first time. The interest is directed to their nature and education.

4. A professional soldier class

373e9-376e1. What type of man is then required, as the defence of the state is one of the most important jobs? 374b6–e8.

These men must have keen perception, speed in pursuit, strength to

---

[1]) 373d9–10, . . . ἐὰν καὶ ἐκεῖνοι ἀφῶσιν αὐτοὺς ἐπὶ χρημάτων κτῆσιν ἄπειρον, ὑπερβάντες τὸν τῶν ἀναγκαίων ὅρον;

[2]) 373e6–7, . . ., ἐξ ὧν μάλιστα ταῖς πόλεσιν καὶ ἰδίᾳ καὶ δημοσίᾳ· κακὰ γίγνεται, ὅταν γίγνηται.

[3]) A. Krohn supposed that Plato originally meant to expose *adikia* in this inflamed or swollen society, pp. 34, 72.

[4]) C. Mossé, *La Fin de la Démocratie Athénienne*, Paris 1962, thinks it quite sure that the *phlegmainousa polis* is Athens, p. 355.

fight, courage, and philosophic disposition, 375a5–376c5. The subject of *andreia* (courage) and *thymoeides* (high spirit) thus enters into the dialogue, 375a2–b2. High spirit is the quality of the soul which makes its possessor (man or animal) eager to fight. This is useful in war, but can men with such a disposition also be good citizens? What if they turn their weapons against the society and break it up! Can gentleness and fighting spirit really be united in the same soul? Do they not contradict each other? A combination of such qualities is undoubtedly required, but is it a realistic desire?

Socrates, playing on the words σκύλαξ-φύλαξ,[1]) had compared in the foregoing (375a2–3) the well brought-up young man with a well-bred watch-dog. Now he observes that such a dog actually has the combination of qualities sought: gentleness to known persons, hostility to strangers, 375e1–4. The combination therefore exists in the realm of nature; it is not contrary to it.[2]) In fact, there actually exist animals which are able to canalize their gentleness and their fighting spirit to different fields of action; you are not unrealistic if you suppose that men of this kind could also be created.

Socrates continues with the dog-comparison. A dog is also a philosopher in some way, 376a2–b1; it recognizes its friends by the test of its knowledge of them 376b3–6; wisdom must then be very dear to him; his wisdom is his knowledge of those to whom he belongs,[3]) 376b6.— Thus the illustrative capacity of the dog image is forced. As a metaphorical animal the dog readily lends itself to different ideological interpretations.[4]) Placed in its context (375a2–376c6) the dog simile depicts the

---

[1]) Cf. Adam, vol. I., p. 106.

[2]) 375e6–7. Τοῦτο μὲν ἄρα, ἦν δ'ἐγώ, δυνατόν, καὶ οὐ παρὰ φύσιν ζητοῦμεν τοιοῦτον εἶναι τὸν φύλακα.—The city of *Bks II–IV* is a κατὰ φύσιν οἰκισθεῖσα πόλις, Adam, vol. I, p. 95.

[3]) Is the argument about the philosophic dog really seriously meant? If it is a joke, what is the point of that joke? T. A. Sinclair thinks that Plato is here parodying the sophists, who constantly referred to *physis* against *nomos*. "... to the unspoken objection that it is not "in Nature" for a courageous and spirited man to restrain his impulses and refrain from attacking others Plato playfully replies "On the contrary, you will find warrant for it in the animal world. Just look at the dog, whose behaviour is according to your own theories *natural*." *CR* vol. LXII 1948, pp. 61–62.

[4]) Visualisers are, says I. A. Richards, exposed to a special danger. Images owe much of their character and detail to sources which are quite outside the author's control. "A quality in an image which seems to one reader quite beside the point

type of character the soldiers ought to have: πρᾷον καὶ μεγαλόθυμον ἦθος, that is to say mildness and great spirit; in 440c7–441a3 the equation shepherd/dog=rulers/auxiliaries=*logistikon/thymoeides* illustrates an element of trust and alliance.

The introduction of the soldiers marks an important stage in the development of the *polis*. They are the much-needed specialists. The political implication of the specialization (giving the carpenters all the saws, and the soldiers all the weapons) involves a serious problem which Socrates treats not as a constitutional problem, but as one of character-building. The soldiers are destined to be the élite. And as, I conjecture, they are not to be found ready-made anywhere, they must be moulded by education, *paideia*. The whole state is moved by one lever, "the education which forms the souls".[1] Socrates forestalls that the educational discourse will be lengthy. He does not want to be tedious, but is now allowed ample time for describing the education of the future guardians. Developing his educational plan, he constantly observes the unsatisfactory cultural conditions of contemporary society. Thus it appears that the case of false education is quite dominating.

5. Criticism of culture, reform of education

376e2-392c5. Education consisted traditionally of literary and physical training, 376e2–4. Socrates thinks it convenient to start from this division. He begins with the stories, which are told already in nurseries.

Homer and Hesiod supply the grand examples of untrue myth-making, 377c7–d6. The gods are represented as indulging in all sorts of vices. The greatest ill-deeds secure Olympic authorization. These stories about unreliable and revengeful divinities, capriciously causing sometimes good, sometimes evil, are retold by less talented story-tellers as fairy tales for children. Impressions implanted at an early

---

may be an essential item to another". Thus we stand before the difficult subject of *relevant connection*. *Practical Criticism*, London 1964, p. 236.—The trouble with the dog as a metaphorical animal is that it is quite ambivalent. (Comparing the metaphorical use of the dog with that of the lion, you find that the latter is always wild, strong, fierce; trying to trick Thrasymachus is as foolish as trying to shave a lion, 341c1–2.) Therefore Plato makes clear that he thinks of the *well-bred* dog (375a2,e2).—As for metaphorical animals I refer to B. Snell, *Die Entdeckung des Geistes*, Hamburg 1955, pp. 258 ff.

[1] *Paideia* vol. II, New York 1943, pp. 199 ff.

age are difficult to uproot.[1]) Children, we may conclude, are steeped in pseudo-culture already on their mothers' laps. The production of stories must therefore be supervised, 377b11–c5; the majority of those in use has to be discarded, 377b5–9.

We can cut down the criticism of culture to the following statements: no unworthy representations of gods and heroes, 377e1–3; no tales about internal fighting in heaven, 378b8–d3; god is author of good only, evil has other causes, 379c2–7, 380c6–9; the gods are truthful and consistent in action, appearance and character,[2]) 380d1–382e11; the horrible tales about Hades should be eliminated, 386c3–387c5; good examples must be set: divinities do not give themselves up to excesses 390b6–c7, and no person of worth should be pictured in fits of lamentation or laughter, 388a5–e7. Poets should not depict unjust men as happy or just men as unhappy, 392a13–b6.

Socrates is concerned with the Hesiod-Homer inspired culture of his own times. He is reading large letters,[3]) and the text is certainly not imaginary; the references to Homer are abundant. Homer had kept his place in the education of the young though society had changed greatly since his times. "The system of value which served the loosely knit Homeric society" no longer agreed with the civic society of Athens.[4]) Still more inadequate was this culture for the Platonic aims. He looked for a cultural pattern which functionally answered to the needs of the united society under construction.[5]) The constructive work is based on a realistic criticism of culture wedded to quite an unbiased view of the human soul: Socrates does not say that true beliefs stick more to

---

[1]) 377a12–b3. Οὐκοῦν οἶσθ' ὅτι ἀρχὴ παντὸς ἔργου μέγιστον, ἄλλως τε δὴ καὶ νέῳ καὶ ἁπαλῷ ὁτῳοῦν; μάλιστα γὰρ δὴ τότε πλάττεται, καὶ ἐνδύεται τύπος ὃν ἄν τις βούληται ἐνσημή-νασθαι ἑκάστῳ, cf. 395d1–3, 401e1–402a4.

[2]) God is ἁπλοῦν, simple in the Platonic sense, 380d5, 382e8.—Plato was definitely not an agnostic, comments in this connection P. Grenet, p. 73.

[3]) 377c7–d1. 'Εν τοῖς μείζοσιν, ἦν δ' ἐγώ, μύθοις ὀψόμεθα καὶ τοὺς ἐλάττους. δεῖ γὰρ δὴ τὸν αὐτὸν τύπον εἶναι καὶ ταὐτὸν δύνασθαι τούς τε μείζους καὶ τοὺς ἐλάττους.

[4]) Cf. A. W. H. Adkins, p. 338.

[5]) Religion is aptly adapted to the interests of the state. There was never a Church presiding over religion, but only states. And "the compact nature of the community" gave opportunities of an active life which may have helped to prevent that overflow of other-worldliness later appearing, when the restraining influence of the city-state was gone. Cf. Guthrie, *The Greeks and their Gods*, London 1962, p. 334.

the soul than false ones. The sad fact that the soul receives bad impressions as easily as good ones, excuses the drastic purification of the swollen state, cf. 491a7–495e2.

6. Formal aspects of culture

392c6-403c8. The topic of *mimesis* and the imitative use of literature is next taken up. The dramatic form of literature must be especially observed. Imitative acting, continually practised, becomes a habit and (second) nature, 395d1–3. Base roles should be avoided. Socrates again refers to the principle of specialization, saying that one must economize with the resources of effort, as men are not capable of doing many things well, 394e3–395b6. One man, one job, 397e4–8. In the state under construction there will be no *double or multiform man.*[1])—The simple and united person, we conclude, must correspond to the simple and united society, cf. 398a4–b4. The endurance of the *polis* is dependent on this principle. It concerns especially the guardians, who from childhood must be modelled on the assumption that they are to be capable defenders of the city, 395b8–d3.

Socrates (398c1–403c8) passes from literature over to music and song. Musical forms sink down into the regions of the soul ($\epsilon i s \ \tau \grave{o} \ \grave{\epsilon} \nu \tau \grave{o} s \ \tau \hat{\eta} s \ \psi \upsilon \chi \hat{\eta} s$) and fasten themselves there, 401d5–e1. Convivial or languid melodies are forbidden.[2]) To express both courage and moderation, the Dorian and Phrygian modes are chosen, 399a3–4, matching the type of character looked for; the music should answer both to the spirited and the gentle side of the personality. In describing this music, Socrates sheds light on the sociability and the peace-time behaviour of the soldiers. We see them praying to the gods, mingling with the citizens, giving or receiving instructions or admonitions, never being arrogant, but always behaving with moderation and reasonableness, 399a5–c4.

Step by step the swollen *polis* is being purged, 399e5–6. The rules of simplicity are applied to rhythms, arts and artifacts of every kind, 401b1–d3. All forms of deformity are expelled. The cultural movement must blow like a healthy wind through society.[3])

---

[1]) 397e1–2. . . . ὅτι οὐκ ἔστιν διπλοῦς ἀνὴρ παρ' ἡμῖν οὐδὲ πολλαπλοῦς.

[2]) Plato is here condemning not Ionian and Lydian, but *slack* Ionian and *slack* Lydian, comments Adam, vol. I, p. 157.

[3]) 401c8. . . . ὥσπερ αὔρα φέρουσα—The passage 401b1–d3 is one of several about the case of a young man in relation to his cultural milieu.

Speaking about educational aims, Socrates returns to the *image of
the letters* (εἰκόνας γραμμάτων, 402b5). To read is to be able to recognize
the letters (few as they are) in all their varying combinations. First
we must know the letters themselves before we can recognize images
of them, reflected as they may be in different mediums. The guardians
are not educated before they have learnt to recognize the essential
features of *sophrosyne, andreia, eleutheria, megaloprepeia*, and other
excellences akin to them, as well as their opposites in all their variety,
402a7–c8.—In its first instance, the letter-image referred to the comparison of two identical texts, (368d1–7). Now (402a7–b3) the image
relates instead to the art of reading, in itself being a condition for understanding any kind of text.[1]) *To the guardians* it is important to be
able to recognize the unvarying features of the essential virtues (and
their opposites) in all social circumstances.

7. *Physical education*

403c9–412b7. The suitably educated soul will have a healthy influence
on the body. *Psyche* is the primary source of strength: it is not the
excellent body which makes the soul healthy, but the good soul that
makes the body capable, 403d2–4.—The soul is the guardian's guardian,
cf. 403e7.

The training of the body (403c9–404e6) is undertaken in accordance
with the rules of simplicity.[2]) Complexity and excess engender illness of
mind and body.[3]) When law courts and surgeries increase in number,
when lawyers and doctors become predominant, this is a big sign (μέγα
τεκμήριον, 405b1–2) that the educational system has gone astray.—
Socrates, we realize, is spelling from the larger text of contemporary
society.

A new step takes us to the *topic of medicine*, 405c8 ff. The art of

---

[1]) The term εἴδη occurs, but it hardly means Ideas in the technical Platonic
sense. Read within the context of *Bks I–IV* it is, says Adam, unwarrantable to
read in Ideas here, vol. I, p. 168. J. E. Raven, stressing that *Bks II–IV* are exclusively
devoted to the primary education of the guardians and the incalculation of right
belief, takes the view that εἴδη refers here to the Socratic universals rather than to
the Platonic Ideas, *Plato's Thought in the Making*, Cambridge 1965, pp. 125–126.

[2]) ἁπλῆ μουσική, 404b4–5, 410a7–9.

[3]) *Sophrosyne* and *akolasia* are antipodes, 402e3–4, 403a7–11.

Asclepius is essentially a political medicine,[1]) working in the interest of the state, 407c7–e4. In the well-governed society everyone has a job to do and has no time for permanently nursing poor health, 406c1–8. Socrates recalls the medicine of the old days before valetudinarianism began to be practised. A tough medicine intended for a sound constitution is recommended. Those who are unhealthy will be left to die, and the spiritually corrupt will (if they are incurable) be put to death, 409e4–410a6.—Finally it is repeated that this simple form of education inspires both the philosophic part of human nature and *thymoeides* so that they become joined harmoniously in the personalities of the soldier-guardians, 410a7–411a1. If the constitution is to survive there must always therefore be someone in charge of education, 412a4–10.

The gospel of unity and harmony is reflected in many ways. Expressions of it are found in the opinions of heaven, society and personality. The gods are simple and trustworthy.[2]) The cultural forms of the state are simple.[3]) In contrast to the two-folded and many-folded men[4]) in other states, the citizens of our state are simple. The dominant idea which runs through all Plato's criticism of culture, says Nettleship, is that of simplicity as opposed to complexity; Plato thought that the Athenians were losing their simplicity in every direction.[5]) The demand for simplicity is, indeed, highly stressed. But, as Socrates was requested to employ the method of the extreme types, we must expect extremity as an outcome of the illustrative use of exaggerations.

8. Conclusions and observations

Turning to *polis* first, we have noted that the *polis*-words abound in the section 368d–374a, where the community is rapidly developed, cf. *TABLE 1*, p. 236.

---

[1]) 407e3. Πολιτικόν, ἔφη, λέγεις 'Ασκληπιόν — In the discussion with Thrasymachus, 342d2–7, we learn, that the physician is unselfishly concerned with the good of his patient. Now we see the good of the patient subjugated to the good of the society. The former saying "does not accord with the basic teaching of Platonism", writes L. S. King. "The physical health of an individual is distinctly secondary to the good of the soul, and the welfare of the individual is incorporated into the welfare of the state." *Plato's Concept of Medicine, JHM*, vol. IX, 1954, p. 46.

[2]) 380d5, 381c9, 382e8; the term ἁπλοῦς being used.

[3]) 392d5, 393d7, 394b1, 404b5,7; ἁπλοῦς is used also here.

[4]) 397e1, διπλοῦς ἀνήρ; 397e2, πολλαπλοῦς ἀνήρ.

[5]) Nettleship, pp. 109 ff.

The stages of the γιγνομένη πόλις are: (1) ἀναγκαιοτάτη πόλις, generated of but a very small number of co-operative men; (2) ἀληθινὴ πόλις, enlarged with a great number of people in various professions; (3) τρυφῶσα πόλις, also called φλεγμαίνουσα πόλις, still more enlarged, this time in order to raise the volume of consumption beyond the proper limit. At the next stage *polis* is purged, and the discussion is engaged on educational matters; the *polis*-words are not so frequent in the section 376e2–412b7 about the primary education of the guardians, but the cultural climate of the *polis* is always in the background.

From *TABLE 1* we see that the *psyche*-words increase considerably in the section 400e–412b. Here are a few illustrations of meaning and usage.

Psyche is made up of several elements. It seems as if human nature is fractional, broken up in small pieces, so that we cannot do many things well, but must specialize, 395b3–6.—Furthermore, souls can be moulded, particularly during youth, 377a12–b3. They receive impressions (377b7), and they are dependent on the social environment: the guardians must not grow up in evil surroundings, as in some unhealthy pasture, "and there browse and feed upon many a baneful herb and flower day by day, little by little, until they silently gather a festering mass of corruption in their own soul."[1]—Using many metaphors, Plato speaks about the plasticity of *psyche*, its delicacy and sensitiveness. *Thymoeides* can, like iron, be softened or hardened; the process is done with different sorts of *mousike*. If one indulges in soft music, the toughness of the soul is dissolved, its sinews are excised, 411a10–b4. Just as the bodies of children are developed by the hands of their mothers, so their souls are moulded by the stories they are told.[2]—Soul and body are interdependent. If these two are joined in harmony under the soul's guidance, then health, strength and gentleness are generated.[3]

Psyche is often exchanged with "self" (ἑαυτοῦ). The occurrence of this pronoun is quite significant. Here are some examples: to mould oneself, to be below oneself, to sin against oneself, the highest part

---

[1] 401b8–c3, quoted in Jowett's transl.
[2] 377c3–4. καὶ πλάττειν τὰς ψυχὰς αὐτῶν τοῖς μύθοις πολὺ μᾶλλον ἢ τὰ σώματα ταῖς χερσίν.
[3] 402d1–4, 403d2–4, 410b10–e3, 411e4–412a7.

of oneself, to master oneself, and to disagree with oneself.[1])—The phrases reflect how complex and variable man's personality is.

We are next obliged to observe how *polis* and *psyche* are matched with each other in order to make the comparison possible. A basic requirement is that both the components of the *polis-psyche* motif are capable of being moulded. The case of the "swollen city", which is being purged, belongs to the man-makes-*polis* motif, whereas the reason for the undertaking of this purging is that *polis* (by means of its general social and cultural environment) forms man.

That the case of the "swollen city" is a study of *adikia* we need not doubt.[2]) From *Bk I* we are familiar with the same technique. A study of *adikia* was inserted there, as well, in the course of the exposition of *dikaiosyne*; the transition into a normal city, observes Shorey, makes a better sociological laboratory.[3]) The "swollen *polis*" is an excessive society, and it is in the nature of excess to be conspicuous. From an expositional point of view, this is of course an advantage. The study of the "swollen *polis*" can be compared with the study of physiological hypertrophy. In the course of observing the relation between excessive nutrition and excessive growth, one learns something about the conditions for organic life and health. By making Asclepius a statesman and by employing the language of medicine, we are invited to look at society as an organism. Plato in this way supplies a model for his analysis of function.

The analogy between medical treatment and social reformwork depends to some extent on what concept of *medicine* one applies to the concept of *society*. The Greek *polis* was small-scaled. The town with its inhabitants, the valleys and slopes with their farmers and shepherds, the harbour with its ships and sailors—all this could be surveyed and, I think, contemplated as a pattern of inter-dependence. Possibly the economic, social, and political interaction of such a closely-knitted social aggregate, fertilized conditions for the development of the organic

---

[1]) 382a7, τῷ κυριωτάτῳ που ἑαυτῶν; 390b3, ἐγκράτειαν ἑαυτοῦ; 396a2 ἁμαρτάνουσιν εἰς αὐτούς; 396d4, ἑαυτοῦ ἀνάξιον; 396d7, αὐτὸν ἐκμάττειν; 409b1, ἔχοντες ἐν ἑαυτοῖς παραδείγματα; 430e11–12, Οὐκοῦν τὸ μὲν κρείττω αὐτοῦ γελοῖον; ὁ γὰρ ἑαυτοῦ κρείττων καὶ ἥττων δήπου ἂν αὐτοῦ εἴη καὶ ὁ ἥττων κρείττων.

[2]) 372e4–8, cf. 373e4–7.

[3]) *What Plato Said*, Chicago 1965, p. 217.

line of thought.[1])—The general feature of ancient medicine to match this view of the Greek *polis* is, it seems, its theory of health and sickness based on the notions of harmony and disturbance of harmony; it is the balance between various forces which rule the organism. Balance is natural. To be cured is to get one's balance restored.[2]) *Sophrosyne* fits very well into such a view of health.[3])

If medicine is the science of harmony and dis-harmony in the human body, politics can be established as the knowledge of harmony and dis-harmony of the social body. The doctrine of balance was by no means new. It belonged to the pre-Socratic heritage. Plato pulled the threads together, writes Guthrie,[4]) and, we may add, intertwined them to suit his version of *sophrosyne,* the nucleus of social cohesion and unity. By speaking of social reform-work in terms of medicine, Socrates is able to give a special flavour of scientific knowledge to the imaginary experiment in which he is involved.[5])

In 376e2–412b7 the *sophrosyne-akolasia* complex is rather more dominant than that referring to *dikaiosyne-adikia. Philia, homonoia* and *koinonia*—the terms for social cohesion—were in *Bk I* grouped around *dikaiosyne.* Now *sophrosyne* has become the head of a family of words comprising friendliness, civility, moderation and temperance. But at 389d9–e2 *sophrosyne* means basically (a) to be obedient to those in authority; and (b) to exercise self-discipline concerning food, drink and sex. This is meant as a first approach.[6])

---

[1]) "Would Aristotle (a sober observer) have asserted that the whole is before the part if his statement had not corresponded to the facts as they still were in his day?" W. Stark, *The Fundamental Forms of Social Thought,* London 1962, p. 95.

[2]) Jaeger, *Paideia* vol. III, pp. 26–27.

[3]) By the help of Homer Plato, however, takes resort to a mythical medicine, 407c7–408b5. This medicine suits to serve the state-interest. Medicine should help to preserve good health, not serve to make sick and useless men live a long time.

[4]) Guthrie, *HGP* vol. I, p. 210.

[5]) Cf. Jaeger, *Paideia,* vol. III, p. 25.

[6]) Cf. H. North, *Sophrosyne. Self-Knowledge and Self-Restraint in Greek Literature.* New York 1966, p. 170. Also Adam, vol. I, p. 138.

CHAPTER VI
MODEL POLIS COMPLETED
(Bk III:412b8–IV:445e4)

1. Fundamental classes of polis

412b8–415d2. The subject of ruling is next taken up, marking a new and important stage in the construction of the *polis*.

The best of the elders should rule. The best means the most guardian-minded, those who are wise, efficient and devoted to the state, 412c9–13. The love of the commonwealth is on firmest ground when one accepts that self-fortune is intimately bound up with common welfare, 412d4–7, cf. 369c6–7. One may, however, be persuaded or forced or charmed to abandon this truth, 412e10–c3. Therefore the candidates must be trained and tested so that the finally selected rulers possess the required persistent love of the *polis*, 413c5–414a7.

The former class of guardians is divided into two fundamental classes: *phylakes*, (guardians in the fullest sense of the word) and their *epikouroi*, (auxiliaries), 414b1–6. The rest of the population make up the third class. At 414d2–4 this three-fold division is indicated by the terms rulers, soldiers and the rest of the *polis* (τὴν ἄλλην πόλιν).

A long discourse (414b8–427c5) then takes place about the precautions for social stability and unity. There are various means at hand to achieve these goals. First there is the use of *pseudos* (convenient fictions),[1] cf. 382c6–d3, 389b2–9. This much-needed propaganda or

---

[1] Cornford, pp. 66, 103, n. 1.—The passage 414b8–c1 has proved troublesome. Jowett translates "royal lie", Shorey "noble lie". Cornford renders it "a single bold flight of invention", thinking "noble lie" self-contradictory. A criticism of Cornford's version is found in G. Thomson, *Aeschylus and Athens. A Study in the Social Origins of Drama*, London (1941), 2. ed. 1946, p. 453, n. 29. Cornford's answer is published in *The Unwritten Philosophy and Other Essays* (ed. by Guthrie), Cambridge 1950, pp. 132 ff.

myth-making[1]) should be used on all the three fundamental classes, 414d1-4. All are to be told that their education and training happened as in a dream.[2]) According to the myth, they were in reality formed, reared and equipped in the earth. The Earth is their mother. They belong to the soil, and the fellow-citizens are to be regarded as brothers born of the same mother, 414d4-e6.

The tale is a modification of the popular belief that the Athenians were *"autochthonous"*, born from the soil, and kin to the city itself.[3]) And this myth is combined with another, the suitably adapted tale about the five races of men.[4]) In order to preserve the right sort of social order, the citizens should be told that there are important differences between them to observe. God has mingled gold in the composition of the guardians, silver in the auxiliaries, and brass or iron in the others, 415a2-7; the presence of iron or brass in the higher levels means destruction of the state, 415a7-c7. Thus a wide social distance should be upheld between superiors and inferiors; all citizens are brothers, but brothers of qualitatively different capacities.

We see thus that the myths are state-supporting. They are suggestive and they provide efficient images, which help to build up useful doctrines and attitudes.[5]) The engineering of myth and religion to the interest of the state was not unpractised in Greek history. From early times state and religion were intertwined in many ways.[6])

---

[1]) 414b8-c2 ... μηχανὴ γένοιτο τῶν ψευδῶν τῶν ἐν δέοντι γιγνομένων, ὧν δὴ νῦν ἐλέγομεν, γενναῖόν τι ἐν ψευδομένους πεῖσαι μάλιστα κτλ.

[2]) Cf. 414d2-4. It is a myth for all the people, Cornford p. 104.

[3]) A parallel is the cult of the heroes who represented a sort of blood-relationship with the city itself. Cf. M. P. Nilsson, *A History of Greek Religion*, Oxford 1956, p. 233.

[4]) About the traditional elements of this myth, cf. P. Frutiger, *Les Mythes de Platon*, Paris 1930, pp. 235 ff.—There is also in this passage a complex of comparisons, observes P. Grenet, p. 169:

$$\frac{\text{Enfants}}{\text{Femme}} = \frac{\text{Citoyens}}{\text{Patrie}} = \frac{\text{Métaux}}{\text{Sous-sol}}$$

[5]) Myths, shaped in accordance with reason, bring the light of reason to the realm of passions. L. Edelstein, *The Function of Myth in Plato's Philosophy*, *JHI*, vol. X, 1949, pp. 463 ff.

[6]) Cults and myths were not seldom administered to political ends. Cf. M. P. Nilsson, *Geschichte der Griechischen Religion*, I, 3:te Aufl., München 1967, the chapter *Religion und Staat.*, pp. 708 ff.

2. Features of a unified polis

415d3-427c5. Plato's holistic views provide cues for further interpretations. Take the stipulation that a person could be moved from
one place of work to another because of his capacity. Calling to mind
how the individual according to Plato is moulded by the social forces,
the possibility of the potter's son to progress seems small. If it, however,
occurred, it would, I think, consist in the rarely undertaken administrative act of putting some stray person in his proper place, an act not
done to please ambition, but to promote the interest of the state, 423c6–
d6. The *polis* is founded on authorized values, and the standard for
judging them is without dispute in the hands of the rulers.[1])

Unification, we conclude, is the statesman's prime office. There is
a closely-related cluster of words (simplicity-harmony-unity-efficiency)
indicating the goal for cultural and social policy.

Social planning aims at the maintenance of inner stability, i.e. to
prevent society from swelling, 422b9–10, cf. 460a2–6.

A strategical place must first be selected from which the city can be
dominated and guarded from assault by both internal and external
enemies, 415d8–e4. The guardians should be adequately housed, clothed
and nourished so that they do not (like badly treated dogs) turn on
the sheep, 416a2–b3. The greatest care must be observed that a friendly
spirit is upheld, 416b1–d1; the internal dangers threatening society
are greater than the external ones, 417a6–b6. The rulers and the soldiers
are forbidden to have valuables or property of any kind. They must
not be men of property. They would then soon become strangers to
the people, severed by hate and envy. The rulers and the auxiliaries
should therefore have what they need, no more—no less. Wealth and
poverty are two evils. The one breeds softness, idleness and passion
for novelty, while the other engenders meanness, bad workmanship

---

[1]) H. D. Rankin, *Plato and the Individual*, London 1964, surveys briefly the
pros and cons of lower-class promotion in the *Rep*. "Plato wanted mobility of
talent within society, but these assimilative tendencies in his society are against
it. These work against his desire for a just allotment of individuals among the
groups of the *Republic*. People become what they do. They become what they
perceive. They are therefore liable to be fixed in the group in which they were
born", p. 76.—On the other hand it might be held that we know too little about
the social stratification of the third class to be able to determine what chances
there could be.

and social destruction, 421d1–422a3. We now come to the celebrated question of Plato's communism, which is here only dealt with briefly: such questions as the possession of wives, marriage and child-bearing should as far as possible be treated according to the proverbial saying "friends have all things in common", 424a1–2.[1])

Adeimantus interposes that those selected men are offered a poor sort of life, and are being deprived of everything which by common consent makes men happy. But, he adds, it is their own fault as they themselves control the state and fail to take advantage of their opportunities, 419a1–420a1. This flash of criticism calls forth the important declaration that the *polis* is not founded to make a part of it exceptionally happy, but to secure the greatest happiness to the state as a whole.[2]) Happiness should be distributed in due proportion according to the pattern of organic unity; painting a statue you must not make one part of it so brilliant that it outshines the other parts and breaks up the total shape, 420c4–d5. Attention is focused internally on the fundamental tripartition of work; if the members of the three classes are compelled and induced to perfect themselves within their functional levels, the *polis* will prosper and each class receives the happiness that nature awards it, 421a3–c6. Such a state—unified, disciplined and efficient—is truly great even if it has but a thousand military defenders, 423a5–8.

For Plato the notion of *polis* implies unity; all other forms of societies are more or less split up into poor and rich people. The best standard (κάλλιστος ὅρος) for determining the size of the *polis* is that it may grow so long as unity can be preserved, 423b9–10. Next (423d2–6) we learn, that when the principle of division of work is respected in such a city, then each citizen becomes one man, and not many, just as the *polis* in this process becomes one city, and not many. Here, in few words, is indicated what strong character-shaping capacity this closely-knitted *polis* is supposed to have.

---

[1]) Apelt here observes Plato's economy of disposition. With calculated art the controversial subject is avoided. "... er will mit einer so verfänglichen Sache nicht wie mit der Tür ins Haus fallen ...", pp. 464–465, n. 13.—Cf. 453c10–d3.

[2]) 420b5–8, ... οὐ μὴν πρὸς τοῦτο βλέποντες τὴν πόλιν οἰκίζομεν, ὅπως ἕν τι ἡμῖν ἔθνος ἔσται διαφερόντως εὔδαιμον, ἀλλ᾽ ὅπως ὅτι μάλιστα ὅλη ἡ πόλις.—And, Socrates goes on, in such a state we thought the chances best for finding *dikaiosyne*, just as we expect to find *adikia* manifested in a city of the contrary kind, 420b8–c4. Again we are reminded of the systematic importance of the *dikaiosyne-adikia* polarity.

The *educational planning* has already been dealt with. It is now stressed that it is essential that the educational system be well preserved and applied; innovations are dangerous, 424b3–c4. Political change is intimately bound up with cultural change, 424c5–6. A powerful metaphor says that the fortress of the state is to be built on the field of education.[1] The cultural policy (like the policies of social welfare and economics) is guided by holistic views.

As a contrast, there are at intervals notices concerning the nature and danger of social and personal dissolutions. Such references are found at 416a2–b3 (about badly treated dogs), and at 417a6–b6, 421a2–8, 421d4–422b3, 422e3–423b2, 424b3–e2, 424e5–425a1 and 426a1–c6 (about the danger of wealth and poverty, acquisition and luxury etc). We further learn (though the matter is only very briefly mentioned, 424a4–e2) that society and personality change in the same cumulative way. If the start is good, the process turns out good, 424a4–b1.[2] If another disposition is introduced the movement runs towards destruction in both man and society, 424d7–e2.[3]

3. Cardinal virtues of polis

427c6-434d1. Finally, and this is a moment of great importance, the foundation of the *polis* is declared completed. *Polis* is now available for its illustrative purpose, 427c6–d7, cf. *TABLE 2*, nr 9. Provide yourself with a light, says Socrates, and try to find where *dikaiosyne* and *adikia* are in the *polis*, and see how they differ and how they stand in relation to happiness.

If the *polis* is rightly ordered it is also completely good, (τελέως ἀγαθὴν). It lacks in no kind of virtue. The constituents which make up the whole of *arete* are four in number, 428a8–9. They are (427e10–11) *sophia, andreia, sophrosyne* and *dikaiosyne*. Earlier on in the *Republic*,

---

[1] 424d1–2. Τὸ δὴ φυλακτήριον, ἦν δ᾽ ἐγώ, ὡς ἔοικεν, ἐνταῦθά που οἰκοδομητέον τοῖς φύλαξιν, ἐν μουσικῇ.

[2] "Etwa nach Analogie eines Organismus, in welchem alles wechselseitig Ursache und Wirkung ist und in welchem, wie z.B. in einer wachsenden Pflanze, durch dies innere Spiel seiner Kräfte das Wachstum zustande kommt: ..." Apelt, p. 465, n. 14.

[3] Little by little morals and manners are undermined until both public and private life are ruined.—Adam (commenting on the word ὑπορρεῖ) writes: "as a gentle river may become a destructive torrent before its course is ended". There is here, Adam means, a loaded reference to the decay of Athens, vol. I, p. 217.

other combinations of virtues have also been mentioned, 395c4–5, 402c2–4. Now, however, the virtues occur with a higher degree of systematization. But Plato does not explicitly tell us why they are just four.—We may, however, assume that these four capacities together constitute what is roughly required from a functional social unit; i.e. they are the essential and co-existing constituents of complete *arete*.[1]) In the earlier educational discourses, *andreia* and *sophrosyne* have played important roles. They mark the need of both fighting spirit and friendliness, and—judging from the preceding sections—they seem unavoidable. The inclusion of *sophia*, the crown of the virtues with a high place in the Attic scale of virtues, is to be expected. With the addition of *dikaiosyne*, which is the subject of Plato's research, the list is complete. From such considerations, the Platonic selection of virtues involves, I think, no surprise.[2]) We can also understand that Plato requires a fixed number of virtues which is not too large; *dikaiosyne* is to be discovered by the method of residues, 428a2–6. The method of elimination is set to work on that table of values which springs from the functional approach, employed in the construction of the *polis*.

a) *Sophia* emerges first. In the light of what we have seen about the importance of functional integration, it is not surprising that a special value is given to the interest of the agent as a unit. *Sophia* is the knowledge (*epistheme*) of *polis* as a whole, judged both from internal and external aspects. This knowledge resides with the smallest class of citizens (τῷ σμικροτάτῳ ἄρα ἔθνει καὶ μέρει, 428e7–9), which consists of the guardians in the true sense of the word (τελέους φύλακας, 428d6–7). The guardians, taken as a fundamental part of the *polis*, deliberate for the good of the whole *polis*, and, in so doing, they exercise wisdom.[3])

b) *Andreia* is related to that part (εἰς τοῦτο τὸ μέρος, 429b2), the task of which it is to defend and fight for the *polis*; notes on the importance of this task have already been found in the preceding sec-

---

[1]) The term "essential constituents of complete *arete*" I have borrowed from R. S. Bluck, *Plato's Meno*, Cambridge. 1961, p. 231.

[2]) The explanation provided results from the pursuance of the motif. There may be other explanations, for instance influences from Pythagoreanism. Cf. J. Ferguson, *Moral Values in the Ancient World*, London 1958, pp. 24 ff. Cf. Adam, vol. I, pp. 224–225.

[3]) 428c11–d3. ἀλλ' ὑπὲρ αὐτῆς ὅλης, ὅντινα τρόπον αὐτή τε πρὸς αὐτὴν καὶ πρὸς τὰς ἄλλας πόλεις ἄριστα ὁμιλοῖ;

tions.[1]) But *andreia* is not only a matter of sword and spear. Its characteristic feature is a kind of preservation.[2]) It consists of a true conservative spirit, 430b2–5. The auxiliaries must under all circumstances preserve the incalculated values, 429c7–d2. The dangers that threaten the *polis* are many. And permanently it runs the risk of having its cultural pattern corrupted. Just as wool must be well prepared if it is to retain its colour, so through education must the souls of the auxiliaries be "impregnated with the spirit of our laws like dye", 429d4–430b5. That *polis* is courageous means that there exists a soldier-class having the engrained capacity of courage to preserve and defend it.

c) *Sophrosyne* well deserves the dignity of a cardinal virtue; we have frequently met the term in *Bk III*. Taking into consideration also other occurrences of the word, *sophrosyne* stands out as the head of a group of civil values, being closely related to friendliness, simplicity and harmony, as well as to obedience and self-control.[3]) Even now (430e6–9) we learn that *sophrosyne* is an important factor in the making of a social *kosmos*.[4]) Another indication of the meaning of the term is found in the puzzling expression "master of oneself" (κρείττω αὐτοῦ), which involves the idea of a structural person, ruled by some principle, cf. 431a3–b2, and p. 93 above. Plato refers here first to the individual aspect of *sophrosyne*, before he gives the political view.[5])—We are then summoned to make use of the newly founded *polis*, cf. *TABLE 2*, nr 10. We may expect to find *sophrosyne* realized in the same manner as in the well-ordered soul. The inferior part (cf. 431a4–5), Socrates tells, consists generally of children, women, servants and citizens from the third class, 431b9–c3. The better part of the *polis* is composed of the few who are of both excellent physical constitution and good education, are simple and moderate, and besides are directed by reason and right convictions.[6]) The conclusion is that the *polis* is self-controlled,

---

1) Cf. 375a11, 381a3, 386a6, 410d6 and 410e10.

2) 429c5. Σωτηρίαν ἔγωγ', εἶπον, λέγω τινὰ εἶναι τὴν ἀνδρείαν.

3) 389d9, 390b3, 402e3, 403a7, 403a10, 404e4, 410a8, 410e10 and 416d8.

4) 430e6–9. Κόσμος πού τις, ἦν δ' ἐγώ, ἡ σωφροσύνη ἐστὶν καὶ ἡδονῶν τινων καὶ ἐπιθυμιῶν ἐγκράτεια, κτλ.

5) "Für die σωφροσύνη ist eigentlich das beabsichtigte Verfahren umgedreht worden: nicht aus der πόλις wird ihr Begriff erkannt, sondern ihr psychologisch festgelegter Begriff wird auf die πόλις angewandt. Apelt", p. 469, n. 41.

6) 431c5–7. Τὰς δέ γε ἁπλᾶς τε καὶ μετρίας, αἳ δὴ μετὰ νοῦ τε καὶ δόξης ὀρθῆς λογισμῷ ἄγονται, ἐν ὀλίγοις τε ἐπιτεύξῃ καὶ τοῖς βέλτιστα μὲν φῦσιν, βέλτιστα δὲ παιδευθεῖσιν.

when the best part rules over the others, 431c9–d8; the ruling should, however, be a matter of agreement, 431e4–5. The relation of *sophrosyne* to harmony and concord is given at 431e10–432a9. It is first stated that *sophia* and *andreia* are departmental, each of them existing in separate parts (ἐν μέρει τινὶ ἑκατέρα ἐνοῦσα) of the *polis*. *Sophrosyne*, however, is distributed in a different way. It pervades all society. All the three fundamental classes have their share of it, 432a2–6.

d) *Dikaiosyne* appears last. The essential constituents of complete *arete* are four. Three are found. The remaining one must be *dikaiosyne*, 432b2–5.[1]) What does it mean?

The question now to be answered is momentous. The whole investigation centres around this question. Socrates holds the attention, and then finally declares *dikaiosyne* to be the very principle on which the state was founded: division of work as expressed in the formula of doing one's own business, and not doing many jobs, 433a8–9. Specialization (natural talent, concentration and training) are the conditions for a good job. But Socrates does not want to be involved in petty aspects, 434a3–7. He directs our attention to the relation between the three fundamental classes of the state. As a first step we are informed that πολυπραγμοσύνη and interchange of jobs between the three classes are harmful to the *polis* and deserve the name of *adikia*, 434b9–c7. Contrary to this, *dikaiosyne* is realized, when each class restricts itself to its proper field of work and abstains from any meddling in other fundamental occupations.[2])

The study of the larger text has brought us to the famous tripartite state. To its three fundamental classes are joined the four essential constituents of *arete*. For the sake of clarity and survey, the socio-ethical pattern can be presented as on the next page.

The table records personal interpretation, and it should not be

---

[1]) The process of elimination is in its closing stage dramatically likened to a hunt. As for the passage 432b7–d7 cf. C. J. Classen, *Untersuchung zu Platons Jagdbildern*, Berlin 1960, pp. 37–38.

[2]) 434c7–10. χρηματιστικοῦ, ἐπικουρικοῦ, φυλακικοῦ γένους οἰκειοπραγία, ἑκάστου τούτων τὸ αὑτοῦ πράττοντος ἐν πόλει, τοὐναντίον ἐκείνου δικαιοσύνη τ' ἂν εἴη καὶ τὴν πόλιν δικαίαν παρέχοι; A. W. Small, commenting on this conclusion, says that it is a skilful process of persuasion, "not a piece of research ending in discovery ... the conclusion was safely packed away in the premises before the argument began." *AJS*, vol. 30 1924/1925, p. 688. See also Ch. L. Stevenson, *Ethics and Language*, New Haven 1953 (and later ed.), pp. 224 ff.

Table F. Socio- cultural pattern

The fundamental classes of *polis*, 434c8, 440e10–441a1	The essential constituents of complete *arete*, 428d7–429a2, 429b1–c3, 431e4–432a9, 434c7–10		
I. Guardians	*Sophia,*	*Sophrosyne*	*Dikaiosyne*
II. Auxiliaries	*Andreia,*		
III. Traders etc.			

forgotten that the pattern given is a controversial question in literature concerning the *Republic*.[1])—Summing up we see that *sophia* rests exclusively with (I), and *andreia* exclusively with (II), while all three classes partake of *sophrosyne*. When *sophia*, *andreia* and *sophrosyne* are distributed in this way, and each of the fundamental classes specializes on its own sphere of activities, then *dikaiosyne* can be predicated to the whole of *polis*,[2]) 434c7–10.

4. Fundamental parts of psyche

434d2-441c3. Attention is now directed to the meaning of *dikaiosyne* in the micro-text. The previous result cannot be accepted as valid before it has been confirmed in *psyche* as well, 434d2–5, cf. 368e7–369a3.

At 434d6–435a3 the double-text method of *Bk II* is referred to. The reading of the larger text was undertaken in order to facilitate the study of the lesser one, cf. *TABLE 2*, nr 11. We must now see if the pattern of righteousness in *polis* agrees with that of *psyche*. If they agree—all is well, if they do not, then the two components of the comparison must be carefully re-examined, each in turn. This process of

---

[1]) Adam, vol. I, p. 236, pictures the distribution of *sophia*, *andreia* and *sophrosyne* (having not yet treated *dikaiosyne*) in a similar way. "Plato's account of σωφροσύνη in other dialogues differs in many respects from this, and is rather a hindrance than a help in elucidating the present passage".

[2]) 435b4–5. ᾽Αλλὰ μέντοι πόλις γε ἔδοξεν εἶναι δικαία ὅτε ἐν αὐτῇ τριττὰ γένη φύσεων ἐνόντα τὸ αὐτῶν ἕκαστον ἔπραττεν, ... — In Praechter-Ueberweg there is an instructive table illustrating the distribution of the cardinal virtues. *Sophrosyne* is there predicated the total community under the leading aspect: Einigkeit des herrschenden und der beiden beherrschten Stände über den Beruf des ersteren zur Herrschaft. And *dikaiosyne* is predicated the total community when jeder Stand τὰ αὐτοῦ πράττει, p. 275.

repeatedly inspecting *polis* and *psyche* is compared with producing fire by rubbing two pieces of wood against each other, cf. *TABLE 2*, a methodological complement. We may observe this procedure as the rationalist's method of comparison and creative confrontation; in the thought-experiment, trial and error are set to work on similarities and polarities.[1])

The guiding properties of the *polis* are its threefold structure combined with the four virtues. Though this pattern might be expected to prevail also for *psyche*, Socrates warns us that we should not be too confident that the double-text method is infallible. There is also a longer way to go.[2]) A valid method involves more than just comparing structural outlines. Accurate comparison and measurement rest on the use of true standards. Socrates does not want, however, to complicate the investigation here with epistemological inquiries. The double-text method suffices for the immediate purpose.—The introduction of a still longer way of examination in the midst of the laborious development of the double-text method, (cf. 369b2–3) seems somewhat strange[3]).

Returning to the analogical mode of investigation it would be ridiculous to suppose that *psyche* is tripartite just because *polis* is threefold. On the contrary, Socrates says, what is found in *polis* emanates from the individuals, 435e1–5. To demonstrate this point Socrates refers to what we call ethnological observations. In different countries one can observe a certain variation of the predominant characters.[4]) There

---

[1]) G. E. R. Lloyd speaks about this confrontation (368d f) as a verification. *Polarity and Analogy*, Cambridge 1966, p. 397.—As the term verification carries with it associations to strictly empirical sciences, it is perhaps safer to regard the technique of confrontation as a control against unchecked analogizing.

[2]) This μακροτέρα καὶ πλείων ὁδός (435d3) does not lead towards empiricism but towards a higher level of speculation.

[3]) Adam thinks that 435c9–d5 was written at a later time, when Bk VI 504a–d was composed, cf. vol. I, pp. 244–45.

[4]) Let us compare Plato's view here with that of an anthropologist. R. Linton says that it cannot be doubted that there is a close relation between the personality configuration and the culture of the society. "Culture, in so far as it is anything more than an abstraction made by the investigator, exists only in the minds of the individuals who compose a society. It derives all its qualities from their personalities and the interaction of these personalities. Conversely, the personality of every individual within the society develops and functions in constant associations with its culture. Personalities affect culture and culture affects personality." *The Study of Man*, New York 1936, p. 464.

are for instance the Attic love of knowledge, the Thracian or Scythian reputation of courage, and the love of money attributed to the Egyptians or Phoenicians, 435e3–436a3. There is a preponderance of one quality here and of another quality there. The concept of *polis* as made up of individuals and as profiled by their basic character, belongs to our *anti-motif*. The illustrative power of the *polis* is due to the fact that a community is made up of men, and that their drives more or less project themselves on to the social body. In other words *polis* is able to illustrate *psyche* because *polis* itself, roughly speaking, is an enlarged reflection of the personalities.[1])

The ethnographical material indicated three main types of drives roughly corresponding to the three classes of the *polis*. But how does the psychological mechanism work? There are at least two alternatives, thinks Socrates. (1) Do we know with one part of ourselves, are angry with another, and desire with a third? Or (2) is the whole soul possibly involved in every act, 436a8–b2? Socrates takes the first alternative to be true. This verdict is upheld by two main arguments, one causal and one introspective.

a) According to Plato's general theory of causality the same thing cannot act at the same time in opposite ways.[2]) From this statement it is derived that a part of the soul is likewise incapable of acting simultaneously in opposite ways. If you are thirsty there must somehow be an urge to drink. And if you are thirsty, but hesitate to drink, there must be another principle which checks the first one, 439a9–c7, cf. 604b3–4. This theory of *pluralistic psychology* is paralleled by the differential social forces of the *polis*.

b) Through introspection we experience ourselves as curiously charged with different inclinations.[3]) To illustrate this, Socrates tells the *story*

---

[1]) "Broadly speaking ... the predominant character of a State depends on the predominant character of the individual citizens." Adam, vol. I, p. 245.

[2]) 436b8–c1, 436e8–437a2. Cf. Robinson, pp. 111–112, and Crombie, vol. i, pp. 365 ff.

[3]) "Diese Seelenlehre wird gewonnen an Phänomenen der inneren Selbstentzweiung der Seele und ist deshalb auf diese Selbstentzweiung des Menschen bezogen." H-G. Gadamer, *Platos dialektische Ethik und andere Studien zur platonischen Philosophie*, Hamburg 1968, p. 216.

of Leontius, who experiences himself as the battle-field of opposite forces.[1])

From a) and b) the conclusion is drawn that *psyche* is moved and modified by different elements working alone or in combinations.—The analysis of the thirsty man who does not permit himself to drink allows Socrates to make a distinction between the reasoning faculty (*logistikon*) and the bulk of appetites (*epithymetikon*), 439d4–8.

Thereby two parts of the soul have been found.[2]) Piloted by the larger text Socrates now asks for a third part, cf. *TABLE 2*, nr 13. That reason and the passions are often found at war was commonplace.[3]) Now we must see why three elements are needed, and how they are exposed.

The rationalistic element is distinguished by its ability to judge and deliberate, and the appetites by their characteristics of violence and blindness. In between these two forces the element of *thymos* is posited, (a fiery, courageous and energetic part) manifesting itself as moral indignation. Thus (if not corrupted by bad education, 441a3) *thymos* is allied to *logistikon*, 440a8–b7. It gives emotional force to the rational element and helps to execute its deliberations about the right course of action.[4]) The conclusion is that *thymos* is different from both *epithymetikon* and *logistikon*,[5]) 441a5–6.

To bring out his point Socrates refers to the behaviour of children.

---

[1]) 439e6–440a3. A man, Leontius, is passing the place of execution just outside Athens. There he observes some dead bodies, and he feels disgust and curiosity. He tries to control himself, but the curiosity urge is stronger, and finally in anger he gives in to this morbid desire.—Concerning the significance of this story, Crombie, vol. I, pp. 346–347.

[2]) 439e2–3, . . . δύο ἡμῖν ὡρίσθω εἴδη ἐν ψυχῇ ἐνόντα.

[3]) It was common in Greece to speak about this inner conflict as a personified fight between two forces. Cf. C. J. Classen, *Sprachliche Deutung als Triebkraft Platonischen und Sokratischen Philosophierens*. Zetemata. Monographien zur klassischen Altertumswissenschaft. Heft 22, München 1959, p. 19.—Also B. Snell, pp. 83 ff.

[4]) 440d2–6, as the dog obeys the shepherd.

[5]) According to Jaeger "Plato took from Hippocrates not only the word θυμοειδές for his concept of the spirited part of the soul, but also the characteristic features of that aspect of the life of the soul. Most significant for this is, according to Hippocrates, the predominance of ὀργή in this type of man." *A New Word in Plato's Republic, Eranos*, vol. XLIX 1946, pp. 129 ff. Cf. *Paideia*, vol. II, p. 407, n. 190.

They display anger at an early age, but only accommodate themselves to the control of reason at a later stage, 441a7–b1. Also in the animal kingdom one can observe the phenomenon of *thymos*, 441b2–3. At last (441b6) Socrates also refers to a passage in Homer, *Od. XX, 17*. —Thus it is shown that, like *polis*, *psyche* has three parts, 441c4–7.

The demonstration rests on an impressive arsenal of arguments. By the aid of the theory of causation, together with observations from ethnology, introspective psychology, child-psychology, zoology and literature, *psyche* is examined on its own grounds. The promise involved in the method is fulfilled in the sense that independent and ingenious reasons are given for the conclusions drawn. The support for the theory of the structured self is of a realistic kind.[1]) By means of this theory of the structured self Plato is able to give (as will be seen in *Bks VIII–IX*) a realistic interpretation of man's character in its varying patterns. The structural similarity between *polis* and *psyche* is so far this: rulers-auxiliaries-traders/reason-spiritedness-appetites, 440e10–441a3, c4–7.

These components are spoken of as parts.[2]) I do not think that it is profitable to try to sort out whether γένη or εἴδη or μέρη or any other expression is the most accurate term. Assuming that it is, in any case, a question of principal parts of functional wholes, I will from now on use the terms *fundamental classes* and *fundamental parts* for the components of *polis* and *psyche* respectively.

---

[1]) Frutiger, takes the term myth in a very broad, perhaps too broad a sense: everything which is in any way symbolic even if it is quite "scientific" but exposed without the aid of dialectics, i.e. things which are probable but not certain, p. 37. By such a definition also 434e–441e turns out a myth in spite of its very unmythical argumentation. This is queer. Frutiger admits that the passage under discussion has such a marked technical character that one at first hesitates to place it among the myths, pp. 88 ff.

[2]) For the fundamental classes the following terms are used; ἔθνος καὶ μέρος, 428e7; μέρος 429b2, 429b8, 431e10; γένος 429a1, 434b9, 434c7,8, 435b5,7; εἶδος 434b2. For the fundamental elements of *psyche* the following terms occur: εἶδος 435c1, 435c5, 437c1, d3, 439e2, 440e8,9; μέρος occurs at 442b11, c5, and γένος by implication at 441a2, and conclusively at 443d3 and (subsidiary to μέρος) at 444b5; referring to both *polis* and *psyche* γένος is used at 441c6 (and 441e1 by implication); εἴδη καὶ ἤθη 435e2; μέρος 444b3.—Thus γένος, εἶδος and μέρος are the three main terms used when either referring to *polis* or *psyche* exclusively or to both of them at the same time in summing-up sentences. What is now said refers to 427b1–444e6.

5. Cardinal virtues of psyche

441c4-444a9. Having found that the three parts of *psyche* correspond to the three classes of *polis*, Socrates reminds us how the virtues were distributed in the society. This pattern, he concludes, is valid also for *psyche*, 441c9–442d9.

(a) *Sophia* displays itself through that principle which rules and deliberates, and has knowledge of what is best for each of the three parts and for man as a whole, 441e4–6, 442c5–8.

(b) *Andreia* results from the activity of *thymoeides*, adhering through pain and pleasure to the directions of *logistikon*, 442b9–c3.

(c) *Sophrosyne* manifests itself through friendliness and concord. Man is self-controlled when there is an internal agreement about ruling and being ruled, 442c10–d1.

(d) *Dikaiosyne*, finally, consists in the maintenance of the division of work, primarily in the aspect of ruler-ruled, 443b1–2.

The finding of *dikaiosyne* in the soul is of course a great event, being one of the two professed goals of the investigation. This happy ending is almost providential, says Socrates, 443b7–c2. What we actually see of specialization in the field of trades is an outward reflection of *dikaiosyne*, 443c4–7. Then comes the so-called long definition of *dikaiosyne*, 443c9–444a2, see p. 221 below. It is asserted that in reality justice is a kind of division of work upheld in the inward self,[1]) 443c9–d1; the functional aspect is embodied in 444c5–e6.

Looking at the distribution of virtues we note that *sophia* and *andreia* are departmental; each has a separate location, both in *polis* as well as in *psyche*. But *sophrosyne* and *dikaiosyne* are distributed in a different way: at 432a2–9 it is expressively said that *sophrosyne* is present in all the three classes of the *polis* and manifests itself through the friendliness between them; that this feature holds good also for the soul is evident from 442c10–d3; and concerning *dikaiosyne* cf. 434c7–10, 443b1–6. —The four cardinal virtues stand out as functional requisites for the unity and stability of both society and man. They are concerned with ruling, preservation, harmony and specialization.

The theory of the tripartite soul was, we have seen, backed up with

---

[1]) The definition of *dikaiosyne* as a matter of the inward self seems, it has been observed, egocentric and alien from that inter-personal field of action which alone fits justice.—This question is treated in the last chapter.

independent arguments. As for the cardinal virtues, the question arises as to whether the preparatory illustrations, carried out in a socio-political context, inescapably lead to *psyche* being politicized. There is much talk of inward ruling and being ruled, of defence and alliance.[1]) At 441c9 ff. it seems as if Plato simply takes it for granted that the ethical pattern holds good also for *psyche*.[2])

I assume that Plato's confidence in the established pattern of comparison is connected with the belief that organic units generally must have certain constitutive traits in common. Specialization of work and reciprocity of services, guided by insight of what is best for the preservation of the unit, calls for the same basic structure and complementary capacities, whether one thinks of *polis* or *psyche*. A special argument for the identity of the ethical pattern is that the ethical qualities found in society come from the individuals who make up the society. Dimly a biomorphic model is seen behind the concepts of both *polis* and *psyche*, cf. 462c10–d3. We have observed the doctrine of the natural balance in the ancient theory of health, a view which in the *Republic* is combined with the conception of *psycho-somatic* unity. By this line of thought *sophrosyne*, the merit of harmony and moderation, is predestined to become a key-term for the integration and balance of organisms. It is symptomatic that Plato, when speaking of *sophrosyne* in the social context (430e3–432a9), first turns to how this virtue is experienced in the person. Looking for the biological prototype, what is more close at hand than man himself? Having a basic, organic outlook, and using the political language in a transferred sense, Plato is able to articulate his theory of the structured self. His re-definition of the cardinal virtues, wedded to the theory of the structured self, stands out, I think, as the main result of the four first books. Also, recalling that man was approached as a social being, I think Plato may be granted to have, within his rational mode of investigation, fulfilled what the double-text method

---

[1]) In the *Rep.* there are many such references: 353d, 432a, 441e, 442a, d, 443d, 444d, 462d, 579c, 581b, 586e, 590c, 591a, c, and 608b. Cf. P. Louis, *Les Métaphores de Platon*, Rennes 1945, p. 107. "Mais l'image la plus fréquente est celle qui assimile la raison à un souverain ou à un magistrat qui gouverne l'âme".

[2]) Reading the passage 441c9–d6 in a detached way you get the impression of a formal analogical conclusion, but read in its context it takes the shape of a summing up of the preceeding discussion.

implies; in all he gives so many reasons for his conception of personality, that he could have developed it without the technical help of *polis* as an illustrative mean.[1]) It is on the other hand difficult to see how Plato, in a precursory inquiry of psychology, could have avoided the use of political and social metaphors in communicating his theory of the structured self; cf. p. 93 above. Simply by the force of language, the concept of *psyche* seems in a sense bound to be sociomorphic.[2])

6. *Some notes on sophrosyne and dikaiosyne*

There is a number of questions related to *sophrosyne*, to one of which we must now turn.

That *sophia* and *andreia* are departmental can not be disputed. *Sophrosyne* has, however, been in this respect a victim of contrary judgements. It is virtually, so it has been said, departmental. There is a certain tension between the description given of *sophrosyne* as a harmony of the whole, and the expectation engendered by the knowledge that the guardians and the auxiliaries have each a special merit. One expects that the third class also should have a special distinction. Those taking this view think that *sophrosyne* is merely the quiet acceptance of being ruled.[3]) There are others who take an intermediary position: *sophrosyne* is departmental in *psyche*, but not quite so in *polis*, where it is given to all three classes, but it is, however, most characteristic for the lowest one.[4]) Thus there is a tendency to expel *sophrosyne* from the higher ranks and establish a symmetry by giving each of the funda-

---

[1]) Joseph thinks that Plato's account of the nature of the soul is based "on a direct consideration of the soul itself", p. 82.

[2]) In describing man's inner nature Plato was bound by the possibilities of the language. Certain metaphorical expressions were used long before to characterize internal conditions. Plato was sensitive to this way of speaking, cf. p. 93 above. Terms like ἐγκράτεια, κρείττων, ἥττων etc. (430e6–12), contain vague political similies, which, holds Classen, may have stimulated Plato in his development of the concept of the tripartite soul, cf. *Sprachliche Deutung*, p. 21.

[3]) Adkins thinks that the explicit description of *sophrosyne* is defeated by the general driving of Plato's political philosophy. Take the image of the watchdogs and the effort by means of myth and education to establish a wide gap between rulers and subjects. Thrasymachus should be delighted. The question about the *manner* of ruling is suppressed and smoothness emphasized, which suits the tyrants well.—*Sophrosyne* is a persuasively formulated pseudo-virtue belonging to the low ranks, pp. 287 ff.

[4]) So for instance Wilamowitz, vol. I, p. 393.

mental parts of the components a merit of its own[1].) But this symmetry is achieved at the cost of Plato's own words.[2])

Earlier (pp. 94 and 101) we have observed that *sophrosyne* in the developing *polis* stands out as the head of a group of civil virtues. Now it is enlightening, I think, to ask what is the function of *sophrosyne* *on the ruling level*.[3]) It would be odd if one of the cardinal virtues should be of less importance for the higher ranks. On the contrary one may be disposed to think that *sophrosyne* (the opposite of *akolasia*) grows in importance with the higher level from which it is practised. The actual explanation as to why the city is not raped by the guardians and their helpers is that they are trained to practise self-control. The notable fact that the weapon-carriers abstain from using their arms to their own advantage, we may assume, sets an example to the lower ranks. The practice of *sophrosyne* on the élite level illustrates the meaning of that virtue, spelled out in large letters.—One can conclude, therefore, that *sophrosyne* is a fully developed virtue as important in the higher as in the lower levels of society.[4])

We now turn briefly to the relation of *sophrosyne* to *dikaiosyne*. As they are aspects of complete *arete* it is not surprising if they somewhat overlap. On the other hand, if only four aspects out of a great number of possible virtues are selected, you are entitled to expect that some main differences between them should emerge.

It has been argued that *sophrosyne* and *dikaiosyne* are essentially synonymous. There is in the *Republic* a tendency to think of them

---

[1]) A. Lesky, *Geschichte der Griechischen Literatur*, Bern 1957/58, p. 497 gives the following pattern:

Polis	Psyche	Polis & Psyche
Herrscher	Die Vernunft	Weisheit
Wächter	Das Muthafte	Tapferkeit
Werkende	Das Begehren	Masshalten

This misconception is of old standing, cf. *Scolia Platonica*, ed. W. C. Greene 1938, p. 224. See also R. Hirzel, *Hermes*, Bd 8, 1873–1874, p. 382.

[2]) 431e10–432a9, 442c10–d3.

[3]) Adam commenting the view that *sophrosyne* is merely otiose and ornamental says that this charge is best refuted by considering whether the city is complete without it. *Sophrosyne*, in Plato's sense, is necessary for the rulers as well as for their subjects, vol. I, p. 236.

[4]) Cf. H. North, *op. cit.* ". . . sophrosyne must be practised by all three parts of the soul; it is never, for Plato, as for many later Platonists, solely the virtue of the appetitive part", p. 173. See also Krämer, p. 93, n. 116.

as one.[1]) To get a reliable notion of what is meant with these terms one must, it has been held, study all of Plato's works and not depend on *Bk IV* alone.[2]) This method—going through all the dialogues and selecting certain formulations as representative of Plato's outlook as a whole—does not agree with our motif-directed approach.

Division of labour is already from the start presented as a conspicuous feature in the constructive plan of the model city. By this scheme everybody gets a job to attend to, and efficiency is promoted by specialization. This outlook is, we have seen, preserved in the definition of *dikaiosyne* given later. Specialization makes men efficient, but efficiency must be combined with friendly co-operation and not with social struggle. We are then led to *sophrosyne*, the ground-pattern of civil spirit, cf. pp. 101–102 above. Joint operations are associated with trust and friendliness. And it is here, I think, that the notions of *sophrosyne* and *dikaiosyne* overlap. From the aspect of *dikaiosyne* we see the citizens as unequals, specialized for different jobs. And from the aspect of *sophrosyne* we see them in trustful co-operation fostered by self-discipline and a general feeling of friendliness.[3]) Thus the two notions are spiritually allied, but they are not identical. They both earn their living in the *Republic*. Plato has, in the course of the reasoning leading up to *Bk V*, made extraordinary efforts to demonstrate the cardinal virtues as functional requisites of the unified *polis*.[4]) At 444b1–8, 609b11–c1 the

---

[1]) Plato's characteristic use of *dikaiosyne* and *sophrosyne* "is a loose one in which the two virtues are essentially synonymous", holds C. W. R. Larson, *The Platonic Synonyms, ΔΙΚΑΙΟΣΥΝΗ and ΣΩΦΡΟΣΥΝΗ. AJP* 72/1951, p. 397. The best example of this is the passage 443c9–444a1 giving a long definition of *dikaiosyne*. Judging the narrower definitions of *sophrosyne* and *dikaiosyne* (432a2–9, resp. 433a8–b5) in the light of the long definition the conclusion is drawn that the former involves harmony explicitly and "doing one's own" implicitly, while the order is reversed in *dikaiosyne*, p. 406.

[2]) "For a reliable conception of Plato's ideas of justice and sobriety one must study all his works, and not depend on book IV of the *Republic* alone." Larson, p. 396.

[3]) R. Demos, wrestling with the complex *dikaiosyne-sophrosyne*, comes to the provisional conclusion that the former stresses *diversity* and the letter *harmony*. *A Note on Σωφροσύνη in Plato's Republic, Ph & Phen R*, vol. XVII 1956, pp. 399 ff.

[4]) Does *sophrosyne* refer to each of the three classes separately or does it refer to the whole of the state? Adam thinks both the alternatives are possible. The same questions can of course be put in relation to *dikaiosyne*.

opposites of the cardinal virtues are mentioned; over against *sophrosyne* there is *akolasia*, cf. p. III above. In chapter IV we proposed that the *letter-aspect* (p. 74) should not be applied too rigorously lest we might be engaged in an unrestricted hunt for similarities. The *established basis of resemblances* does not, we see, consist of a very large number of common properties. The analogy holds between two highly functional systems endowed with tripartite structures and a similar distribution of four essential virtues.

Approaching the *polis-psyche* relation as an *analogy* we meet in the literature different opinions as to its content and meaning. "If states are like persons, persons are like states."[1]) Socrates' way of speaking about the fundamental parts of the soul as being "allied" or "agreed" implies a "personification" of these elements. Pursuing the *polis-psyche* motif, we see that the analogy brings with it a political way of speaking about *psyche*; even common and literary language contains basically political metaphors referring to man's inner constitution. This manner of speaking, now systematized, allows Socrates to describe his views about the nature of personality.[2])

The analogy has also been interpreted in the reverse sense. The citizens, it is now held, are wholly absorbed in their functions. Instead of real persons we get conditioned drives: the persons are "depersonified".[3]) The answer Murphy offers is that, by speaking of the city as a person, Plato uses personality as a *metaphor* by which he can stress his idea of the *polis* as a single and unified agent.

From such interpretations we learn the advisability to be restrictive and not to allow extensions beyond what is explicitly warranted.[4])

[1]) Murphy, p. 68.

[2]) Speaking in this way about rights and interests of the component parts of man "Plato can bring out vividly his main ethical idea of the best life as one in which all the agent's different interests and opportunities of satisfaction have been brought to a single focus and a balance struck between them in the light of what will be best for him on the whole", Murphy, p, 69.

[3]) Murphy, p. 69.—Grote holds that "the perfection of the commonwealth ... consists in its being One: an integer or unit, of which the constituent individuals are merely functions, each having only a fractional, dependant, relative existence", vol. III, p. 124.

[4]) "But an analogy is the finding of some points of resemblance between things that in other respects are dissimilar, and Plato's comparison of states and persons in some respects seems to give us no serious ground for further comparisons in those respects in which it is clear to everyone that states and persons differ", Murphy, p. 70.

In the course of the next chapter we will meet some important dis-
analogies which help to point out irrelevant comparisons. It is also
important to locate the place and functions of various metaphors and
illustrations; metaphors running loose, I. A. Richards has taught,
provide entrance for capricious interpretations.

7. Transfer to the topic of adikia

444a10-445e4. We have maintained (chap. II) that the *polis-psyche*
motif is expanded through a continued discussion about the polarity
between *dikaiosyne* and *adikia*. We have repeatedly taken the opportunity to observe the important role played by *adikia* in the *Republic*.
When now *dikaiosyne* has been discovered, we recall that Socrates had
promised also to reveal the nature of *adikia*. He now turns to that
matter. And he does it in a very calculated way, cf. 444a4–e6. *Adikia*
is an internal disorder, a confusion of functions, an unlawful uprising
of the properly subordinated elements. As a result of this derangement
of the tripartite pattern, the cardinal virtues are transformed to what
we might call cardinal vices: instead of *sophia* prevails *amathia* (ignorance), and *andreia* is replaced with *deilia* (cowardice). Similarly *sophrosyne* is exchanged with *akolasia* (licentiousness) and *dikaiosyne* with
adikia, 444b1–8, cf. 609b11–c1.—That this inversion holds also for
polis cannot be doubted. That we are introduced likewise to an extension
of the basis of resemblances is quite clear. We observe that this extension is not executed by adding more fundamental elements. It is by
arranging the three elements in a new relationship that new analogical
results occur. By putting the established hierarchical order on its
head, the four virtues become as many vices. To the rationalist this
result serves as a confirmation of the truth of the previous reasoning.
The illustrative capacity of the analogy is increased by an inversed
use of the structural elements once selected. It will be part of our undertaking to see how skilfully Plato succeeds in fitting his descriptive
sociology to the extended analogy.

We are thus soon forced to admit an extension of the analogy.
It will facilitate our inquiry to distinguish between (a) *the established
analogy* (which exposes the right structure) and (b) the *extended analogies*
(exposing the main forms of disorganization). Sometimes we will have
reasons to speak of both (a) and (b). We will then use the term *general analogy*.

Plato's general analogy is supported by his doctrine of the nature of health and disease,[1]) ὡς ἐκεῖνα ἐν σώματι, ταῦτα ἐν ψυχῇ, 444c5–6. Health corresponds to the order of the established analogy, and disease to the disturbed order of the extended analogies. The medical theory of Plato defines the nature of health with due observance of the contrary cases of diseases. Similarly, the general analogy illustrates health in souls and states against the contrasting background of diseased forms. Platonic medicine propounds the well-being of the total man, soul and body. In a like manner, his political medicine takes care of the whole of *polis*. The general analogy works hand in hand with the theory of health.

We are now in a position to see that the comparison between *polis* and *psyche* is carried out within a system of important analogies and polarities. There are the two contra-posited analogies (a) *dikaiosyne/* health and (b) *adikia/*disease.[2]) Joined to these one has the general analogy of *polis/psyche* which in its *established version* corresponds to (a) and in its *extended* version to (b). Enclosed in such a system—and with the ancients' propensity to look for recurring patterns—the probability of being charmed by its magic must have been great.—Add to this that justice-health is κατὰ φύσιν, while injustice-disease is παρὰ φύσιν, 444d3–11. And health and virtue correspond to beauty, disease and vice to deformity, 444d13–e2.

Socrates is now about to make the final step and examine also the case from the position of *adikia*. Glaucon thinks this unnecessary. But Socrates insists on a fulfilment of the programme: the remaining work is perhaps not needed for saving or confirming the truth of the conclusions, but it is worthwhile for the sake of clarity, 445b5–7.[3])

---

[1]) As for Plato's frequent use of the term *physis* in *Bks II–IV*, cf. A. Krohn, pp. 59–62.—The complex meaning of the term *physis* is explicated by D. Mannsperger, *Physis bei Platon*, Berlin 1969, esp. pp. 295 ff. See also Krämer, p. 119.

[2]) Robinson distinguishes a third important analogy, viz. that between the guardians of the model city and the dog, p. 205.—It is true that Plato makes extensive use of this illustration. I prefer, however, to keep it apart from the field of the general analogy, and instead observe it as an important additional picture with a special function.

[3]) If *adikia* follows as a corollary from the definition of *dikaiosyne*, its value as a proof is only formal. Now Socrates does not actually say that he is going to prove the matter. He will expose it more clearly; that there may be a surer way he has already interposed, 435d3 ff.—Tentatively we may, however, venture that a study of the corollary brings us closer to existing societies and social realities, which in their turn help to frame the plausibility of the table of the established virtues.

The preceding discourses have led to a strategical point of circumspection from which a commanding view over the territory presents itself, seeing both the nature of *arete* and *kakia*, 445c4–7. This Socratic insistence of inspecting also the nature of unrighteousness is important for our study. *Adikia*, the great antipode of *dikaiosyne*, is now announced for a thorough treatment. This wholly agrees with the plan of the total investigation.

There are within the limits of the general analogy five distinct forms of *polis* and as many forms of *psyche*. The true form is either a monarchy (βασιλεία) or an aristocracy (ἀριστοκρατία); this difference is of minor importance as long as the fundamental principles are carried out, 445d3–e4. The remaining four forms are vicious.

Bk IV ends at 445e4. One expects that the subject of the diseased forms would be exposed in the next book, but this is not the case. Socrates is interrupted by Adeimantus who brings in other subjects into the discussion.

8. Conclusions and observations

Within *Bks II–IV* the model city is developed to serve as a convenient instrument for the study of *dikaiosyne* in *psyche*. And in *Bk IV* it is also used for its purpose. Let us collect the main features paralleled in the soul and at the same time draw attention to some important disanalogies.

Graph E. ILLUSTRATIVE LIMIT OF MODEL POLIS

Disanalogical features further developed in Bk V		Analogical features Socio-cultural pattern		
Do not live in private families, and do not possess private property	I	**Rulers**	SOPHIA	SOPHROSYNE / DIKAIOSYNE
	II	**Soldiers**	ANDREIA	
Live in private families and possess private property	III	**Rest of the Polis**		

The hierarchical order of classes and values in *polis* must now be observed. This feature (using Plato's own metaphor 424d1–2, 560b7–8, 561b7–8) we may denominate acromorph. Figuratively *sophia*, represented by the rulers, resides on the *acropolis*. The rulers (not yet called philosopher-kings) know what is best for the *polis* as a whole. United in natural alliance with *sophia* there is *andreia*, embodied by the soldiers, also called auxiliaries. The distance between the two higher classes and the rest of the population is pronounced. The élite commands respect but also trust, we may suppose, when the people recognize that it is not subjected to the law of the grab, cf. 416a2–b3. On this point the function of *sophrosyne* emerges. Traditionally it denoted self-control, moderation and balance, now it includes also concord, harmony and order (430e3–6), being attributes which gain their meaning in the context of interdependence and mutual interest, 412d4–7. Unlike *sophia* and *andreia*, which are departmental, *sophrosyne* extends to all the three classes, 431e10–432a6. Politically *sophrosyne* is manifested when there is agreement between the naturally superior and the inferior on the question of who should rule whom, 431d9–e2, 432a6–9. Ruling requires natural gift, expert knowledge, long training and a lasting devotion to the long-termed interest of the *polis* as a whole. This brings us to the need for specialization and division of work; the definition of *dikaiosyne* springs from this idea. The stress is on complementary work, the skill and efficiency—especially on the ruling and the defending levels—which makes the *polis* a well-run unit. *Sophia, andreia, sophrosyne* and *dikaiosyne* are defined in relation to each other. As they serve to establish and support the model *polis*, I have called them functional requisites. *Dikaiosyne* does not specify acts, but a characteristic condition of the *polis* as an agent. Each class is just, when the principle τὸ τὰ αὑτοῦ πράττειν is respected. But Plato does not think that this principle can operate on its own; he does not believe in the existence of an invisible hand harmonizing the actions. Division of work must be operated from above, by *sophia*, and this is the Burg-aspect.

The socio-cultural pattern holds also for *psyche*. Man's structure is hierarchical. Self-command means that *sophia* rules, helped by *andreia*, and that there is an inner balance (*sophrosyne*). To accomplish this *dikaiosyne* is needed—without it there is no order.[1] *Psyche* is in analogy

---

[1] Dikaiosyne is, writes Krämer, "die Bedingung der Möglichkeit aller übrigen ἀρεταί, weil sie die Tätigkeit aller einzelnen Teile und die zwischen ihnen waltenden Bezüge auf das Ganze des Gefüges hin ausrichtet. Sie ist, mit anderen Worten, das Prinzip der Einheit in der Vielheit und damit der Inbegriff der Ordnung, des οἰκεῖος κόσμος der Seele selbst", p. 94.

with *polis* conceived as a functional unit. *Psyche* is an acropolis, not an agora.—As for the use of the analogy Plato is cautious. The guiding properties found in *polis* should be confirmed in *psyche*; by means of arguments from different branches of knowledge, the tripartite structure of the soul is discovered.

In *Graph E*, p. 116, above some disanalogical features are indicated.[1]) They make a passage to *Bk V*, where the political study is pursued beyond what is required by the analogy.[2]) Now we may merely note that Plato does not enumerate a great number of detailed correspondences between society and man. The traits, economically selected, are instead the more intensively utilized.

The definition in 443c9–444a2 of *dikaiosyne* as an internal order in the soul, has been observed by scholars as being egocentric. Reading the passage in the light of our anti-motif we find that the just person is the creative centre from which just acts flow into the society, cf. 443d7–444a2. A main reason for thinking that *polis* can illustrate man, is that the prevalent characteristics of a society come from the persons who compose it, cf. 435e1–436a3.

The *polis-psyche* motif says that *polis* illustrates *and* forms man. As can be seen from *TABLE 2*, nrs 9–25, *Bk IV* abounds in illustrative use of *polis*. The sub-motif *polis forms man* is manifest in different ways. The citizens are acted upon by the rulers, now viewed as a fundamental class and as an institution. Through radical social and cultural reforms the citizens are bound up in a closed social system, which creates personalities of the same unified type. Employing the *polis-psyche* motif we are warned against the tendency to freeze the analogical features and regard them as two detached sets of properties.

---

[1]) Adam notes that the rulers are recruited from the soldier-class but *logistikon* is not a select part of *thymoeides*. Thus the difference is in this respect greater in *psyche* than in *polis*, vol. I, p. 255.

[2]) "There are cases where the political study is persued beyond what the analogy requires, for example in the investigation of marriage and the education of women in Book V. That is a political or social problem and has no obvious analogy in the relation between the parts of the soul." Murphy, p. 76.

PART FOUR

INTERLUDE

CHAPTER VII
TOWARDS AN IDEAL COMMUNITY
(Bk V:449a1–471c3)

1. Preliminary notes

Bk II began with the provocative speeches by Glaucon and Adeimantus. Their contribution was important and their scepticism a salt. Socrates then proceeds briskly, and the two brothers have little to say. But they are not entirely passive. Their doubt breaks through occasionally. The true and healthy city of Socrates they call a community of pigs, and the proposed life for the guardians they think is destitute of happiness. Socrates cuts such opposition short. He leads the way alone. He determines what is relevant, because he—and no one else—knows what is asked of the *polis* in its illustrative capacity. The model city is thus completed, the dream accomplished, 443b7.

But in *Bk V* (449c2) a change occurs. The participants in the discussion demand information on various subjects which deserve consideration *from a social point of view*; they will not be cheated of a whole chapter of the story. And Socrates agrees to take up these questions. Before we turn to these matters, let us, however, add a few observations on the composition of the *Republic*.

The topics to be discussed this time do not belong to the established analogy. Thus the subject of the sexes, for instance, has no counterpart in the lesser text, nor do matters such as marriage and child-rearing extend the analogy.[1]) Reading the *Republic* without a proper pause

---

[1]) As for the question about dis-analogies between *polis* and *psyche* Adam has noted (vol. I, p. 255) that the guardians are selected from the auxiliaries, but the *logistikon* is not selected from the *thymoeides*.—Another difference worth mentioning is, I think, that the third class lives in families, a condition which is not paralleled in the structure of the soul.—R. Demos, *Paradoxes in Plato's Doctrine*

before *Bk V*, the impression is easily obtained that Plato becomes so interested in the details of the *polis* on its own account, that he forgets that it was introduced as an instructional device.[1])

Keeping to our motif we have reason to call the three following books an interlude.[2]) Finding that *Bks II–IV* make a complete section of the *Republic*, one now expects it to be counterbalanced by an impressive antithesis. Towards the end of *Bk IV* the intention to take up *adikia* for inspection is also mentioned, 444a10–11. We have reached, says Socrates, the summit of our reasoning.[3]) From there, both goodness and various forms of wickedness can be studied. We now expect the antithesis to be introduced. It would well answer to the method of the extreme types. The demonstration of the deformed system is postponed, however, to *Bks VIII–IX*. Thus it looks as if the planned dispo-

---

of the Ideal State, CQ., N.S., vol. VII 1957, p. 169, rejects the attempt to look for symbolic meaning in this part of *Bk V*. These details of the ideal city seem to have no counterpart in *psyche*. ". . . what could possibly be the symbolic meaning of the communistic elements in Plato's state: the community of property and of children among the two upper groups".—A tentative defender of a contrary view is R. G. Hoerber: "Plato's purpose was not to advocate seriously the institution of such a community, but merely to illustrate the characteristics and proper spheres of the rational and appetitive elements of the soul." *Note of the Structure of the Republic*, Phron. vol. VI 1961, pp. 37 ff.—The position taken in the present study is that *Bks IV* and *V* structurally belong to different discourses. The established analogy between *polis* and *psyche* is completed in *Bk IV*. Instead of involving ourselves in exegetical difficulties about the hidden meaning of *Bk V*, we may accept it as a political portion of the *Rep.* having, however, a special function in the total argument, cf. p. 114 above.

[1]) Cf. R. Demos, *A Note on Plato's Republic*, RM., vol. XII, 1958, p. 307. O. Utermöhlen writes: "Die Ausgestaltung und Ausmalung dieses Staates nimmt im Laufe der Bücher II–V jedoch einen solchen Umfang ein, und die Details der idealen Polis treten so sehr in den Vordergrund, dass man mit Recht die Frage aufwerfen kann, ob das ursprüngliche Thema überhaupt noch fungiere, . . ." *Die Bedeutung der Ideenlehre für die platonische Politeia*, Heidelberg 1967, p. 12. See also Murphy, p. 76.

[2]) See for instance Crombie, vol. I, p. 100.—Formally it is a digression, says Adam, but in reality *Bks V–VII* "fulfil the hopes held out in sundry parts of III and IV", completing the picture of the perfect city and the perfect man "by giving us Plato's third or crowning effort—the philosophic City and the Philosopher-King", p. 274.— Still more important is, however, that Plato himself at 543c5–6 (*Bk VIII*) calls the inserted three books a digression; . . . ἀναμνησθῶμεν πόθεν δεῦρο ἐξετραπόμεθα, ἵνα πάλιν τὴν αὐτὴν ἴωμεν.

[3]) 445c4, . . . ὥσπερ ἀπὸ σκοπιᾶς μοι φαίνεται, . . .

sition of the *Republic* has been altered.[1]) Anyhow, it is by the existence of the two main sections *II–IV* and *VIII–IX* that the method of the extreme types is manifested. The ground-pattern of polarity rests on these two balancing blocks.[2])

Bearing this in mind one is apt to look at *Bks V–VII* as an inserted section of the *Republic*. As a matter of fact, critics have since long observed that it is possible to read the dialogue jumping from the end of *Bk IV* to the beginning of *Bk VIII* without "noticing any break in the subject or any great difference in the philosophy or psychology".[3]) And Lutoslawsky has by means of stylometric methods concluded that *Bks V–VII* seem to be composed somewhat later than *II–IV* and *VIII–IX*.[4]) Possibly there existed an early version that did not include *Bks V–VII*.[5])

2. *Social reconsiderations*

451c4-461e4. The preceding discourses concerned mainly the male sex. Delving now into social questions more specifically, it is natural that the subject of women should be taken up, 451c1–3.

Socrates again returns to the nature and behaviour of dogs. Watch-dogs of both sexes, fed and bred in the same way, hunt and keep watch together.[6]) If men and women are therefore going to do the same kinds of jobs, they must be given the same education, 451e6–7. Conven-

---

[1]) See above p. 91, Adam's judgement about "the longer way" as an editing note written at a later time than *Bk IV*.

[2]) H. Ryffel, *ΜΕΤΑΒΟΛΗ ΠΟΛΙΤΕΙΩΝ*, has in a graph, p. 253, brought out this balance between *Kultur- und Staats-Entstehungs-Lehre* and *Meta bolé- und Verfalls-Theorie der Verfassungen*.

[3]) Nettleship, p. 162.

[4]) Lutoslawsky says that, generally speaking, *Bks VIII–IX* belong to the same period as *II–IV*, "showing a later style only to such an extent as might be expected in a continuous work of these dimensions". The bulk of *Bks V–VII* are probably added later, at least after *Bk IX*, pp. 323–324.

[5]) Nettleship thinks it possible that *I–IV* were published first, "and that criticism which fastened on the most obviously paradoxical suggestions in them induced Plato to work out at fuller length the consequences of his conception of an ideal state", p. 163.

[6]) Plato is guided by an analogy from animal life but does not forget to argue the point, observes Barker, p. 220.—A. Krohn enumerates 452e, 453b, c, e, 454b, c, d, 455a, d, e, 456a, b, c, 466d, 470c, 473c, 474b, 476b as examples of "ein naturalistischer Geist" in *Bk V*, pp. 102–104. Also Adam, vol. I, p. 280.

tionalism must on this point give way to rationalism, 452a7–e3. Determining the place of women in society we must look, says Socrates, for those distinctions which are vital for the subject under discussion, 454a4–b9. In other words, we should look for that distinctive mark (τὸ εἶδος) which is relevant to the work to be done, 454c7–d1. This mark of relevance is the ability to learn. Some learn easily, others with difficulty, 455b4–c2. The capacity to absorb instruction is not reserved for men only. There is in principle, therefore, no agency of the state which belongs to someone by merit of sex. Natural abilities are distributed similarly among men and women, and as far as nature is concerned, women can participate in all occupations equally with men.[1] Thus, if a woman has the qualities of a guardian, she should be selected to do that job. This would mean, of course, that training possibilities open to capable men should also be open to capable women, 455d6–456b11. The reform is *kata physin*; similar capabilities, similar employment. The existing, conventional order is *para physin*, 456b12–c2. What promotes the functional unity of the *polis* is natural. Women are thus admitted to the highest of offices.

The next step is still more notable, 457c3–5. The case for communism is now taken up. Private families are abolished among the élite. Men and women guardians should live together in camps, and be forbidden to withdraw to private households. Both wives and children are to be held in common. No parent shall know his child, no child its parent, 457c10–d3.[2]—Socrates knows that he is open for attack, but wants to postpone for the moment all discussion concerning the practicability of the project until later. He wants to follow up his vision first, 458a1–2.

---

[1] What is in 451c ff. said on the subject of women lends itself to different conjectures: should Plato be hailed as a champion of the modern idea of equality between the sexes with the right for women to engage in professional life? Or did perhaps Plato anticipate modern anthropology in maintaining that feminine nature is largely culturally conditioned? Cf. Y. Brès, *La Psychologie de Platon*, Paris 1968, p. 223.—R. Lagerborg suggests that Plato was primarily interested in the emancipation of the philosophers from the nuisance of private families. In its context, however, the project is first and last in the interest of the state, holds Lagerborg, *Den Platoniska Kärleken*, Stockholm 1915, pp. 27 ff.

[2] It is impossible, says Aristotle, to avoid the fact that resemblances between parents and children to some extent reveal their relationships to one another; the objection is supported by both ethnographical and biological observations. *Politics*, II, 1262a14–24.

A new institution of marriage promoting social unity is introduced, 458d2–e1. The methods used in animal breeding is advisory. The best individuals in each sex should be mated to one another. To prevent ill-feeling from those rejected, the selection must be manipulated as a false lottery; lies, we remember, are allowed as a medicine of the state. Controlled weddings of this nature aim to raise the quality of the race and to regulate the number of the population. The population policy also involved other means; i.e. transposition of ranks according to metal-value. Infanticide is now sanctioned in certain cases of inferiority and unfitness.[1]) To relieve the female auxiliaries from maternal chores and help to maintain collective parentage, public nurseries are instituted, 460c1–d5.

3. Stress on unity

461e5-471c3. We have had rich opportunity to study how highly Plato values unity. The opposition between unity and disunity is now stressed to the utmost in the section 462a2–e6.[2]) There is no greater evil to the society than division, and no greater good than cohesion.[3]) This insight is strategical for the statesman, 462a2–4. The rulers must find a common ground for the feelings of the citizens. It is bad when some citizens mourn and others rejoice over the same public events, 462b8–c1. Therefore, Socrates says, the society must be almost like an individual; if a finger is hurt, the pain effects the whole man.[4]) In the respect to pleasure and pain, the social body can be compared

---

[1]) Cf. 459d9–e3, 460c3–5, 461b1–7.—It is disputed whether Plato really recommended infanticide. The text, however, seems to refute attempts to read in modern humanitarian ideals.—At 460c3–5 we are told that the children of inferior guardians plus other defective offspring will be taken to a secret place to be concealed there; "ein verschleiernder Ausdruck für Kindermord", comments O. Apelt, p. 482, n. 46. See also Adam, vol. I, p. 299.

[2]) This "almost morbid insistence on the unity of the staet" (Sinclair, p. 118) is subjected to severe criticism by Aristotle in *Politics* II.

[3]) 462a9–b2. Ἔχομεν οὖν τι μεῖζον κακὸν πόλει ἢ ἐκεῖνο ὃ ἂν αὐτὴν διασπᾷ καὶ ποιῇ πολλὰς ἀντὶ μιᾶς; ἢ μεῖζον ἀγαθὸν τοῦ ὃ ἂν συνδῇ τε καὶ ποιῇ μίαν;

[4]) 462c10–d3. οἷον ὅταν πού ἡμῶν δάκτυλός του πληγῇ, πᾶσα ἡ κοινωνία ἡ κατὰ τὸ σῶμα πρὸς τὴν ψυχὴν τεταμένη εἰς μίαν σύνταξιν τὴν τοῦ ἄρχοντος ἐν αὐτῇ ἤσθετό τε καὶ πᾶσα ἅμα συνήλγησεν μέρους πονήσαντος ὅλη, καὶ οὕτω δὴ λέγομεν ὅτι ὁ ἄνθρωπος τὸν δάκτυλον ἀλγεῖ· Cf. Adam, vol. I, p. 306, and Jaeger, *Paideia*, vol. III. pp. 26 ff.

to the human body, 464b1–3. In these statements we have explicit the nucleus of Plato's *psycho-somatic* model of the society.

The social unity should be reflected in the way the citizens address themselves. The appellations must express the general fellowship and the inter-dependence of the limbs of the social body, 463a1–c4. The two higher classes constitute a great family, and the family terms should be applied accordingly, 463c5–e2. Because of the functional inter-dependence (the community of interest and feeling) some differences between the words "ours" and "mine" vanish, 463c3–464a6. In the context of collectivity, the meaning of "mine" undergoes a change and comes to denote something of the individual's participation of the whole. Again we note the importance Plato attaches to the force of language.[1]

Domestic communism is linked with communism of property, 464b5–c3. The function of this kind of communism is to prevent the *polis* from being torn to pieces (διασπᾶν) by private and group interests, 464c5–e2. As a special check against social strife on the higher level, the task of ruling is given to the elders. The auxiliaries and all others then come into son-father relationship to the rulers.[2] Common decency, respect (463c8–d8) and fear of repraisals of the numerous relatives of the victim, will prevent the young from attacking the guardians, 465a5–b3. Plato has thereby made provisions in many ways for concord between the two elite classes. That these special provisions for unity among the superiors are very important, will be effectively demonstrated in *Bks VIII–IX*. Rivalry within the ruling class has devastating consequences for the whole of *polis*. On the other hand if there is concord in the higher regions of the community, the risk for divisions in the lower strata is minimal, 465b5–10; this upper class communism also relieves the rulers from many petty pecuniary troubles, 465b12–c7.

At 419a1–420a1 the objection was raised that the guardians and their helpers were not very happy, because they were deprived of property,

---

[1] Cf. Adam, vol. I, p. 307.

[2] This son-father relation also appears as normative in the *Crito*, 50e1 ff. Sinclair in this connection observes that "the comparison of the πόλις to a father or mother, to whom all citizens owe love and allegiance, is not peculiarly Platonic. In the great days of the city-state the relationship was not unlike that of benevolent parent and loyal son, and the πόλις, while encouraging and recognising family obligations, had taken over or canalised much of the power of the family", p. 128.

comfort and privacy. Socrates now repeats the motivation for founding the city: the *polis* as a whole should be made as happy as possible, 465e4–466a6. Separatist tendencies must be stopped, 466b4–c3. The guardians, permanently engaged in preserving the rightly formed *polis*, stand for triumphs finer than even the Olympic victors, 466a8–b2. Private business is futile in comparison with the work of the guardians.

The position of women is defined. Both men and women keep watch and hunt together, 466c6–d4. Their children will be taken to see the encounters. From early life they should be acquainted with soldiering. Courage in the field is promoted in different ways. In the presence of their children the parents will fight with inspiration; animals fight best when protecting their offspring, 467a10–b1. As the father labours for his family, so the soldier fights for his *polis*. Sexual gratification, honours, and other rewards are given for distinction in the field; cowards are degraded to some third class job, 468a1–469b3.

After having thus depicted how the parents go to war in the presence of their children, Socrates passes over to the subject of war and humanity. Greek states should observe the codes of humanity when engaged in internal fighting. They should not enslave each other, nor rob the dead, or burn houses, or ravage the land. As all Greeks are akin, a conflict between Greek cities is not really war (*polemos*), but civil war (*stasis*) 470b4–9, 471a1–2. The model *polis* is Greek. It is good and civilized. Its citizens love Hellas, having the same enemies and sharing the same temples, 470e4–10. Discord ought to be judged as temporary quarrels not without prospects of reconciliation. The term *polemos* is reserved for war with the barbarians, 471b6–8.

4. Conclusions and observations

The section of *Bk V* (449a1–471c3) which has now been treated constitutes according to our introductory divisions *the fourth main part*. It does not, I think, add new features to the structure of the analogy. But it offers complements which make the *polis* more convincing as a model. The full significance of these reinforcements stand out more clearly when the disorganized societies of *Bks VIII–IX* have been surveyed.

The task of creating a completely unified *polis* requires the rejection or exchange of existing institutions that counteract unification. Plato knows perfectly well that some of his reforms are outrageous. They provoke indignation even today.[1])

In the very first stage of the γιγνομένη πόλις we meet the notion of συνοικία, a catchword for the social idea of living together in one place as partners, exchanging work for a common end, 369c1–7. Κοινωνία is another word for co-operation and inter-dependence. And in the term ἁπλοῦς βίος the ideal of a simple, peaceful and healthy way of life can be compressed, 372a5–c1. Later, in the full-grown city, σωφροσύνη (with the sister-concepts φιλία, συμφωνία, and ἁρμονία) expresses the nature of the internal relationships which characterize it. Culture and social organization mirror the gospel of unity and simplicity; the myths are state-supporting and every precaution is taken to prevent wealth and poverty to enter the city causing social struggle. Communism is a conspicuous topic. If one believes in the abolition of private property for the two upper classes, it seems logical also to renounce private family life in these classes, because private households tend to become nurseries for egoism and group interests. As for the emancipation of the élite women from the bondage of the household, this reform is not motivated by the cause of women's rights, but for the unity and strength of the *polis* as a whole.[2])—Thus, fostered by emotional, intellectual and practical engagement, individual wills are submerged under the call of the *polis*.

In 422e7–423b2 Socrates makes a rough distinction between his complete community (ἡ μία πόλις) and other (existent) types of societies. Each one of the latter should be mentioned in the plural, πόλεις, because such a society is in fact not one but many, being engaged in class-struggle and other forms of competition. Its corresponding kind of personality, we may infer, is of a double or multiform type, cf. 397d10–e2. It is

---

[1]) Crombie recommends the relevant pages for reading by "connoisseurs of *a priori* absurdity", vol. I, pp. 100–101.

[2]) The additional social reinforcements of *Bk V*, heavily stressing the unity of the model *polis*, were destined to a life of their own in many commentaries. So the dictum at 462a9–b2 about unity, as the greatest good of the society, seems to have invited Aristotle to much of his celebrated criticism of the Platonic notion of unity, *Politics, II* 1261a10 ff. If one carries the demand for unity too far, says Aristotle, one combats the natural aim of the *polis* which is the mutual exchange of services between different kinds of people endowed with different capacities.— In *Bk II* we have, however, seen that Plato discusses the function of men's natural inequalities within the frame of reciprocity and specialization.

otherwise in the model *polis*. Involved in co-operative activities, and directed by the principle of the division of work, the citizen becomes one man, and not many. Similarly the *polis* becomes one society, and not many.[1]

Gemeinschaft is, I think, an expressive term which bears out what the model *polis* represents in the tradition of sociology. *Community* (the English equivalent) indicates in this context "forms of relationship which are characterized by a high degree of personal intimacy, emotional depth, moral commitment, social cohesion, and continuity in time. ... Its archetype, both historically and symbolically, is the family, and in almost every type of genuine community the nomenclature of family is prominent."[2] F. Tönnies, who coined the term, derived the type from his study of the mediaeval village, family and clan. *Community* (meaning far more than mere local community) makes according to R. A. Nisbet one of five essential unit-ideas of sociology.[3] Like Plato's μία πόλις, *Gemeinschaft* is systematically opposed to all those more loose and contractual bonds which stem from individualism.[4] Thinking of the model *polis* with its strong value-implications[5], it is interesting to observe that there has been found in the writings of Comte, Tönnies, Durkheim and Weber—to mention only a few of those who have explored the community—a preference for moral and conservative values such as order, organic solidarity, corporate tradition and the like.[6] "Community begins as a moral value", affirms Nisbet; only

---

[1] 423d4–6, ὅπως ἂν ἐν τὸ αὐτοῦ ἐπιτηδεύων ἕκαστος μὴ πολλοὶ ἀλλ' εἷς γίγνηται, καὶ οὕτω δὴ σύμπασα ἡ πόλις μία φύηται ἀλλὰ μὴ πολλαί.

[2] R. A. Nisbet, *The Sociological Tradition*, New York 1966, pp. 47–48.—On this point of family and kin I refer to 414d1 and 463c5–e5, where family terms are applied to express the general fellowship and close relations which hold between the citizens.

[3] Nisbet, p. 6.

[4] "Gemeinschaft ist das dauernde und echte Zusammenleben, Gesellschaft nur ein vorübergehendes und scheinbares", writes F. Tönnies in *Gemeinschaft und Gesellschaft*, Berlin 1926, p. 5.

[5] We must of course not forget that the model *polis* is constructed in order to illustrate *dikaiosyne*.

[6] That Comte, Durkheim and others more or less deflected from scholarly objectivity does not mean, writes W. Stark, that they should be jumbled together with the hackwriters of conservative interests, *The Fundamental Forms of Social Thought*, London 1962, pp. 102–103.

gradually does the term become secularized.[1]) Introducing his distinction between community and association, F. Tönnies writes: "Alles vertraute, heimliche, ausschliessliche Zusammenleben (so finden wir) wird als Leben in Gemeinschaft verstanden. Gesellschaft ist die Oeffentlichkeit, ist die Welt. In Gemeinschaft mit den Seinen befindet man sich, von der Geburt an, mit allem Wohl und Wehe daran gebunden. Man geht in die Gesellschaft wie in die Fremde. Der Jüngling wird gewarnt vor schlechter Gesellschaft; aber schlechte Gemeinschaft ist dem Sprachsinne zuwider."[2])

The idea of community and related concepts did not originate in the nineteenth century. It is a question of re-discovery. "They may", writes Nisbet, "be seen in the ancient world: in, for example, Plato's Athens, when Greece, like Europe two thousand years later, was searching for new foundations of order to replace those that had seemingly been destroyed by the ravages of war, revolution, and *stasis*. Plato's concern with community, alienation, authority, hierarchy, the sacred, and with social generation and degeneration is, of course, profound, and it is hardly extreme to say that all the essential elements of subsequent Western social thought are to be found in, first, Plato's development of these ideas and, second, in Aristotle's responses to them."[3])

The model *polis* is constructed in thought. Its aim is to illustrate *psyche*. In *Bk V* (as *TABLE I* indicates) it is not used in this capacity. Instead it is developed along its own lines. But still it is a construction in thought. At this point we see its kinship with (a) sociological constructs of the ideal-type character, (b) utopian thought. To the former I shall return later. As for the latter, it has inspired the literary genre of the Utopias. It would still be wrong to think of the model *polis* as a community of nowhere.[4]) It is settled on Greek soil and in the circumstances of Plato's own times, 470b4–c3. It is, observes Barker, both a deduction

---

[1]) Nisbet, p. 18.

[2]) *Gemeinschaft und Gesellschaft*, pp. 3–4.

[3]) Nisbet, p. 7.

[4]) "Plato's commonwealth is not the City of Zeus or the Kingdom of Heaven. It is a reformed Greek city-state, surrounded by other city-states and by the outer world of barbarians, against which it may have to hold its own. Hence he does not contemplate the abolition of war, which figures in all modern Utopias." Cornford, *The Unwritten Philosophy*, p. 61.

from first principles and an induction from the facts of Greek life.[1]

But the real task that the model *polis* performs in the *Republic*, as discussed now, is to explain how perfectly integrated, harmonious and righteous personalities can be formed. And it is in this field of socio-cultural thought, that our *polis-psyche* motif can also be established as an important motif of ideas.

---

[1] Barker, p. 239.

CHAPTER VIII

POLIS AS IDEAL AND REALITY

(Bk V:471c4–VI:502c8)

1. Polis as a political standard

471c4-473b3. At 471c4–e5 Glaucon agrees that the *polis* will function very well in theory. Tired of details he wants, however, to know if the model is possible to realize.

The interruption is decisive. It marks a new structural division in the argumentation of the *Republic*.

Socrates then finds it instructive to remind us of the subject, purpose and method of the investigation. The subject is the nature of *dikaiosyne* and *adikia*, 472b3–5. The method used so far was to contrast the perfectly just man with the most unjust one. And the purpose was to use these extremes as standards for finding out our own personal stand-point in relation to happiness or misery, 472c4–d2.—It may be noted in passing that it seems as if Plato had forgotten that the pattern of *adikia* has not yet been presented in its radical shape; on the hypothesis that *Bks V–VII* are inserted books, this omission is natural enough because then *Bks VIII–IX* were written earlier.

When the two extremes are now mentioned again, it happens in the twilight zone (472a8–475e2), before the method of the Forms is introduced. The pattern of *dikaiosyne*, attained by a painstaking thought experiment, dawns to a higher dignity.

But the aim of developing a perfectly just city in thought did not imply a demonstration also of its practicability, 472d1–2. The achievement of finding a useful model for the illustration of *dikaiosyne* in *psyche* was important enough. Take for instance a painter who has painted with great skill an ideally beautiful man. The beauty of the painting is not reduced because one is unable to find such a person in real life, 472d4–7. The same argument speaks for the model city, 472d9–e5. If nevertheless the question of its practicability is taken up, let us not forget, maintains Socrates, that practice always falls short of theory.[1]) The ideally perfect pattern can only be approximated, but never completely realized in actual life, 473a5–b2. With these explicit ideas about the difference between making a model for an illustrative purpose and trying to realize the model actually in work, Socrates points out that a new topic is brought into consideration, a topic lying outside that which Glaucon and Adeimantus originally requested him to explicate. If the social excursions of 449a1–471c3 serve to make the *polis* more convincing as a model, the new demand stirs up questions of a different kind.

2. *Philosopher-kings, a necessary requirement*

473b4-487a8. There is a change—not very small or easy—by which an existing state might be transformed to something approximately like the ideal state, 473c2–4.

The philosophers must become kings, or *vice versa*, the rulers must be philosophers. Politics and philosophy must meet in the same persons, 473c11–d3. If on the contrary these two branches of activity remain divorced, there will be no end to our public and individual troubles, 473d3–e2. The demand that philosophers should rule, seems indeed presumptuous. Socrates calls it paradoxical, 473e3–5. And Glaucon thinks that such a demand would be outrageous to public opinion if it was openly proposed, 473e6–474a4.

Whatever one thinks of the proposition, the term philosopher must be defined, 474b4–6. This leads to the much discussed distinction between philosopher and non-philosopher.

Philosophos literally means friend or lover of wisdom. Socrates takes advantage of this meaning, stressing first *philia*, then *sophia*. A philosopher has a strong passion for knowledge, 475c6–8. He loves the whole of it, not merely a part; the genuine philosopher has a passion to see the truth.[2])

Glaucon, living up to the role of a critical interlocutor, asks what "seeing the truth" means.

To an outsider it might be difficult to explain, says Socrates, but he

---

[1]) 473a1–3. Referring to this passage J. Gould speaks of "the characteristic belief that the achievements of thought may grasp hold of more of truth than those of action", *The Dev. of Plato's Ethics* p. 155. Also Adam, vol. I, p. 328.

[2]) 475e4. Τοὺς τῆς ἀληθείας, ἦν δ᾿ ἐγώ, φιλοθεάμονας.

is confident that Glaucon will understand him.[1]) The theory of Forms is then briefly introduced.

Accordingly Socrates enumerates a number of attributes. There are, he says, *beauty* and *ugliness, justice* and *injustice, good* and *bad*, etc. They are, we observe, presented as pairs of opposites. So for instance *beauty* is opposite to *ugliness*.[2]) And, he goes on, as such opposites are two in number they are consequently each of them one,[3]) 476a2. By this process of separation we arrive at one single *Form of Beauty*, one single *Form of Ugliness*, one single *Form of Justice* and so on, 476a4–6.[4]) The *Form of Ugliness* emerges as manifestly as does the *Form of Beauty*, and similarly *adikia* and *dikaiosyne* leap into awareness.[5]) And now for the first time in the *Republic* the term *eidos* (476a5) appears in such a context that one is bound to conclude it means something different from merely "visible shape", "kind" or "species", in which senses the word has earlier occurred. The context brings forth the difference between (1) the ordinary world of things and actions and (2) the true and real world of Forms. The majority of men take delight in the former mistaking the particulars for the real objects. Such men are dreamers whether they are awake or not, 476c5–8. The world of Forms, on the other hand, stands for reality. It is accessible only to the philosophers, who alone have the power to uphold the distinction between "the beautiful itself" (αὐτὸ τὸ καλὸν) and the many beautiful particulars (τὰ πολλὰ καλά) which share or participate (κοινωνίᾳ, 476a7, μετέχοντα, 476d2) in the Form of Beauty.

Corresponding to the difference between the Forms and the particulars there is first the difference between philosophers and non-philosophers.[6]) Secondly there is the distinction between *epistheme* (scientific

[1]) Speaking, says Adam, as one Platonist to another, vol. I, p. 335. Cf., however, 533a1–10, where Glaucon, not being a dialectician, is told that he has asked for more than he can grasp.

[2]) 475e9. Ἐπειδή ἐστιν ἐναντίον καλὸν αἰσχρῷ, δύο αὐτὼ εἶναι.

[3]) This manner of analysing pairs of concepts seems to be paralleled in mathematical reasoning, 524d7–525a2. Cf. A. Wedberg. *Plato's Philosophy of Mathematics*, Stockholm 1955, p. 23.

[4]) Taking advantage of the explications of Cross and Woozley, p. 140.

[5]) As for the nature of some of the contraries, see D. Ross, *Plato's Theory of Ideas*, Oxford 1961, p. 38.

[6]) The non-philosophers constitute formally a rest-class of people. They should

and reliable knowledge) and *doxa* (belief or opinion). Thirdly *epistheme* and *doxa* are related to different powers or capacities (*dynameis*) operating with different objects in different fields, 478a3–b5. The one is turned to the Forms, the other to the particulars.

That *epistheme* is founded on metaphysical objects is, in its dialectical setting, clear enough. Curiously it is the ontological status of our ordinary things (*ta polla*) which causes difficulties. Their half-reality is puzzling, 479b11–d5. Socrates is therefore bound to discuss this matter. Again we have occasion to see the dialectic leap from the notion of pure existence to that of absolute non-existence. But as the negative extreme is unfit for any epistemological use, Socrates must posit a midway status between knowledge and ignorance for the apprehensions of the non-philosophers.[1])

The subject of *doxa* and *epistheme* is difficult to unravel. Plato treats the matter briefly. He is mainly concerned with pointing out the most important characteristic of the philosopher, and does not feel obliged to present the various reasons for the theory of Forms. The important thing is that the philosophers command reliable knowledge.

Bk VI begins with the conclusive remark that now we know what a philosopher is.[2]) We know his capital merit. At 485a10–486e3 Socrates enumerates some complementary virtues necessary for the

---

not, however, be taken at too low a level, says Murphy. Plato is not making an unnecessary attack on the uneducated. It is the cultural leaders who are being criticized, p. 101.

[1]) The passage 475e–480 is puzzling in more than one way, sum up Cross and Woozley. This portion can be divided into two main parts: 475e–476d directed to those accepting the theory of Forms, and 476d–480 directed to a wider audience. The total passage contains a) the distinction between knowledge and belief, b) the corresponding distinction between two different classes of objects. The Forms are truly real and the many particulars (e.g. things and acts of the everyday world) "fluctuate between existence and non-existence" and are only semi-real, pp. 164–165.—Lately J. Gosling, discussing the meaning of 479a, has advanced the view that τὰ πολλὰ καλά etc. does not refer to "the many particular beautiful objects" but "the many kinds of colour, shape etc. commonly held to be beautiful", *Republic, Book V: τὰ πολλὰ καλά etc., Phron.* vol. V 1960, pp. 116 ff. Thus it is the various beliefs that "roll about between reality and unreality".

[2]) The stretch of text from 484a1–487a8 could as well have belonged to the end of *Bk V*.

ruling philosopher.[1]) These virtues are summed up in 487a1–5.[2]) Some of them (*mneme, eumathia, megaloprepeia, aletheia*) are intellectual capacities, and may be understood as belonging to the sub-structure of *the logistikon* of *Bk IV*. Of the cardinal values three are mentioned: *dikaiosyne, andreia* and *sophrosyne*, but without reference to the systematics of the earlier treatment of this matter; at 504a4–6 Socrates indeed refers to the cardinal virtues in order, this time however, to discard as imperfect the results of the earlier investigation of *Bks II–IV*. Recalling the pains taken to establish the meaning and range of the cardinal virtues in *polis* and *psyche*, one may find the missing integration a bit discomfiting.[3])

The notion of *philosophos* is now dressed with the additional excellences, and there can be no doubt that the task of ruling must be entrusted to this class of men, (487a8). In this way the paradox of the philosopher-king is lessened. The best men should rule.—We may here note that the subject of the importance of the philosopher-kings stresses the anti-motif, i.e. the discourse on how capable personalities determine the society.

3. How polis moulds man

487b1-502c8. But Adeimantus cannot help observing the clash between the standard of the nominal and the actual philosophers, 487b1–d5. Step by step the Socratic arguments are surely binding, but the final result of the reasoning is not convincing. As a matter of fact, the actual philosophers seem to be either totally useless or otherwise really bad men. By what merit can we combine the hope for society with such men? Adeimantus thus holds on to the requested tough line of argument with which we are acquainted in *Bk II*. And, we may add, it is due to a few such important objections that the *Republic* can be reckoned among the

---

[1]) Here we meet some virtues belonging to the *sophrosyne* family of values; remembering the earlier discussion (see pp. 110 ff. above) whether *sophrosyne* is departmental or not, our conclusions now seem to be confirmed. This merit is as important to the rulers as to the ruled.

[2]) At 490c10–11, 494b1–3 and 503c2–7 the enumeration of virtues is continued.

[3]) J. Gould observes that the *Republic* often gives the impression of great effort resulting only in anticlimax and disappointment, p. 154.—This experience is, I think, to some extent due to the fact that three different methods are tried in the *Republic*. First there is the Socratic method of the *elenchus*, then the method of the double text, and, finally, the method of the Forms.

dialogues, and is not merely a pseudo-dialogue intersected with monosyllabic affirmatives.[1])

Socrates thinks that Adeimantus is right in his estimation of the present state of the philosophers. Their situation is really tragic. What the potentially best men suffer in society is sad beyond words, 488a2–4.

To illustrate this the simile of the ship and its crew is told, 488a7–489a2.

There is a ship, a captain and his crew. The captain (symbolizing the people) is taller and stronger than any sailor on board. But unfortunately he has defective sight and hearing, and his knowledge of navigation is not of the best. The crew, divided in mutinous groups, has no knowledge of navigation, nor do they believe in such knowledge. They have no conception of the skills demanded from a competent pilot. Finally they take over the ship (the captain has been drugged), and they feast themselves on the stores. The able pilot is doomed to passivity, being considered a useless star-gazer. The state of philosophy is analogous to that of navigation. The pilot should not ask the crew for permission to pilot them, any more than the doctor should beg the sick to let him cure them,[2]) 489b3–c7.

How is it that the philosophers have become such worthless men? The story is told in 490e2–497a5. The pages contain a piercing criticism of the contemporary (Athenian) society and include as well much of the social thought of *Bks VIII–IX* in a nutshell. They tell how *polis* determines *psyche*.

From the earlier books we know well that unhealthy socio-cultural conditions have a depraving effect on man (see p. 87 ff. above). This lesson is now (491b7–e6) enforced in a dialectical way. Bad cultural conditions are, strange as it sounds, particularly corrupting to the most gifted. For it is generally the case, that the more vigorous a growing

---

[1]) There is a distinction to make between the *dialectic analysis* of concepts (cf. 475e9–476a7) and the *dialectical structure* of the *Republic* resting on the *pro* and *contra* method of disposition of the arguments.—For a short history of dialectic before Plato, see G. Ryle, *Plato's Progress*, London *1966*, pp. 110 ff. As for the place of dialectic in Plato's development, see Robinson, pp. 61 ff, and Ryle, pp. 193 ff.

[2]) The parable of the Ship is discussed by R. Bambrough, *Plato's Political Analogies*, in Plato, Popper and Politics, Cambridge 1967, pp. 103 ff.

organism (plant or animal) is, the more it will lack those proper conditions in nourishment, climate or soil, which are required for natural development, 491d1–8. This applies also to man: lacking the proper environment, the best-endowed suffer most. They turn out the worst, for it is with great crime as with great virtue, that nothing powerful comes from weak natures.

The good man is demoralized by the general cultural environment in which he is enclosed. The public is the greatest of the sophists, fashioning everyone after its heart. In public places the masses are clamouring their approval or disapproval,[1] "booing and clapping till the rocks ring and the whole place redoubles the noise of their applause and outcries"[2] Private instruction cannot help the individual to withstand such torrents of opinion. "In the teeth of public opinion" noble character-building is foredoomed to failure.[3] The multitude commands the law-courts to help the general sentiment to prosper. The influence of the many on the individual is irresistible. With private standards of education one cannot hope to produce a character different from the one which prevails in society at large; such a thing does not happen, has never happened, and will not happen, 492e2–493a2. Thus man—even the best-endowed—is moulded by the *polis* in which he lives.

Socrates does not think that the so called sophists primarily are to be blamed for this state of things. No, it is the entire social and cultural environment,[4] voiced by public opinion, which is depraving. The sophistic movement is merely symptomatic; the sophist himself is a product of his times. He merely studies and nurses the dispositions of that "large and powerful animal", which produces public opinion, 493a6–c8.

Now take the case of the young man, a potential philosopher, who has all those gifts that a philosopher should have; the case is stated in 494b5–495b6. Outstanding already as a boy, he will be nourished from the beginning of his career by flattery and admiration. People, anxious to influence him for their own purposes, will fall at his feet. Growing up in a great city he will be intoxicated with unlimited aspirations, and his self-conceit will censor every honest advice, thus preventing him

---

[1] 492b9–c2. . . . πρὸς δ᾽ αὐτοῖς αἵ τε πέτραι καὶ ὁ τόπος ἐν ᾧ ἂν ὦσιν ἐπηχοῦντες διπλάσιον θόρυβον παρέχωσι τοῦ ψόγου καὶ ἐπαίνου.

[2] Cornford's translation.

[3] Adam vol. II, p. 21.

[4] "The general character and tone of a city", to use Murphy's words, p. 151.

from listening to sober reason. Should he be inclined towards philosophy, his friends will do anything to stop him. Thus, concludes Socrates, the very gifts which are required for a good philosopher conspire against him, if he is placed in the wrong kind of society. His talents are utilized for the wrong goals. Accordingly his greater capacity brings a greater amount of evil to his society.

By this law of social influence, the promising youths are drawn into the whirls of the mass-dominated society. Philosophy is abandoned by her own kind of natures, "like a maiden deserted by her nearest kin". Philosophy is usurped instead by the unworthy, allured by the glitter of her name. Only sophisms are produced by such people.

The last passage has a personal ring. And it holds good for the whole span of text stretching from 487b to 497a, that there are many allusions to Athens, her political system, cultural circumstances and ways of life.[1] It is true that there is left a small remnant of worthy disciples of philosophy. They are those very few honest persons who, by exile or other intervening circumstances, have been saved from the corrupting influence of the city; Socrates mentions also his own case, but he happens to be an exceptional case. Thus there may be a small group of friends of philosophy. But this group, small and disconnected, has no good social force with which to unite—and unassisted they are destined to perish "like a man thrown among wild beasts", 496a11–497e2. Under such conditions they are left alone, trying to protect themselves in the best possible way from the evil influence of the corrupted society.[2]

The painful fact is that there is no existing constitution which is congenial to philosophy, 497b1–c4.[3] The proper socio-cultural frame is given in the model city, but one further point must be made clear. The constructed *polis* should have an authority, which is on level with its plan and intentions and which is able to maintain the city in the right condition, 497c5–d2.

But the heart of the matter now is whether the plan of the *polis* is possible to realize. There is nothing absurd in the plan itself, 499d4–5.

---

[1] See for instance Adam vol. II, pp. 9, 19, 22, 25, 26 etc. See also W. S. Ferguson, *CAH*. vol. V, pp. 351–352, and Jaeger, vol. II, p. 270.

[2] Plato powerfully compares their situation with that of a man sheltering from a storm of dust and hail, 496d5–8.

[3] 497b3–6. Under the present conditions like a seed sown in foreign soil; ... ὥσπερ ξενικὸν σπέρμα ἐν γῇ ἄλλῃ σπειρόμενον κτλ.

But can the prejudice of the people be overcome? Even this is not impossible. The people are accustomed to the game of word-fighting and individual rivalry. They have never experienced the consistent argument of word and practice exemplified when a good man governs a community as good as himself, 498d6–499a2. Only a few of the citizens are really bad, the great majority of the people are not downright perverted but only misled. The chances are that they might be persuaded to adopt a sympathetic attitude towards the rule of the philosophers.[1]) If they discover the truth their hostility will disappear. But the possibility of the realization of the project still rests with this one assumption: that our philosophers (one or few) take over the rule, 499a11–c2.

The real difficulty lies in the foundation of the community. But even on this point Plato is optimistic. It is not impossible that in the infinity of time a few men of the highest gift for philosophy will find themselves compelled to take part in politics; when this happens—here or in some other place—the new community will be realized, 499c7–d6.

500b8–501c2 signifies a passage which is important in different ways. First it can be read as a clarifying complement to the long definition of *dikaiosyne*, given as an internal order at 443c9–444a2. We now learn that the philosopher contemplates a world of divine order and tries to imitate it. Having reproduced that order in his soul he, now as a statesman, sets out to shape also the characters of his fellow-citizens to conform with his vision of the ideal. Here (501a2–c2) Socrates returns to the simile of the painter. Taking *polis* and the manners of men as his canvas, the philosopher will first begin to clean it.[2]) Looking frequently at the model-types of the different virtues, he then begins to reproduce them in the personality and in the society.[3]) The features of the anti-motif are here conspicuous.

---

[1]) At 499d10–500a2 Adeimantus is admonished not to condemn the masses too sweepingly. This actualizes the topic of Plato's attitude towards the people. In the ship allegory the role of the captain is given to the people. But the captain is surely not first rate: he is a little blind, a little deaf, a little misinformed and destined to be drugged at the critical moments.

[2]) 501a2–7. λαβόντες ... ὥσπερ πίνικα πόλιν τε καὶ ἤδη ἀνθρώπων πρῶτον μὲν καθαρὰν ποιήσειαν ἄν, κτλ.—About the political meaning of this canvas-cleaning, cf. Popper, *OSE*, vol. I, pp. 166–167.

[3]) 501b1–7. Ἔπειτα οἶμαι ἀπεργαζόμενοι πυκνὰ ἂν ἑκατέρωσ' ἀποβλέποιεν, πρός τε τὸ φύσει δίκαιον καὶ καλὸν καὶ σῶφρον καὶ πάντα τὰ τοιαῦτα, καὶ πρὸς ἐκεῖν' αὖ τὸ ἐν τοῖς ἀνθρώποις ἐμποιοῖεν, κτλ.

4. Conclusions and observations

In the previous chapter we saw how Socrates was driven to discuss social aspects outside the general analogy between *polis* and *psyche* in order to demonstrate the tenability of his construct. Whereas the earlier part of the investigation was theoretical, the present chapter concerns the practicability of the *polis*. This matter also takes us beyond the analogy. The *polis* is now not an instrument for the inspection of souls, but a model for the realization of the best possible community. Thus the aim of the *polis* is extended in the middle books.

There are impressive strokes of both the motif and the anti-motif. To take the former (in its *polis-forms-man* version) first, we learn that practically no one can escape the bad effects of noxious surroundings; an educational ideal, contrary to the taste of the public, was never allowed to exist; and the strong natures, the potential philosophers, suffer most, because their gifts are biased towards the wrong ideals; in 494b5–495b6 Plato describes the particular case of a promising youth who is spoiled by his society. All in all, the section 491d1–495b6 is of paramount importance for the *polis-forms-man* motif. The passage 492b5–c8 (cf. 138 above) is interesting from the point of view of collective behaviour. Material for such a study, Plato indicates, was richly available from the citizen assembly, the law courts, the theatres and the military camps. Plato pictures, writes A. Menzel, "den Lärm, die übertriebenen Äusserungen von Lob und Tadel und vor allem die *Suggestion*, welche von der Masse ausgeht. . . . Hier wird also das wichtigste Problem der Massenpsychologie, die ansteckende Kraft der Äusserungen und Handlungen der Masse, bereits angedeutet."[1]

In these pages which describe how the general cultural environment and the public and collective behaviour mould man, there is also interspersed an element of thought that carries us over to the opposite motif, i.e. the *man-forms-polis motif*. Just as in the animal or vegetable world, writes Jowett in his analysis, "the strongest seeds most need the accompaniment of good air and soil, so the best human characters turn out the worst when they fall upon an unsuitable soil".[2] Such natures are rare at any time. Within their ranks you find the individuals who harm the society most, but also—if the tide turns—those who do it the

---

[1] *Griechische Soziologie*, p. 47.
[2] *The Dialogues of Plato*, vol. II, p. 70.

greatest good. From small minds no great achievement in either way can be expected; σμικρὰ δὲ φύσις οὐδὲν μέγα οὐδέποτε οὐδένα οὔτε ἰδιώτην οὔτε πόλιν δρᾷ, 495b5–b6. Out of this opinion concerning the decisive importance of the strong and well-endowed natures for the career of the *polis*, springs the project of selecting such men, educating them, and making them philosopher-kings. The passage at 473c11–e5, which speaks about the necessity for the rule of the philosophers, if the cities are to be saved from their evils, is the keystone of our anti-motif in its *man-forms-polis* version.

The motif and the anti-motif are thus, in the versions mentioned above, very much alive also in the middle books.

CHAPTER IX
DIALECTIC METHOD
(Bks VI:502c9–VII:541b5)

1. The knowledge of the Good

502c9-505b4. Why, we may now ask, is the method of the double texts, so vigorously used in *Bks II–IV*, considered unsatisfactory?[1])

The reason for a complementary study is given in 504a4–c7.[2]) The system established by combining the tripartite *psyche* with the cardinal virtues does not suffice for the philosopher-kings, who must possess accurate ethical knowledge.

Then from 504c ff we meet goodness in a new key. Goodness is something more than just the cardinal virtues, defined in relation to each other in order to create a functional unity. The greatest knowledge is about something higher than *dikaiosyne* and its allied virtues, 504d4–8. They all derive their usefulness and value from the Form of the Good.[3]) If we are ignorant of the Good, the rest of the virtues, however much they are praised, are of no consequence, 504e4–505b3.—This does not mean that the earlier exploration was futile. It resulted, we know, in a perfect city. But goodness should not emerge, we may conjecture, as a by-product from the analysis of subordinated virtues.[4]) In ethical discourse, the notion of goodness is the most vital thing, (τοῦ ὄντος τὸ φανότατον, 518c9). Goodness, then, must be given the priority in a careful study of ethics.

---

[1]) That a new subject is taken up is evident from 502c9–d2.

[2]) This new study is called the larger circuit, μακροτέρα περίοδος, (504b2, cf. 504c9) and μακροτέρα καὶ πλείων ὁδός, 435d3.

[3]) 505a2–4. ἐπεὶ ὅτι γε ἡ τοῦ ἀγαθοῦ ἰδέα μέγιστον μάθημα, πολλάκις ἀκήκοας, ᾗ δὴ καὶ δίκαια καὶ τἆλλα προσχρησάμενα χρήσιμα καὶ ὠφέλιμα γίγνεται.

[4]) 504d6–8. It does not suffice with merely an outline (ὑπογραφή) of the virtues. This is, writes Adam, a clear proof that the cardinal virtues of *Bk IV* are not transcendental, vol. II, p. 50.

2. Sun-Good analogy

505b5-509b10. Socrates briefly records some well-known experiences of ethical reflection. It is difficult to say what that mysterious word "good" (τὸ ἀγαθόν) means. Some define it as pleasure, others as knowledge. But nobody can in the end avoid to use the tricky word "good" to designate what he earnestly thinks worth having. The general experience of ethical reflection is, according to Socrates, that the good is the object of our aspirations, though, at closer examination, the notion is found perplexing and difficult to grasp, 505b5–d3.

The rulers then must know the good, 505e4–506b1. But what is it?— Socrates cannot give a straightforward answer, but he is willing to illustrate the matter, 506d8–e5. First a preparatory step.

According to the distinction at 475e9–476d6 there are many beautiful particulars, but only one Form of Beauty. This is now (507b2 ff) confirmed and explicated. To each of the classes of particulars a single Form can be posited.[1] This Form is predicated "that which is". The particulars are visible but not apprehensible by thought; the Forms are apprehensible by thought but not visible, 507b9–10. There follows a note on seeing. To the relation between the eye and the perceived object, one must add light as a necessary condition, 507c1–508a2. Without light one cannot see. The sun is the ultimate cause of light. Our eyes are the most sun-like of the sense-organs. The power of sight flows, so to speak, out from the eye (508b7), but this capacity comes from the sun. Finally, with sight we can see the sun itself, the prime cause of vision; the sun is the offspring of the Good, 508b12–c2.

We are thus supplied with the components of the famous analogy between the sun and the Good, 508b12–509c4. Several equations are involved in it.[2] The sun stands in relation to sight and visible things, as the Good stands in relation to intelligence and intelligible objects. A primary message is that Goodness alone confers truth and being (ἀλήθειά τε καὶ τὸ ὄν) to the objects of knowledge, 508d4–6, 508e1–509a5. The analysis thus says that the Good is not produced by our thought of it; the sun does not spring into existence because of our sight.

---

[1] 507b6–7, ... πάλιν αὖ κατ᾽ ἰδέαν μίαν ἑκάστου ὡς μιᾶς οὔσης τιθέντες, "ὃ ἔστιν" ἕκαστον προσαγορεύομεν.

[2] Adam, vol. II, p. 60, enumerates eight points of similarity; Murphy concentrates on five: the sun/the Good, the light/the truth, sight/knowledge and that which comes into being/that which really exists, and the eye/the soul. p. 154.

In the ethical context this means that the cardinal virtues hang in the air if they are not co-ordinated with the Form of the Good.[1]) The Good is not an intellectual construction. It is rather the opposite: as one apprehends the Good, the configuration of the virtues emerges.

3. Nature of dialectic thought

509c1-511e5. The sun and the sunlight are well chosen symbols for Plato's aims;[2]) in the history of ideas this symbolism, firmly settled in the *Republic*, has had a great career.

Next, in the end of *Bk VI* 509d6–511e5, we meet a new illustration, that of the divided line. I shall not enter into its particulars.[3]) It contains, however, the following. There is (A) the realm of sight and (B) that of thought. In (A) you can distinguish between (1) seeing merely images (reflections, shadows etc.) of things, and (2) seeing the physical objects themselves. Thus a difference of authenticity can be extracted.[4]) Passing over to (B) we find two different kinds of thinking: (1) to reason as the mathematicians do, i.e. by the help of visible constructions (models, diagrams etc.), and (2) to reason by pure thought. This difference in thinking can be brought down to a difference in the handling of hypotheses. In the mathematical arts, the student starts from certain unexamined postulations, taken as known and self-evident; their truth is never doubted. Mathematics, thus, falls below the highest level of knowledge as it fails to include full reflection on its own principles,[5]) cf 510c1–d3, 511c3–d5.

With the transition to the procedures of pure thought, we are brought to the main subject, explained in 511b3–c2. The hypotheses are now

---

[1]) Cf. Ross, p. 42.

[2]) Cf. J. A. Notopoulos, *The Symbolism of the Sun and Light in the Republic of Plato, CPh.,* vol. XXXIX, 1944.

[3]) For a thorough treatment of this illustration, see Raven, pp. 142 ff.

[4]) Murphy has urged that shadows are not to be held as being less real "but of being less intelligible and explicable than the solid originals which are not only, visually, firmer in outline and more vivid in tone, but are bound to each other by causal nexus in a way in which shadows are not", p. 197. Also Raven, p. 149.

[5]) Though mathematics in many ways is a model of intelligent thought, it lacks as a science, comments Murphy, self-criticism in that it does not concern itself either with the examination of its own logic nor with the real nature of its objects, cf. pp. 99 and 196.

not taken for granted but are literally used as *hypo-theses*[1]) (or "under-positions", Adam). They are positions laid down as steps which the *logos* "mounts upon and takes off from" in order to arrive at an un-hypothetical and all-inclusive first principle, ἵνα μέχρι τοῦ ἀνυποθέτου ἐπὶ τὴν τοῦ παντὸς ἀρχὴν ἰών, 511b6–7. When this climb is fulfilled the *logos* turns back (descends), clinging all the time to the consequences which emanate from the first principle. This process of (1) critical (cf. 534b8–d1) and hypothetical thinking which deliberately aims upwards; and (2) deductive thinking aiming downwards,[2]) is throughout operated with Forms; it also ends with Forms.[3])

The divided line has of course been interpreted in different ways. Understood as an analogy the following points emerge: as there are two kinds of vision, there are two kinds of thinking; the physical objects of the one correspond to the Forms of the other; each of the regions has its highest object, the sun and the Form of the Good respectively. The sun analogy thus pervades the divided line. The light symbolism also extends to the allegory of the cave, coming next.

4. Science and social duty

514a1–521b11. *Bk VII* begins with the cave illustration, 514a1–517a6. The allegory describes the path from darkness to the vision of the sun, and the descent again into the cave and its region of shadows. The cave is at 517a8–c5 linked to the divided line. The upward path stands for the progress of the soul into the intelligible region. The ascent is painstaking: critical positing of assumptions towards the un-hypothetical principle, predicated as the cause of rightness and goodness, author of light, intelligence and truth.

The explication of the cave allegory leads to some important remarks about the nature of education, 518b6–518d1. Knowledge cannot be

---

[1]) 511b5, . . . τὰς ὑποθέσεις ποιούμενος οὐκ ἀρχὰς ἀλλὰ τῷ ὄντι ὑποθέσεις, . . .
—Robinson goes thoroughly into the matter of hypothetical thinking in Plato. "'Ὑποτίθεμαι or 'hypothesize' is to posit as a preliminary. It conveys the notion of laying down a proposition as the beginning of a process of thinking, in order to work on the basis thereof", p. 95. See also Murphy, p. 195.

[2]) Robinson comments: "Plato surely conceives of the downward path as a proof, a deduction, a demonstration, in which conclusions are drawn from the anhypotheton as from an axiom", p. 164.

[3]) 511c1–2, . . . ἀλλ' εἴδεσιν αὐτοῖς δι' αὐτῶν εἰς αὐτά, καὶ τελευτᾷ εἰς εἴδη.

put into the soul; one cannot put sight into blind eyes. Every man has the power to learn, each of us has an organ for this aim.[1] Accordingly *paideia* consists in turning the observation in the right direction: one must turn round from the image world. Pondering the cave allegory from this aspect, the returning cave-dweller becomes a liberator summoning the cave-men to try to be free.

Thus wisdom seems to be different from the ordinary virtues, which are a matter of training and use like physical excellences. With reason it is otherwise. It is something one possesses, but whether it is used for good or for evil depends on how the soul is turned, 518d9–519a1. Notice the perverted intelligence of the shrewd but dishonest man, cunningly observing his narrow interests, 519a1–6.

The sun-line-cave discourses relate to the way *polis* should be governed. Only properly educated men, gazing resolutely in the right direction, could function as rulers. The best men must be compelled to climb the upward path, 519b7–d2. After having sufficiently studied dialectics, they are to return to social life from philosophy and put their knowledge into action for the welfare of the society as a whole.[2]

Glaucon (519d8–9) doubts whether a man should be made to live under conditions which are below his natural status. Then Socrates again (cf. 419a1–420a1) impresses upon his friends that the *polis* was not founded in order to make a special class happy, but to ensure the welfare of the whole society. The aim of the legislation is (using persuasion or compulsion) to unite all citizens and make them share together the benefits they| contribute to the society; the purpose of the rulers is not to please themselves, but to be instruments for the interest and unity of the whole *polis*, 519e1–520a4.

Good rulers (earnestly longing for science and learning) do not turn to politics as soldiers of fortune, but because of their duty to the society. Those who love power should not rule; competing for power, they will ruin the state by internal fights, 520e4–521a8.—This is brought out in large letters in *Bks VIII–IX*.

---

[1] 518c4–6. Adam notes the optimistic ring of this pedagogic "well fitted to inspire the teacher with indomitable courage and inextinguishable hope", vol. II, p. 97.

[2] "This strong sense of social duty distinguishes Plato's ideal of spiritual culture from the philosophy of the pre-Socratics." Jaeger, *Paideia*, vol. II, p. 300.

5. Ideal of science

521c1-530c5. The earlier *paideia* proves unsatisfactory. It is no longer a matter of implanting right beliefs but of stirring the mind to self-activity. The purpose of the propaedeutic studies, which we now approach, is to turn the soul from a kind of night-like day to a true day, ἀλλὰ ψυχῆς περιαγωγὴ ἐκ νυκτερινῆς τινος ἡμέρας εἰς ἀληθινήν,521c6–7.

In the sensible world we are often confronted with perplexities (e.g. relational facts, such as big and small, one and many) which call for the attention of the reason, 523e3–524b2. Mathematical reflection then often proves useful, 524b3–525b1. Furthermore the mathematical arts (theory of number, geometry, astronomy and harmony) have a noble and elevating effect on the mind, facilitating the liberation from the bondage of the senses, 525d5 ff. The reason is more valuable to the soul than a thousand eyes, 527d6–e6.

Plato's under-estimation or disregard of the role of the sense-perceptions in science reaches, I suppose, its highest degree in the treatment of astronomy.[1] One cannot base knowledge on sensible things; sense-perceptions are sense-perceptions, even if one looks at the stars, 529a9–c3. The true astronomer leaves the starry skies alone, operating instead— like the true geometer—with absolute standards, using the heavens only for illustrative purposes, 529c7–530c1.

---

[1] 529c4–530c1 is a remarkable passage, observes Raven; it has, "not without some justification", been used to reproach Plato as anti-scientific, p. 179. J. Mittelstrass discusses the topic of astronomy in the *Republic* in *Die Rettung der Phänomene, Ursprung und Geschichte eines antiken Forschungsprinzips*, Berlin 1962, pp. 117–130. Plato's exhortation to turn away from the phenomena cannot be reconciled with a dominating feature in astronomy since the times of Eudoxos, expressed in the formula σῴζειν τὰ φαινόμενα; i.e. by means of mathematical models reduce seeming irregularities to tolerably reliable regularities.—When this position of Plato's has been observed, we may ask what could have fostered this extremely high expectation of the powers of mathematics and pure thought. Jaeger reminds us of the rapid progress of mathematics in these times. Within comparatively few generations a small number of brilliant scientists "created an atmosphere of victorious confidence which was bound to produce reactions on philosophical thought, in the general excitement of the intellectual life of fourth-century Athens. To the philosopher, mathematics looked like an ideal science: a solid and exact structure of logical inference and proof, something undreamed-of in the days of the pre-Socratic natural philosophers." *Paideia*, vol. II, pp. 305–306. See also Adam's commentaries, vol. II, pp. 130–131.

6. Route of pure thought

530c5-535a2. The propaedeutic studies have brought us to the threshold of dialectics. By now we should be able to see that the mathematical arts are bound together by certain relationships and affinities, 531c9–d4. But mathematics alone does not make a dialectician, 531d7–e1.

Socrates thus again approaches the topic of dialectics, 532a1. We now expect additional information. Socrates (532a5–b2) says that dialectics is the progress of pure thought towards ultimate reality, succeeding in the end to grasp the very nature of Goodness itself.[1] This route is called *dialektike*, 532b4.

Being now at the journey's end, Glaucon asks for closer information about the power, structure and ways of dialectical thinking, 532d8–e3. This demand, which, I think, has been accumulating during the long speeches on dialectics, meets, however, with an anticlimax. Glaucon is simply told that he has asked for more than he is able to grasp, 533a1–10. A straightforward demonstration would be to exhibit the vision of truth and reality directly, but this can only be done to the qualified dialectician. Thus Glaucon (and with him the student of the *Republic*) are shut off from further information respecting the nature of higher speculation.[2]

Socrates adds, however, that he is not sure that his version of reality is the true one. But on the other hand, he is confident that there is some such reality to take into consideration, 533a4–6. And the dialectical method (ἡ διαλεκτικὴ μέθοδος, 533c7) is, at any rate, the only known way of inquiring into this matter, 533a8–b3, 533c7–d4. The dialectician, then, is expected to be able to give an account of the real nature of everything, 534b3–4; and in the structure of Forms he can distinguish the Good, 534b8. To do this he must critically, step by step, carry out his examinations by the true standard, not giving way to appearance or convention.[3]

---

[1] 532a5–b2. οὕτω καὶ ὅταν τις τῷ διαλέγεσθαι ἐπιχειρῇ ἄνευ πασῶν τῶν αἰσθήσεων διὰ τοῦ λόγου ἐπ' αὐτὸ ὃ ἔστιν ἕκαστον ὁρμᾶν, καὶ μὴ ἀποστῇ πρὶν ἂν αὐτὸ ὃ ἔστιν ἀγαθὸν αὐτῇ νοήσει λάβῃ, ἐπ' αὐτῷ γίγνεται τῷ τοῦ νοητοῦ τέλει, ὥσπερ ἐκεῖνος τότε ἐπὶ τῷ τοῦ ὁρατοῦ.

[2] Plato conducts us to the chamber wherein the precious secret is locked up, but he has no key to open the door, Grote, vol. III, p. 241; see also Adam, vol. II, p. 139.

[3] 534b8–c3. ὃς ἂν μὴ ἔχῃ διορίσασθαι τῷ λόγῳ ἀπὸ τῶν ἄλλων πάντων ἀφελὼν τὴν τοῦ ἀγαθοῦ ἰδέαν, καὶ ὥσπερ ἐν μάχῃ διὰ πάντων ἐλέγχων διεξιών, μὴ κατὰ δόξαν ἀλλὰ κατ' οὐσίαν προθυμούμενος ἐλέγχειν, ἐν πᾶσι τούτοις ἀπτῶτι τῷ λόγῳ διαπορεύηται, . . .

7. Education for dialectics

535a3-541b5. The program of studies takes us from 535a3 to the end of *Bk VII*. From early years dialectics is taken into consideration as a future goal for the gifted. The disposition for dialectics is tested in the advanced stages by the student's ability to practise abstract thinking and to proceed by pure thought to the reality itself, 537c9–d7.

Dialectics is, however, a dangerous instrument. Incompetent and irresponsible disputations create a bad environment from which only evil results; young disputants arguing, contradicting, and refuting for the sake of amusement, give philosophy a bad reputation, 537d7–539c3, cf. 490e2–497a5. There is a distinction to make between dialectics proper and the technique of contradicting (*antilogia*, 539c5–d1, 454a5). The selected pupils study dialectics from 30 to 35; this study is thus for mature years. Ambition is set in finding the truth, and the instrument of dialectics must be used only for the best purposes.

In the last two pages of *Bk VII* (540a4–541b5) we return from the topic of dialectics to the situation of the best possible state. Compared with philosophy, even administrative work in the good society is a cave job. At 35, the aspirants return to practical work. After 15 years the faultless can be promoted to rulers. They are now able to apply the paradigm of Goodness to the affairs of society and men.[1]

Socrates finally insists that the *polis* and its constitution is not an idle dream, though the realization of the project is difficult. The political power must necessarily be given to the philosophers, one or several. The quickest way of reorganizing *polis* would be to send out into the country all citizens over the age of ten, and remove the children from the influence of their parents, so that one can begin to practise the educational rules and methods earlier described,[2] 540e5–541a7.—We have now, says Socrates, said enough about this type of *polis* and its corresponding man, cf. *TABLE 2*, nr 29.

---

[1] 540a9–b1, . . . παραδείγματι χρωμένους ἐκείνῳ, καὶ πόλιν καὶ ἰδιώτας καὶ ἑαυτοὺς κοσμεῖν τὸν ἐπίλοιπον βίον ἐν μέρει ἑκάστους, . . .

[2] This is a grand example of what Popper calls "Utopian social engineering", *OSE*, vol. I, pp. 22, 166.

8. Conclusions and observations

The *polis-psyche* analogy is abandoned in *Bk V* for a detached discussion on social topics,[1]) 449a1–471c3. The questions of the philosopher-kings and the practicability of the *polis* is then raised, 471c4–502c8. The shortest way to the good society is to introduce ruling philosophers. Their outstanding merit is dialectical philosophy.

Dialectics is pure thinking. Abstaining from sense-perceptions, the dialectician deliberately uses hypotheses. Critically treated they constitute the upward path. The aim is the attainment of the unhypothetical and all-inclusive principle, providing the vision of the co-ordinated Forms headed by the Good. From here the thinking is no longer hypothetical. The downward path consists of proposition linked to proposition in a deductive and fully reliable way. All this movement is within the realm of the Forms.

The crucial point, i.e. how a succession of uncertain hypotheses can end in perfect certainty, remains unanswered. On the other hand, Socrates has with ingenious illustrations (sun, divided line, cave) told us what kind of knowledge the philosopher-kings must possess.

It is not our task to examine the doctrine of dialectics. It is commonplace to think that the *Republic* reaches its highest peak with *Bks VI–VII*. But it is relevant to our discussion to see dialectics in relation to the *polis* and its ruling class.[2]) It is the duty of this class mould the society in conformity with the Form of the Good; to be happy, *polis* must be fashioned after this pattern.

If such a city could be established, it would constitute a text in large letters to read for all those citizens, who are not able for themselves to contemplate its original pattern in the sphere of Ideas.—In this way the keyword *polis* regains something of the illustrative meaning that was lost in the middle books. The ideal *polis*, fashioned as a social *kosmos*, sets an example for the citizen.

---

[1]) "Der ideale Staat erweist sich als Lebensraum des philosophischen Menschen. Beide, so zeigt sich jetzt, bedingen sich wechselseitig". Krämer, p. 105.

[2]) Dialectics is by commentators often separated from its social function. We get the impression that *Bks II–IV* serve mainly as an excuse to take up the subject of Ideas, and in this way help to create the *acromorph* effect of *Bks VI–VII*. "Die drei Gleichnisse der Bücher VI und VII bilden den Höhepunkt der Politeia, sie sind es, auf die die Bücher II–V vorbereiten und zu welchen die Bücher VIII–X eine Nachlese bilden", cf. O. Utermöhlen, p. 9.

Finally, the ideal *polis* furnishes a standard not only for character-building but also for community-building. There is here only a short step to the topic of the *Republic* as a work in the tradition of utopianism.

Some works of political theory aim to make society tolerable, others aim to make it perfect.[1]) The *Republic* belongs to the latter class.

The utopian features of the *Republic* are partially eclipsed in *Bks II–IV* by the function of *polis* as an illustrative instrument in relation to *psyche*. Division of work, co-operation and social cohesion form, however, conspicuous features of the perfect society. More information is supplied in the middle books. Our attention is drawn to the presentation of the philosopher-kings. We are also told of their particular kind of knowledge and wisdom. In utopias one may well meet wise men. By equipping his wise men with the power of dialectics, and discussing the purpose and method of this science, Plato leaves other utopian writers far behind. A new ideal of knowledge and science is sketched.

There is also another characteristic feature to note in Plato's ideal city. *Polis* consists of men, and good men are required. They must be formed by the state-builder. But the basic facts of human nature cannot be ignored. Personality is a delicate thing, easily changed. The appetites must not be left unbridled. Social happiness does not consist in a multiplication of our wants, and in a corresponding increase in our means to indulge them. Plato's examination of human nature does not allow him to conjure away what he considered realistic and fundamental facts of *psyche*. In planning the good society, human nature must be taken for what it is. A. W. Gouldner writes in this connection that Plato, far from being tender-minded, "was among the more tough-minded of social theorists ever to write. He may have wanted the best from men, but he certainly expected the worst."[2])

---

[1]) Cf. G. Kateb, *s.v. Utopianism, IESS.*
[2]) Gouldner, p. 293.

PART FIVE

THE DOUBLE TEXT STUDY (II)

CHAPTER X

TIMOCRACY

(Bk VIII:543a1–550c3)

1. Types of disorganization

543a1-545c7. Now and then in the course of our study we have met a number of references to the disintegrative nature of *adikia*. These passages, containing flashes of realistic social thought, have heightened our expectation of that more systematic examination, which the method of contraposing *dikaiosyne* and *adikia* demands.

Towards the end of *Bk IV* Socrates was about to enter upon this task, 444a10–11. In the next few lines (444b1–8) he puts *adikia* down as internal disorder. A synopsis of the planned examination is next given (445c4–e4), but later in *Bk V*, the conversation is diverted into a new direction.

In *Bk VIII*, Socrates refers back to the synopsis. Glaucon is given the task of recapitulating it, 543c7–544b3. In this way the end of *Bk IV* and the beginning of *Bk VIII* are linked; the books in between are at the same time mentioned as being off the track.[1] *Bk VIII* thus takes its place in the continued application of the double text method,[2] cf. *TABLE 2*, p. 249.

The synopsis given at the end of *Bk IV* indicates how *polis* and *psyche* are related, even in cases of the disorganized patterns. There are many types of badness. Four are worth looking at. Thus, including the good pattern (called *basileia* or *aristokratia*), one gets five distinct types of both societies and personalities.

---

[1] 543c5–6, ... ἀναμνησθῶμεν πόθεν δεῦρο ἐξετραπόμεθα, ἵνα πάλιν τὴν αὐτὴν ἴωμεν.

[2] *Bks VIII–IX* form a strange contrast to the preceding digression (*V–VII*), observes Lutoslawski. Except the recapitulation at the outset in *VIII* there is no direct allusion to the middle books, p. 311.—Krohn comments that the first lines of *Bk VIII*, 543a1–3, correspond inadequately with what is said in *Bk IV*; "Als Verknüpfung mit dem IV. Buche passt dieser Satz nicht, da gerade das besonders hervorgehoben wird, was in diesem nur flüchtig genannt war", p. 198.

The typology of the degenerated states is given at 544c1–d4. Common labels are used, and there is no difficulty in mentioning them.[1] The principal kinds are: (1) the Cretan or Spartan type, commonly admired; (2) oligarchy, burdened with many evils; (3) democracy, opposite to (2); and (4) tyranny, the final disease of society.—There are also many intermediate forms to be found within as well as outside Greece; the modern reader is by this note reminded that there were a great number of Greek city-states in classical times. Rich possibilities for comparison were offered by this wealth of examples. The very abundance of states made it, I think, necessary to treat the matter in some general way, cf. 548c9–d4. A typology was required.[2] Plato does not say much about its construction.[3]

The most characteristic feature of Plato's typology is that it is valid for both states and persons; there are as many types of constitutions as there are differing personalities 544d6–e2. And constitutions do not develop from stocks and stones, but are determined by certain preponderant characters in the population.[4]—Quite clearly this assertion is important for the foundation of the anti-motif; *polis* ultimately consists of persons having certain dispositions.

In the development of the typology the two illustrative methods introduced in *Bk II* are employed, i.e. the method of contrast and the method of the double texts. Socrates first intends to explain how the inferior constitutions develop one from the other (449a7–b1), which implies (545a2–b1) that the types are exhibited in a descending order of merit, beginning with the Spartan-Cretan type and ending with the worst, tyranny. Thus in the end the worst type can be confronted with the best one. As for the double-text method Plato is very explicit, cf. *TABLE 2*, nr 34. This passage is of strategic importance for our

---

[1] Cf. 544c1–3. Οὐ χαλεπῶς, ἦν δ' ἐγώ, ἀκούσῃ.

[2] Cf. K. Vretska, *Typische und Polare Darstellung bei Platon*, SO, XXX 1953, pp. 42 ff. In Almberg, *op. cit.*, pp. 310 ff., there is a discussion on Plato's construction of types.

[3] "We may take it", comments Adam, "that these are, in Plato's view, the four most conspicuous landmarks in the history of political degeneration, as well as the most important and clearly-outlined varieties of existing states", vol. II, p. 198. Also the subject of political change was not originally raised by Plato; of long it had been discussed, and names such as Protagoras. Herodotus and Thucydides are connected with the so-called *metabole*-theories. Cf. T. A. Sinclair, and H. Ryffel.

[4] 544d7–e2. Cf. *TABLE 2*, nr 32.

motif. For the sake of clarity, Socrates proposes that we stick to our earlier procedure and first examine the qualities of the states and then proceed to the individuals. Thus timocracy is bound to be examined first, followed by timocratic man 545b2–c5.

Before leaving the topic of theoretical typology for its practical application let us note that in *Bks II–IV* Plato has hammered out so effectively his positive values of society and man that a survey of the opposite ones becomes superfluous. If *dikaiosyne* is health, then *adikia* is disease. It is ridiculous, says Glaucon, to begin an examination of *adikia* on such assumptions, for no one prefers sickness to health, even if he was offered all the wealth and power in the world, 445a5–b4. Socrates admits this, but insists nevertheless on a demonstration of *adikia*, 445b5–7. To Glaucon it looked as if further examination was destined to end in trivialities. Socrates is, however, allowed to continue. —For this we must be grateful. Otherwise we should be missing those social analyses on which Plato's fame as a sociologist are justly founded. Plato's *polis-psyche* typology is an ingenious achievement. By this merit he stands out as a great precursor of the technique of studying man in his social context.[1]

Objections have been made, however, that the succession of states given in Plato's typology is not historically accurate. In substantiation of this criticism no less an authority than Aristotle can be invoked.[2]

We do not know what Plato thought on the relationship between history and his typology. But we do know that he chose the latter method, and we can even see the arguments which prompted him to employ typology. The choice of a typological exposition postulates that what is lost in respect to historical accurateness is counterbalanced by the rational scope, the psychological insight and the heuristic possibilities offered by the typological system.

In *Bks II–IV*, we saw how the model city was built up in a combined

---

[1] In its way "Plato's *Republic* contains a systematic typological classification which may well be taken as a model for contemporary research in the field of 'personality and social structure' . . . Not only are all the essential features of the methodology of typological classification contained in this seminal work, but it also provides the theoretical model of social change by specifying conditions under which change from one type of polity to another occurs". E. A. Tiryakian, *s.v. Typologies* in *IESS*.

[2] *Politics, Bk V*, 1316 a ff.—See also Popper, *OSE* vol. I, p. 40 and n. 11, pp. 220–221. Against such a verdict there is Adam, vol. II, p. 199.

rational and evolutionary manner: first the productive class was introduced, then the warrior class, and, finally, the governing class at the
top of the pyramid. Now in *Bks VIII–IX*, Plato sets out to demonstrate
how the pyramid is decomposed. This also is done in successive steps.[1]

2. Fall of the ideal polis

545c8–547b1. How is timocracy generated out of *aristokratia*, 545c8–9?
As far as the general principle for constitutional change is concerned,
the answer is quite simple: all change comes from dissension within the
governing class; as long as the members remain united, even if they
are few, no change is possible.[2] This is a sociological principle, and we
shall see that Plato adheres to it throughout the recorded changes.

But the difficulty lies in getting started. The best society is perfectly
united. How does a disunited ruling class come into being? Had Plato
been writing history in the conventional sense, he would not have had
to explain the degeneration of an ideal state. Now the thought experiment must be continued and Socrates has to invoke the help of the
Muses to tell how strife first occurred in the best of societies, 545d5–e3.

Cyclic periodization was a time-honoured idea in ancient mythopo-
etic, religious and philosophic speculation. To this idea Plato now
reverts. The story is told in 546a1–547a7.

The rhythm of the cycles is shorter or longer in proportion to the
length of life of each species. When the limit of evolution is passed,
decay inevitably begins. Everything (plants, animals, man) is subject
to this law. Children, born in unfavourable times, are destined to be
somewhat less excellent than their parents.[3] As before, the best will

---

[1] "Just as before we witnessed the logical construction of a State, in which each
psychological factor was successively introduced, not in order of time, but in order
of importance, so we now witness a destruction of the State, in which each psychological factor is successively taken away, again in order of importance", Barker,
p. 244.

[2] 545c9–d3. ὅτι πᾶσα πολιτεία μεταβάλλει ἐξ αὐτοῦ τοῦ ἔχοντος τὰς ἀρχάς, ὅταν ἐν
αὐτῷ τούτῳ στάσις ἐγγένηται· ὁμονοοῦντος δέ, κἂν πάνυ ὀλίγον ᾖ, ἀδύνατον κινηθῆναι; cf.
465b8–10.—Cf. Popper, *OSE* vol. I, p. 38.

[3] The myth of the cycles is bound up with a complicated mathematical cal-
culation (546b3–d3) ending with a geometrical number, which determines the
quality of the births. For a thorough treatment of this matter I refer to Adam,
vol. II, pp. 264 ff. Cf. K. Gaiser, *Platons Ungeschriebene Lehre*, Stuttgart 1963, pp.
271 ff., and n. 251, pp. 409 ff.

be promoted to the governing class. The rulers are inclined to care a little less for their educational duties. The effect of this is apparent in the next generation. Gradually the standard of the governing class is lowered. By misapplication of the selective principles, iron is mixed with silver, and bronze with gold.—From the view of the anti-motif we observe that the decline of the *polis* is traced to the degeneration of character.[1])

Thus we know how *stasis* (strife) was born. On the super-human level there is the destiny of the cyclical course, and on the social level there are the effects that spring from negligence of education and inability to pick the right people.

3. Timocratic polis

547b2-548d5. The fall of the *polis* is then explained in social terms. Among the rulers and their helpers there are now two kinds of persons each pulling in opposite directions. The iron and brass persons are set on acquiring money and land, while the remaining gold and silver persons (having riches in their souls), stick to the aristocratic pattern of values. Violent tensions take place, but civil war is avoided, and a compromise is achieved. The negotiations are of an internal nature between the members of the higher classes—the third class being unable to defend its rights. The outcome of the clash is told in few words: 1) the men in power agree to distribute land and houses for private ownership 2) they enslave their own people who had previously been free under their guardianship and who had given them sustenance, 3) they keep the people as serfs and menials, and they devote themselves to war and to keeping guard over those whom they have subjected, 547b8-c4.—Thus the property of the society is radically redistributed, and shifted from the third to the upper class; the greater part of the citizens, we conclude, are not only plundered, but also enslaved.

That the new form of government is midway between aristocracy and oligarchy, 547c6-d2, is most carefully demonstrated.

Timocracy is similar to the good society in this respect: authority is upheld; soldiers stick to soldiering and abstain from professional moneymaking; common meals are provided; and gymnastics and training for war are kept going, 547d4-8.

---

[1]) Cf. Adam, vol. II, p. 202.

Timocracy's own peculiar trait is the fear of admitting wise men to power; wise, and at the same time earnest and simple men, disappear; a fiercer kind of man—better suited for war than for peace—predominates; the tricks and stratagems needed in war are highly valued, 547e1–548a3.

The oligarchic feature of timocracy is love of money; the timocrats have a fierce and secret passion for gold and silver, they have private treasure houses[1]) and expensive nests for their wives or anyone else they like, 548a5–b2. Because they are not allowed to acquire money openly, they will be mean; but they are quite ready to spend other people's money for their own interests and are otherwise disposed to the enjoyment of secret pleasures, 548b4–c2. The most characteristic feature is no doubt the dominance of *thymoeides*, the fiery part of human nature. From it emanates *philonikia* (rivalry) and *philotimia* (desire to excel), 548c5–7.—So far, concludes Socrates, an outline of the timocratic society has been given; it would be too great a task to fill in all details and enumerate all the varieties of societies and men, 548c9–d4.

4. Polis moulds man

548d6-550c3. What kind of man corresponds to timocracy? cf. *TABLE 2*, nr 35. How is he produced? What is he like, 548d6–7?

He is rather self-assertive, but somewhat estranged from culture, and though he is a poor speaker he is a good listener, 548e4–549a1. In dealing with people, this kind of man is rough with the slaves, civil with free men, and most obedient to authority, 549a1–3. Power and honour are in high esteem; the claim for ruling is not based on argument, but on force. Athletics and hunting are among the things preferred, 549a3–7.

In his youth, the timocrat is not much concerned about money, but the older he becomes, the more he is attracted by riches. This development is explained by the touch of acquisitiveness which adheres to his nature; he is no longer purely virtuous, since he has lost the guidance

---

[1]) From a historical point of view it is of interest that in 483 B.C. the prospectors at Laureion made rich finds of metal for coining. The precious metals spread over Greece. "But as fast as they come into circulation they were withdrawn from it, especially gold, by the practice of hoarding", a primitive method of capitalization which persisted in many forms. G. Glotz, *Ancient Greece at Work*, London 1965, p. 231.

of the rational element in his soul, 549a9–b4, cf. *Bk IV* 441e4–442b9, also *III* 411c4–e2. Such is, Socrates concludes, the timocratical young man corresponding to timocracy.[1]) The correspondence between *polis* and *psyche* thus concerns the relatively small number of men who belong to the ruling class. Plato says nothing about the personality of the great majority of people.

How is the young timocrat formed?

The father is an excellent man, but the *polis* in which he lives is not well-governed, 549c2–3. He therefore avoids public life with its struggle for honour and office; he would rather give up some of his rights than lose his peace of mind, 549c4–6.

His wife thinks that the social prestige of the family is declining. She feels it humiliating that her husband holds no ruling office; he is not very ambitious in making money, nor is he noticeable in politics or in the law-courts. She is despised by other women. But the husband takes not much notice of her troubles. He gives her neither much regard nor disregard. She is therefore annoyed and tells her son what she thinks of his father: he is not much of a man, being too easy-going. And the criticism is followed up with the usual complaints women make in such circumstances, 549c8–e1. A tedious lot of home-truths, Adeimantus adds, 549e2.

This section has a realistic ring. But it has been objected by critics that the narrow-mindedness of the women is inconsistent with the position given them in *Bk V*.—If we, however, assume that *Bks II–IV* and *VIII–IX* are conceived together, and that the middle books are inserted, this inconsistency is easily explained. It can be reduced, I think, to a matter of inadequate description of how the fall of the *polis* changed the conditions for women. Plato is very brief in his narrative of the changes. But it seems plausible to conjecture that, when private property and private family was introduced, some member of the family had to be detached as a caretaker, and that this role was awarded to the woman. Living within the frame of the household, she becomes family-centred.

But let us proceed. The wife is not the only one to complain. There are also the servants, who—loyal to the house—make the same ac-

---

[1]) 549b9–10. Cf. *TABLE 2*, nr 36.

cusations against their master. If they see him failing to prosecute some dishonest person who has harmed the interests of the family, they will urge the son to be more of a man than his father and try to stand up for his rights, 549e3–550a1. Outside the home the son gets these conventional opinions confirmed, 550a1–4. Naturally, concludes Socrates, these experiences affect the development of the young man.

On the other side there is, near at hand for the son to see, the counter-example of his father. The son can listen to his father's conversation and compare his way of life with those of other men, 550a4–7.

With this in view the young man is "torn in two opposite directions".[1] The father is tending the *logistikon* while the others nourish the *thymoeides* and the appetites.[2] As the young man is not really bad at heart, but is merely influenced by the wrong sort of people, he will steer a middle course between the two ways of life.[3] Thus he will be ruled by *thymoeides*, the middle element of the soul, and he will turn out to be a high-minded and ambitious man.[4]

5. Some historical notes

Briefly and systematically, Plato has outlined the timocratic form of society (547b2–548d5), characterized its corresponding man (548d6–549b10), and sketched his personality development (549c2–550b7).In this way *polis* and *psyche* are presented in their timocratic shapes, cf. *TABLE 2*, nr 36.

The Lacedaemonian ground-pattern is easily recognizable, cf. 544c2–3, 545a2–3.

The question concerning the historic foundations of *Bks VIII–IX* is an extra-textual matter. But we cannot altogether avoid the topic about the historical counterpart to this section of the *Republic*. A resort in this situation is the *Politics* of Aristotle. Even if Aristotle is not

---

[1] 550a4–b1. τότε δὴ ὁ νέος πάντα τὰ τοιαῦτα ἀκούων τε καὶ ὁρῶν, καὶ αὖ τοὺς τοῦ πατρὸς λόγους ἀκούων τε καὶ ὁρῶν τὰ ἐπιτηδεύματα αὐτοῦ ἐγγύθεν παρὰ τὰ τῶν ἄλλων, ἑλκόμενος ὑπ' ἀμφοτέρων τούτων, . . .

[2] 550b1–3, . . . τοῦ μὲν πατρὸς αὐτοῦ τὸ λογιστικὸν ἐν τῇ ψυχῇ ἄρδοντός τε καὶ αὔξοντος, τῶν δὲ ἄλλων τό τε ἐπιθυμητικὸν καὶ τὸ θυμοειδές,

[3] 550b3–5, . . . διὰ τὸ μὴ κακοῦ ἀνδρὸς εἶναι τὴν φύσιν, ὁμιλίαις δὲ ταῖς τῶν ἄλλων κακαῖς κεχρῆσθαι, εἰς τὸ μέσον ἑλκόμενος ὑπ' ἀμφοτέρων τούτων ἦλθε, . . .

[4] 550b5–7, . . . καὶ τὴν ἐν ἑαυτῷ ἀρχὴν παρέδωκε τῷ μέσῳ τε καὶ φιλονίκῳ καὶ θυμοειδεῖ, καὶ ἐγένετο ὑψηλόφρων τε καὶ φιλότιμος ἀνήρ.

unbiased, we may reckon on his general passion for detailed inquiry and manifested capacity for criticising Plato.

Aristotle reviews in *Bk II* some actual states which more or less approach the ideal. The section about Sparta (1269a6–1271b7) can easily be read alongside the timocratic section of the *Republic*.[1])

First Aristotle speaks about the institution of serfdom as being a troublesome system; in Sparta the Helots have often rebelled, involving their masters heavily in guard duties and in suppressing revolts; in this way valuable free time is lost for constructive statesmanship, 1269a29–1269b12.

The position of the Spartan women is then observed. They were given too much freedom. A characteristic Aristotelic passage runs as follows: just as husband and wife are each a part of every family, so the state is roughly divided into men and women. If now the position of women is badly regulated, half the city can be considered as having no laws. This is what actually happened in Sparta, Aristotle goes on. The legislator's aim was to make the whole state hardy. He carried out his intention in the case of the men, but neglected the women, who came to live in licence and luxury, 1269b12–23. This licence, Aristotle continues, seems to have existed from the earliest times, and was only what might be expected since the men were away for long periods. And when they came home, they obediently accepted the laws proposed by the legislator, 1269b39–1270a8.—Aristotle further says that wealth was highly valued, and that there existed avarice and inequality of property, 1270a15–1270b7. The political system involved bribery and favouritism, 1270b7–1271a18. There were common meals, but they were not provided at public cost, 1271a28–37. The constitution aimed at a single virtue—the virtue of the soldier; by such a system one obtained excellence in war, but ignorance in the arts of peace, 1271b1–6.

Thus on the whole we find that Plato and Aristotle agree on the character of the Spartan society. It seems as if timocracy *as a type* captures representative features of Sparta.

Plato is anxious to point out that timocracy is midway between

---

[1]) *The Works of Aristotle*, Vol. X, transl. by Jowett and ed. by W. D. Ross. All refs. are to the Oxford Classical Texts.

aristocracy and oligarchy.[1]) His arguments are listed at page 159 ff above. Because Plato provided a special type for the Spartan-Cretan kind of constitution and placed it first in his record of disorganized cities, he has been accused of idealizing the Laconian way of life.[2]) We shall not engage in this discussion. We must, however, realize that timocracy is a divided state. It is also a state made for the happiness of one special class. Plato has repeatedly stressed that this is a grave mis-construction. Timocracy is neither a friendly state, nor is it attached to science and learning. It is rather a bad state.

6. Conclusions and observations

Bk VIII immediately takes us back to the *polis-psyche* analogy and the method of studying personalities by help of the political and social structure of the society, cf. *TABLE 2*, nrs 30–36. This is also the beginning of the promised study of *adikia*. A typology is presented and timocracy is its first type. The established analogy is extended by a re-arrangement of its three fundamental classes. On next page, the structure of timocracy and timocratic man is presented in brief.

The general fault with existent states is that they are divided, 422e7–423a5. Timocracy is not organically united. Its order is forced. In the model *polis sophrosyne* signified a friendly and co-operative spirit to be found in all the society; the image of the watch-dog was chosen to illustrate that kindness and fighting spirit should exist side by side. The timocrats have got the wrong kind of education: persuasion is substituted by force, intellectual training by physical drill, 548b7–c2.

Plato's record of how the timocratic type of man is produced is most

---

[1]) According to Adam the portrait of timocracy is mainly drawn from the Sparta of the fifth century. During the fourth century the oligarchical element "began to acquire an undue predominance, owing to the temptations of empire and other causes . . .", vol. II, p. 211.

[2]) A discussion on the topic of Plato's idealization of Sparta is found in F. Ollier, *Le Mirage Spartiate*, Paris 1933, pp. 233 ff.—The matter has later been treated by E. N. Tigerstedt, *The Legend of Sparta in Classical Antiquity*, vol. I, Stockholm, 1965, pp. 244 ff. According to Tigerstedt "the Spartan ideal was never exposed to a heavier attack than in the *Republic* and the *Laws*". In timocracy, *sophrosyne*, the prerequisite for the happiness and welfare of the individual and the community, is missing. In Callipolis the rulers rule by the force of their insight and virtue for the good of everybody, willingly obeyed by their own people. Not so in timocracy, where the rule of force triumphs, p. 273.

Timocratic pattern of polis and psyche.

Polis, 547b2–548d5.	Psyche, 548d6–550c3.
Political structure	*Personality structure*
The soldier class in power.	*Thymoeides,* the second part of the soul, dominates.
The philosophers removed from their position as rulers.	*Logistikon,* reason, dethrowned.
The people is enslaved, and its property seized by the soldier class	*Epithymiai,* the bulk of appetites, are suppressed, but the love of wealth, property and pleasure is secretly expanding.

interesting. We are taken into an ancient household consisting of man and wife, a son, and some slaves. The household is divided, and the son is involved in a drama. There is the noble father, sticking to the old values, admonishing the son by word and deed. Against the father and husband stands his wife, the leader of the household chorus, reciting the prevailing opinions of the society. Growing up in this environment, the son is torn in different directions. He becomes a divided man, though he may appear resolute enough. The importance of the small groups, such as family and friends, in forming man's character should be observed.

The study of how the personality of the timocratic young man is formed belongs to some extent to the classic father-son motif: the son looks up to his father and tries to imitate him. The standard pattern is found in the Odyssey, where Telemachus develops as the true son of his heroic father. In the *Republic* we have the story in a new key. Unlike Telemachus the young timocrat is the product of divided parents, and he does not receive divine instructions. He simply and consequently becomes what the divided social forces make him.[1] The *polis-moulds-man* motif is here manifest. The institutions of private family and private property are the main instruments by which the timocratic society executes its influence on the personality.

---

[1] There is a study by E. M. Grossmann on such divisions, *Die Problematik des Dazwischenstehens*, München 1967. In order to illustrate the subject the author has used examples from literature, where such situations are related.—The *Republic* offers, we may add, the earliest systematic study of such "Zwischenpositionen".

The fault with the timocratic women is that they are not taking part in the common interest of the *polis*. They live a detached life in their domestic world. They become family centred, judging happiness only in relation to property, social prestige, and well-being of the family. The servants' interest is bound up with those of the household. Private property and private family constitute a private world which stands in the way of the happiness of the *polis* as a whole.

Having thus studied the destructive results of private interests on the higher levels of existing types of societies, Plato might well have felt the need of strengthening the model *polis* of *Bks II–IV* with a more thorough-going discussion about the requirements for social unity. At 423e4–424a2 (*Bk IV*) Plato explicitly says that he is omitting a good many subjects, such as wives, marriage, and childbearing; the short formula is that "friends have all things in common". This communistic formula is supplemented in *Bk V*. Acquainted with timocracy, we can see the reason for this supplement. This addition does not add new corresponding features to the *polis-psyche* analogy. But it helps to explain how the demanded unity of the model *polis* can be accomplished; and a unified *polis* is a necessary requirement for creating unified men.

CHAPTER XI
OLIGARCHY
(Bk VIII:550c4–555b2)

1. Oligarchic polis

550c4-552e11. In the oligarchic state wealth is the supreme good. The rich rule, the poor are ruled, 550c11–d1.

Timocracy is ruined by the accumulation of gold in the private stores. Money is spent in new ways, and the laws are modified for such purposes, 550d9–12. In the competition to become rich, capital is rapidly circulated. As one citizen sees his neighbour become wealthy, he is eager to be equally successful. The love of wealth expands in the city. In the struggle for prosperity virtue is inconvenient. A change of values can soon be noted: the rich rise in social prestige, the virtuous sink, 550e1–551a2. The oligarchy is fully developed when a statute is passed restricting office to the rich; the régime is established by force in one way or another, 551a7–b7.

The defects of oligarchy are listed at 551b8–552e11.

(a) It is absurd to think that ruling capacity necessarily goes with wealth. If the captain of a ship was chosen on such grounds, the poor but able sailor would never have command. What reasonably holds good for navigation is far more important in politics, ruling a *polis* being the most difficult and important task a man can be given, 551b8–551d2.

(b) The *polis* is no longer one, but two: the city of the poor, and the city of the rich. Though they live together they are constantly plotting against each other.[1]

(c) The oligarchs are unable to carry on a war if needed. By themselves they are too few, and they dare not arm the common people. Their avarice makes them also disinclined to spend money on war, 551d9–e4;

---

[1] 551d5–7. Τὸ μὴ μίαν ἀλλὰ δύο ἀνάγκη εἶναι τὴν τοιαύτην πόλιν, τὴν μὲν πενήτων, τὴν δὲ πλουσίων, οἰκοῦντας ἐν τῷ αὐτῷ, ἀεὶ ἐπιβουλεύοντας ἀλλήλοις.

in *Bk II* 372e2–373e8 Plato has already described the predicament of the swelling city.[1])

(d) Oligarchy breaks up the natural division of work. The same person has too many callings: agriculture, business, soldiering, 551e6–552a2; cf. what has been said previously about *polypragmosyne* (434a9–c6).

(e) The worst defect is, however, the possibility for a man to dispose of all his property by sale. By such a transaction he loses his social function, and is neither tradesman, nor artisan, nor soldier, but becomes just a common pauper. This is an evil which now appears for the first time in the decline of the *polis*, 552a4–b1. We may even ask, Socrates continues, if this new pauper was in his great days, when wealthy and powerful, anything more than a spender and a consumer of goods, who was never really concerned with ruling, though he belonged to the ruling class, 552b2–c1. Such a man is like a drone, and his house is like a drone's cell. As the drone is a plague (νόσημα) to the beehive, this man is a plague to his society, 552c2–4.

The comparison with parasitic bees is further elaborated.[2]) There are both flying and walking drones. The former are without stings, but among the latter some are armed with dreadful stings and some have no stings. In society, the stingless end up as beggars, while the stingers recruit the criminal class, 552c6–d1. Socrates concludes, that whenever one sees paupers in a state, then one can expect to find a variety of thieves operating somewhere, even though they are not in evidence. Criminality is due to lack of education, bad upbringing, and bad government, 552d3–e7.

---

[1]) New demands and the growing population forced the swelling city to war. An inherent weakness of the oligarchic *polis* is, we conjecture, that it develops those very conditions which cause war, without providing the necessary means for waging one, when compelled.

[2]) It might be of interest to note that "bee-keeping had the same importance for non-tropical antiquity from palaeolithic times onwards as sugar production has now. . . . The practical experience of many generations of Greek and Roman bee-masters was finally codified by a number of Greek and Latin authors, . . ." *s. v. Bee- keeping* F. M. Heichelheim in *OCD*.—In the survey of the imperfect societies Plato makes extensive use of illustrations taken from bee-keeping. About *Griechische Tiersoziologie* in general, cf. A. Menzel, pp. 31 ff.

2. Polis moulds man

553a1-555b2. The origin and nature of the corresponding type of man is next examined, cf. *TABLE 2*, nr 38.

Again we are taken to a family. The attention is this time concentrated on the relation between a father and his son. The former is of timocratic character. The son is devoted to his father and follows his example. Then all of a sudden the son sees his father economically and politically wrecked; the father may for instance have held high military command or some other office of importance. Now he is accused by informers, and brought before the law courts. Perhaps he is executed, perhaps not. If he survives, he is exiled or deprived of his civil rights and all his property, 553a6–b5.

The son's personality is changed by these disastrous experiences. Plato describes this process in most picturesque language. *Philotimia* and *thymoeides*, the drives dominating the timocratic character, are recklessly thrust from the throne of the soul.[1] Impoverished and humbled, the young man now mobilizes all his energy in getting rich. By the utmost thrift and hard work he collects a fortune. Another spirit, made up of sensual appetites and love of money, is installed on the vacant throne.[2] There, this spirit reigns like a Great King (oriental style), with diadem, chain and sword.[3] *Logistikon* and *thymoeides* are reduced to slavery. Crouching at the feet of the sovereign[4], the one is allowed only to calculate how lesser money may be turned into bigger money, while the other has to work up an enthusiasm for wealth, 553d1–7.—This is how the young man quickly and violently is transformed into a lover of money, 553d8–9.

The metamorphoses of the young man and the state correspond,

---

[1] 553b7–c4. Ἰδὼν δέ γε, ὦ φίλε, ταῦτα καὶ παθὼν καὶ ἀπολέσας τὰ ὄντα, δείσας οἶμαι εὐθὺς ἐπὶ κεφαλὴν ὠθεῖ ἐκ τοῦ θρόνου τοῦ ἐν τῇ ἑαυτοῦ ψυχῇ φιλοτιμίαν τε καὶ τὸ θυμοειδὲς ἐκεῖνο, καὶ ταπεινωθεὶς ὑπὸ πενίας πρὸς χρηματισμὸν τραπόμενος γλίσχρως καὶ κατὰ σμικρὸν φειδόμενος καὶ ἐργαζόμενος χρήματα συλλέγεται.

[2] The account of the genesis of this man is typical of Greek life, writes Nettleship, p. 307. See also W. S. Ferguson, *CAH*, vol. V, pp. 349 ff.

[3] 553c4–7. ἆρ' οὐκ οἴει τὸν τοιοῦτον τότε εἰς μὲν τὸν θρόνον ἐκεῖνον τὸ ἐπιθυμητικόν τε καὶ φιλοχρήματον ἐγκαθίζειν καὶ μέγαν βασιλέα ποιεῖν ἐν ἑαυτῷ, τιάρας τε καὶ στρεπτοὺς καὶ ἀκινάκας παραζωννύνται;

[4] "Plato makes them squat like servile Oriental courtiers", writes Adam, vol. II, p. 226.

TABLE 2, nr 39. It remains to be seen if he really has the same characteristics as the *polis*, 553e4.

A point of resemblance, first and foremost, is that wealth is valued above everything, 554a2–3, 554b5–6, *TABLE 2*, nr 40.

Moreover, this man is thrifty and hard-working. He satisfies only his necessary appetites; the other desires he represses as unprofitable and vain, 554a5–8. Furthermore, there is something squalid about him, and he is always on the look-out for a chance of profit. He is admired by the multitude, and he corresponds well to the oligarchical constitution, concludes Socrates, *TABLE 2*, nr 41.

It is evident that the oligarchical man has neglected *paideia*. Otherwise he would not have promoted the blind thrift for wealth as a leader of the chorus inside him.[1]

In the next passage (554b7–e5) Plato again demonstrates the double-text method, *TABLE 2*, nr 42. There are two classes of drones: 1) the stingless ones, ending as beggars, and 2) the stingers, being criminals. Owing to lack of education, two similar kinds of appetites are generated in the oligarchic person. As the criminals are restrained by force in the *polis* (552e2–3) so, in the person, criminal dispositions are checked by his diligence, 554b7–c2. But if one wishes to discover his hidden inclinations, he should be watched in a situation when free to act dishonestly without any risk of being found out. Observe him for instance in the role of a guardian of orphans; his reputation as a just man is only based on a sort of enforced respectability. Base desires are alive in him. Because he has no moral conviction, his bad dispositions are never tamed. His hidden inclinations are repressed only by fear and anxiety for his possessions, 554c4–d3. But he is not thoroughly disciplined. Whenever he has other people's money to spend, his dishonest instincts make themselves known, 554d5–7.

Naturally such a man does not escape being torn by inner conflicts. He is not one person, but two.[2] On the whole, his better inclinations prevail over the baser ones. Hence you find him more respectable than

---

[1] 554b5–6. Οὐ δοκῶ, ἔφη, οὐ γὰρ ἂν τυφλὸν ἡγεμόνα τοῦ χοροῦ ἐστήσατο καὶ ἐτί ⟨μα⟩ μάλιστα. — The earliest references to the blindness of Plutus, god of riches, are from Hipponax and Timokreon. From then τυφλός is proverbially predicated Plutus, s.v. *Plutus* by J. Zwicker in *RE*, 1036.

[2] 554d9–e1. Οὐκ ἄρ' ἂν εἴη ἀστασίαστος ὁ τοιοῦτος ἐν ἑαυτῷ, οὐδὲ εἷς ἀλλὰ διπλοῦς τις, ἐπιθυμίας δὲ ἐπιθυμιῶν ὡς τὸ πολὺ κρατούσας ἂν ἔχοι βελτίους χειρόνων.

many men. But genuine virtue, which goes with a truly united and harmonious *psyche*, is far beyond his capacity, 554e3–5.

Though successful in money transactions, this type of man is a loser in the race for official distinction. Love of his property does not allow him to invest money for such purposes. He is also afraid of encouraging expensive tastes. Thus, the oligarch fights only with a small part of his resources. Usually he loses the prize, but remains wealthy, 554e7–555a6.

We cannot doubt, that this thrifty money-maker is like the oligarchic state, *TABLE 2*, nr 43.—From this pronouncement we may infer that the oligarch is not an ordinary person. He is thriftier than most men. He is also more disciplined in his way, and not without a certain respectability. Thus our attention is focused on that small class of people which dominates the *polis* economically and politically, i.e. its leading or representative personalities. But the attitudes of the leading class set an example for other people, so that the oligarchic values expand in society, cf. 554a10—b1.

3. Some historical notes

Oligarchy means literally the rule of the few.[1]) Historically there is a connection with landed aristocracy and the rule of the nobility. But new groups of people later acquired political influence. First the hoplites were made important by the new military tactics, then economic evolution resulted in new sources of wealth (mines, trade, industry) raising the non-aristocrats to prominence. Wealth finally replaced birth as the decisive merit.[2]) As an alternative to oligarchy one can employ the term *plutocracy*.[3]) But as the wealthy in fact were few, the term oligarchy nevertheless retains its significance.[4]) In the *Republic* oligarchy means the rule of the wealthy class, being at the same time a minority.[5])

The place of wealth in man's life is discussed already in the beginning of *Bk I*, 329e1–331b7. Old Cephalus, though a rich man, does not seem over-fond of money, Socrates observes. And, he adds, this is generally

---

[1]) *S. v. Oligarchia, LSJ.*

[2]) I refer to the resumés on *aristocracy* and *oligarchy* by V. Ehrenberg in *OCD*.

[3]) Cf. Cornford, p. 267, Ehrenberg above. Sinclair p. 162.

[4]) Cf. Aristotle, *Politics* 1280a1–6.

[5]) 550c11–d1. Τὴν ἀπὸ τιμημάτων, ἦν δ' ἐγώ, πολιτείαν, ἐν ᾗ οἱ μὲν πλούσιοι ἄρχουσιν, πένητι δὲ οὐ μέτεστιν ἀρχῆς.

the case with men who have inherited their wealth. Self-made men, on the contrary, love their money as poets love their poems, and fathers their children. Such money-lovers are bores, because they are unable to appraise anything but wealth.

In *Bk VIII* Plato studies the money-lovers as the fully developed product of the oligarchic society. The over-emphasis on wealth in this kind of society implies an under-estimation of virtue, 551a1–2. In other words, how one gets rich is of little importance. The main thing is to be successful and become rich, cf. 550e4–8. Overtly the rules of honesty are respected, covertly they are disregarded. In such a society, criminality grows. Plato's account of the change of values sounds convincing, and the relation he sees between the generally accepted goal of economic success and criminality brings to mind the modern sociological concept of *anomie*.[1])

From a psychological point of view, also, the motivations are well recorded. The oligarch is industrious and calculated in his ways. Anxiety for his possessions makes him disinclined to take great risks. For those who recruit the criminal class the situation differs. Among them envy and hatred urge for revenge, and, I conjecture, dispose for the use of more risky methods. Finally, the general effects of the speedy circulation of property in a contest- and opportunity system is plausibly demonstrated. Acquisition is linked to new consumer habits. With new pleasures, there are new temptations. And with more spending, there are more bankrupts[2])—all making favourable conditions for the progress of the thrifty oligarch, cf. 555c1–5.

Corresponding to the dual society there is a dual personality. The divided society emanates from those leading personalities whose genesis

---

[1]) *Anomia* (lawlessness, opp. *dikaiosyne*) introduced in modern sociology by Durkheim, meaning normlessness.—In the study of aberrant behaviour *anomie* is a central concept, symptomatic of a divorce of highly and generally accepted success-goals from the institutionally prescribed conduct by which the goals can be attained. Cf. R. K. Merton, *Social Theory and Social Structure*, Glencoe Ill. 1951, pp. 125 ff.

[2]) The Greeks did not think of economy as an expanding system in the modern sense. To Plato increase in wealth on one hand seems to mean corresponding decrease on some other hand. Accumulation of wealth could only be done, directly or indirectly, by taking it from someone else. Cf. G. C. Field, *The Philosophy of Plato*, London 1949, pp. 89–90.

we know. *Psyche* determines *polis*, which in turn impresses its super-values on the individuals. Hence *polis* also determines *psyche*. The latent layer of criminal tendencies in the person is held alive and nour-ished by the forces the oligarchs themselves have let loose in society. Disregarding *paideia*, the acquisitive spirit prevails. When social prestige is wedded to monetary success, the gifted social climber is restricted to deeds rather than word; what other people do is more important than what they say; words can be used to conceal one's inmost inten-tions. With the sophistic movement, as exemplified by Thrasymachus, this attitude of looking more to acts than to words was, it seems, co-dified as the realistic approach. The young man, placed in a plutocratic hierarchy, and influenced by the primary groups of family and friends, is destined to be like his society.

Timocracy was, we found, to some extent modelled on Sparta and Crete. Oligarchy is not introduced by means of such references. Yet one cannot doubt that there is a wealth of empirical observations under-lying the oligarchic type of constitution. The money-lover, already mentioned in *Bk I*, was, it seems, a well-known figure of a man. This type of personality was certainly not confined to Athens, but could be observed in any of the Hellenic states in the time of Plato, when trade and industry based on monetary transactions were flourishing.[1] With this picture of the oligarch, it has been said, Plato held up a mirror not only to the ancients, but also to the moderns.[2]

As for the oligarchic *polis* there was no need to specify names. Oligarchy, together with democracy and tyranny, belonged to the three principal forms of rule among which Greek societies were continuously tossed. Every *polis* more or less had a first-hand knowledge of oligarchy. There are, however, many guesses as to which particular *polis* Plato had in mind. Taylor suggests Carthage.[3] Barker thinks of Sparta, not the earlier and glorious Sparta, but that of the fourth century, when the citizens had begun to accommodate themselves to the new

---

[1] Adam, vol. II, p. 225.

[2] Plato's picture of the oligarchic man, combining moral puritanism and dubious business methods, calls to mind satiric portraits of our own times, writes Barker, p. 253.

[3] Taylor, p. 297.

ways of living.[1]) Wilamowitz points out Corinth as a probable model.[2]) Adam proposes Athens just before Solon's reform.[3]) Luccioni thinks that the reign of the Thirty is hinted at, which, however, does not exclude the incorporation into the picture of traits also from other cities.[4])—Let us only conclude that features of actual cities have been recognized behind the picture of oligarchy. In this respect the oligarchic type answers to what is implied in typological method: to characterize generalities, not depict individuals.

4. Conclusions and observations

The last traces of the ideal *polis* have now vanished. There is no trained leadership, no specialized soldier-class; the scheme of the division of work is totally blurred. The power of the sword has given way to the power of the money-bag. The disrupting forces, latent in timocracy, are now manifest. The interest of the whole *polis* is subjected to a small and wealthy class. In the struggle for wealth, the society has become sharply divided into the rich and the poor.[5]) Oligarchy is afflicted

Oligarchic pattern of polis and psyche.

Polis, 550c4–552e11.	*Psyche*, 553a1–555b2.
The wealthy class in power.	*Epithymiai*, dominate, represented by the passion for money.
The philosopher-kings and the merited soldier class extinct.	*Logistikon-thymoeides* degraded to serve the passion for money.
The society split up in two factions, the rich and the poor.	The personality divided between necessary and unnecessary appetites.

[1]) Barker, p. 252.

[2]) Wilamowitz, vol. I, p. 430.

[3]) Adam, vol. II, p. 224.

[4]) J. Luccioni, *La Pensée Politique de Platon*, Paris 1958, pp. 14 ff.

[5]) A. Krohn, who found the *Republic* crowded with inconsequences, argued that Plato had already forgotten the law established at 545d1–3, i.e. that all revolutions are caused by *stasis* within the leading class. — This judgement is, I think, rash. Though it is true that the rich agree that they should rule, we must on the other hand see that they are competing within their own class. In this struggle some are impoverished and fall for the money-limit. Thus they come to recruit the poor class, of which, again, the ablest of the impoverished, stimulated by the urge for revenge, become revolutionary leaders.

with several serious faults; it is explicitly a bad constitution, cf. 551b8–552a10.

Corresponding to the dual *polis,* there is a dual personality. The oligarchic features common to *polis* and *psyche* are tabled on p. 174.

As economic success is of the highest value, the energies of the oligarch are concentrated on economic activities; *gymnastike* and *mousike* are neglected, 552e5–7.—Rulers and ruled are alike swayed by the appetites, but the distinction of the oligarch is his thrift. Though his better inclinations mostly prevail over the baser ones, he is, however, internally a divided man.

Plato adheres to the double text method, cf. *TABLE 2,* nrs. 37–43. Oligarchic *polis* illustrates oligarchic man. The individual is also in this section interpreted in relation to society. One notes the institutions of private property and private family, and the cultural goals are focused on acquiring wealth. Through these agencies, *polis* forms man. Wherever the individual is, he feels the impact of the current values. But we can also see a trend in the opposite direction, i.e. from man to society. The leading personalities guide the ordinary men, set the examples, and strengthen the consumer spirit in society. In this process the gulf widens between rich and poor. But when the oligarchs have encouraged the consumer habits in the society they cannot prevent these habits from rebounding upon their own families. There is, we realize, a reciprocity of influence between man and society, society and man.

In the light of Plato's penetrating analysis and unsparing criticism of oligarchy, we are better equipped for understanding the function of communism as found in *Bk V.* Already in timocracy the disintegrative effects of private ownership and hoarding is demonstrated. In oligarchy we find these disintegrative features still more elaborated. If, from these powerful illustrations, we turn back to *Bks III–IV* (416d3–417b8, 423e4–424b1) where are laid down the stipulations for the guardians' way of life, we may well find this treatment somewhat inadequate; the realism of *Bk VIII* makes the educational program of *III–IV* a bit over-optimistic. Building a new society, more stress must be laid on creating those social circumstances which are pre-conditional for the success of the educational program.

CHAPTER XII
DEMOCRACY
(Bk VIII: 555b3–562a3)

1. Democratic polis

555b3-558c7. The democratic city and the democratic man are next inspected. In accordance with the program of research *polis* is first demonstrated, cf. *TABLE 2*, nr 44.

Initially we are reminded that the highest good in oligarchy was to become as rich as possible, 555b9–10. The free spending of money of the younger generation is a pre-condition for the accumulation of wealth in the hands of the oligarchs, who wish to buy up more property and increase their power by the bond of more loans, 555c1–5. In this way also men of quality are impoverished.[1]) Disenfranchised, burdened with debt, they long for revenge. Being stingers, hating those who acquired their property, they dream of revolution, 555d7–555e1. The money-makers, however, proceed as before. Blind to anything but profit, they acquire more money, generating at the same time more drones and paupers, 555e3–556a2. Even when this evil process threatens to blaze up like a fire, the oligarchs are unwilling to fight it, 556a4–7.

The rich are as indifferent to the traditional set of virtues as are the paupers. But the loose way of living, which furthers the economic interests of the oligarchs, cannot be expelled from their own families. The taste for luxury and idleness spreads to the new oligarchic generation. While the fathers, energetic and hardworking, are absorbed in business, their own sons become soft, 556b6–c6.

---

[1]) Men "of no common stamp", translates Adam, vol. II, p. 230. They are the more capable of the impoverished, destined to carry on the revolution when time is ripe.

Sometimes the rich and the poor are brought in personal contact with each other, the *polis* being a small place. In a campaign, for instance, the pauper, lean and sunburnt, used to out-door life, proves the better soldier. Observing the distress of his wealthy and overfed fellow-soldier, the poor discover their own strength and the weakness of the rich. The oligarchic society is in this stage utterly frail. Like an unhealthy person it falls sick at the slightest occasion. Civil war, perhaps, breaks out as one party calls in help from allies in a neighbouring state, 556c8–e9.

When the poor win, they establish democracy. Some oligarchs are killed, others banished. An equal share of rights and offices are distributed to the rest of the citizens, the officials being mostly appointed by lot, 557a2–5. This is, concludes Socrates, the origin of democracy. Revolution was inescapable, we must realize, because the cult of Plutus and *Sophrosyne* cannot exist side by side, cf. 555c7–d1.

What are the characteristics of this new society? This must first be stated in order to elucidate what a democratic man may be like, 557a9–b2, cf. *TABLE 2*, nr 45.

Freedom, *eleutheria*, is the conspicuous feature. The individual has freedom of speech and action, παρρησία and ἐξουσία; he can order his life as he likes, 557b4–10. Accordingly, the greatest variety of men is to be found. The democratic display of characters and life-patterns is likened to a many-coloured cloak, 557c5–7. Most people are attracted by this diversity: every type of constitution is represented. You can stroll around "as in a bazaar", picking the pattern which suits you best, 557d1–e1. Peace or war, you are not forced either to govern or to be governed, but you do as you like. In the short run, this is a good way of life, 557e2–558a3. Generosity is sometimes extended to the condemned; persons sentenced to death or exile may be found sauntering about in town at random, 558a4–8. No one bothers about trifles. And the principles of education, carefully adopted in the model *polis*, do not matter any more. Any man, whatever life he has led earlier, may now enter into politics, provided he declares himself a friend of the people, 558b1–c1. *Demokratia* makes a pleasant form of living together, it is anarchic and picturesque. A sort of equality is given alike to equal and unequal, 558c3–6. Adeimantus nods his assent; Socrates is speaking about well-known things, 558c7.

2. Polis moulds man

558c8-562a3. So much for the *polis*. Now for the lesser text. We have noted the change in the *polis*, now we shall see how the democratic man is generated, *TABLE 2*, nr 46.

We are again faced with the domestic circle. The father, now an oligarch, is thrifty and miserly, and trains his son in the oligarchic virtues. The son, like his father, forcefully subdues all those pleasures which are expensive to gratify, 558c11–d6. Socrates breaks off for an excursus on necessary and unnecessary desires. It is given in 558d4–559d2.

First there are desires from which one cannot rid oneself, and also desires to which it is useful to submit. These can be called necessary. As an example, the desire to eat enough to preserve health and strength for productive work is mentioned. On the other hand there is a variety of more or less luxurious appetites, which could be suppressed by early training. They are either not useful or directly harmful for body and soul, and can be labelled unnecessary.

After this distinction we are led back to an account of how the democratic personality is generally formed. The following section, 559d7–562a3, is worthy of the highest attention in connection with the *polis-psyche* motif.[1]

The son has grown up without much education, influenced mainly by the thrifty side of his father. When the son has tasted the honey of the drones, and has been conducted to all sorts of pleasures by competent guides, then his inner government begins to change towards the democratic pattern.[2] The political change of the *polis* is now being paralleled: the factions, we remember, had resource to aid from other cities. In the same way now, the licentious desires in the young man are helped by similar desires in his drone-friends, *TABLE 2*, nr 47. But the oligarchic desires are also assisted; the son is admonished by his father or some other person in the household with an oligarchic

---

[1] Adam praises this section as "one of the most royal and magnificent pieces of writing in the whole range of literature, whether ancient or modern", vol. II, p. 240.

[2] 559d10–e2, . . . ἐνταῦθά που οἷον εἶναι ἀρχὴν αὐτῷ μεταβολῆς . . . ὀλιγαρχικῆς τῆς ἐν ἑαυτῷ εἰς δημοκρατικήν.

turn of mind. Attack and counter-attack are exchanged—and the son finds himself at war with himself.[1])

In the course of this battle, it sometimes happens that the democratic faction gives way to the oligarchic, and some unnecessary desires are killed, others banished; the young man feels a sense of shame, and the internal order is restored, 560a4–7. However, other desires, akin to the exiled ones, then spring up and through lack of education become numerous and strong. They draw him back to his old acquaintances, with whom he secretly associates, thus increasing the number of unnecessary passions, 560a9–b5.

The end of this drama is painted in the grand style as a battle about a *polis*.

In the end, the new passions occupy the acropolis of the young man's soul; Τελευτῶσαι δὴ οἶμαι κατέλαβον τὴν τοῦ νέου τῆς ψυχῆς ἀκρόπολιν, 560b7–8. The citadel is defenceless, found empty of knowledge, noble passions and true maxims, which are the sentinels and guardians of the inner man, 560b8–10. In their place false and presumptuous notions storm in. To prevent oligarchic assistance from family and friends, the gates of the fortress are now shut. The unnecessary passions triumph. *Aidos* (self-respect or shame) and *sophrosyne* are both exiled, the one is held foolish, the other unmanly; moderation and order are likewise insulted and expelled. The young man now openly belongs to the Lotus-eaters, 560c2–d6.

In rich allegory, Socrates next describes how the soul is cleansed of the old virtues and prepared for the great mysteries of the new fashion of life. With the use of honorary names, insolence is called good manners, anarchy becomes freedom, extravagance means magnificence, and shamelessness is taken for courage, 560d8–561a4.—Looking back we see the change of values given in relation to social change: the aristocratic sham-culture of *timokratia*, the economic value-system of *oligarchia*, and the relativization of the values in *demokratia*.[2])

From now on, as much money and energy is spent on the satis-

---

[1]) 560a1–2, . . . στάσις δὴ καὶ ἀντίστασις καὶ μάχη ἐν αὐτῷ κτλ.

[2]) The charge that popular politicians were upsetting the given moral standards seems to have been quite common. It would be an interesting study, both ethical and linguistic, writes Sinclair, to follow these transvaluations; Hesiod, *W.D.* 271–272, Thucydides *III* 82, Plato *Rep. VIII*, 560d, Isocrates *VII* 20, *XII* 131, *XV* 283 and the παραχαράττειν τὸ νόμισμα of Diogenes the Cynic, cf. p. 139, n.3.

faction of unnecessary appetites as is spent on the necessary ones. But if our young man is lucky, he may escape absolute destruction. With passing years the internal tumult may subside and some of the banished desires may be allowed to return. All pleasures will be regarded as equal. He will successively yield to them one after another as if his inner government were subject to the chance of the lot, 561a6–b5. But the citadel is well guarded against reasoning involving qualitative distinctions between the desires. The prevalent creed is that one appetite is as good as another, 561b7–c4. As a consequence his life becomes most capricious; one day he indulges freely in sensual pleasures, the next he is engaged in ascetic exercises.[1] Periods of physical training, indolence, and study alternate whimsically. Sometimes he throws himself enthusiastically into politics, sometimes his aspirations are of a military or business nature. This life without firmness and order is esteemed pleasant, free and happy, 561c6–d7.

The conclusion is that the democratic man, like the democratic state, is manifold and many-coloured. He contains a variety of constitutional patterns. From him men and women can always pick something to admire, *TABLE 2*, nr 48.

3. Some historical notes

Oligarchy and democracy are both, says Aristotle, subject to questions of degree; a government may be more or less oligarchic, more or less democratic, *Politics* 1301b14–17. Plato ignores intermediary forms of democracy. By his method, he is bound to concentrate on the typical. The extreme is the most illustrative. Contemporary radical democracy is portrayed, but Athens is not mentioned by name. However, interpreters have more or less seen the shape of her political experiences behind Plato's record. Though such an attitude is natural one should not forget that Plato was widely travelled, well-connected with different cities, and addressed himself as much to Hellas as to Athens.[2]

The term democracy sounds modern and up to date. It is therefore something of a paradox that it is this term which is in most need of

---

[1] "One day it's wine, women, and song, the next bread and water", translates Lee. Apelt renders it ". . . jetzt zechend und von Flötenklang umrauscht, dann wieder mit Wasser zufrieden und bei schmaler Kost darbend, . . ."

[2] Cf. Field, *Plato and his Contemporaries*, London 1967, pp 128–129. K. Vretska, *Typische und Polare Darstellung bei Platon, SO*, Vol. XXX, 1953, p. 46.

comment. A few remarks of a historical nature may therefore not be irrelevant.

In ancient democracy, even in its radical form, citizenship was restricted to a relatively small part of the adult resident population.[1]) Not only the slaves, but also the economically important class of the *metics*, were left un-enfranchised. To this must be added the low social standing of the women. Furthermore, ancient, unlike modern democracy, was not representative, but based on the direct participation of the citizens. It means that ancient democracy often worked as a town-meeting democracy.[2]) In *Bk VI* (492b5–c2) there is a picture of such a mass-meeting. In addition to direct participation, popular influence was promoted by three instruments: ruling in turn, appointment by lot, and payment for public engagement. The popular supremacy was also extended to judicial matters.

This political system is upheld by the credo of equality. Under Pericles it seems to have worked well enough, but after his death, under the strains of the Peloponnesian War, a note of brutality and fierceness is reported in the social relations.[3]) Swaying under the changing moods of the *demos*, subject to the influence of questionable leaders, the Athenian democracy appeared unstable.[4]) To Plato the application of equality as a fundamental principle stands out as the very opposite of his functional view of society, which rested on the reciprocity of unequals in the service of the whole *polis* under the guidance of the best-informed.

The other key-term of democracy is of course liberty. It included freedom of speech and freedom of action. High degrees of equality and liberty made radical democracy very much a reality; it has been ventured that "the Athenian *demos* had more *kratos* (power) than any other people

---

[1]) Judged from a modern point of view, writes Glotz, even extreme democracy was never in Greek cities anything but a kind of aristocracy. So in Attica its citizens were but a minority, *The Greek City*, p. 127.

[2]) G. Sartori, *s.v. Democracy*, in *IESS*.

[3]) Thucydides *III* 82–83. Loeb ed. vol. II, pp. 143. ff.

[4]) Greek direct democracy was threatened, writes A. Verdross-Drossberg, by two dangers: *Scheinführertum* (Demagogie) und *Massenpsychose*. Cf. *Grundlinien der Antiken Rechts- und Staatsphilosophie*, Wien 1946, p. 57. And C. Hignett, *A History of the Athenian Constitution*, Oxford 1958, writes that "the dangers inherent in the sovereignty of a mass-meeting were intensified when the demos, in the middle of a struggle for its very existence, turned for guidance to leaders who like itself were technically accountable to no other authority", p. 264.

since".[1]) To Plato democracy appeared as "a large and powerful animal", (*Bk VI*, 493a9–10), the embodiment of public opinion, whose preferences could well be studied and nursed (493b1–7), but from whom you could not expect reliable standards of good and bad. A régime which invites everybody to be a pilot of the *polis* was an absurdity to most of the Greek political thinkers. The crisis of leadership, following upon Pericle's death, was often acute in the times of Plato; we may think of the activities of the sophists and the demagogues and the course of democratic imperialism.

The criticism of democracy is severe. Democracy is denounced both as a form of rule and a way of life. Satire and downright disapproval alternate. Plato has an eye for the kaleidoscopic variety of the democratic *polis*,[2]) but he turns it down as vulgar. Unrestricted by communal obligations the citizens enjoy the bliss of the moment, while convicts, slaves, foreigners and animals (sic) walk around with all the air of equality and freedom. In short the democratic *polis* is lawless and anarchic.—With such phrases Plato seems to overshoot the mark. Barker, thinking of Athens, says that democratic government in the fourth century did not mean anarchy.[3]) And Adam, also with Athens in mind, thinks it difficult not to believe that Plato is exaggerating when talking of lawlessness.[4])—Lawlessness and anarchy are most probably not the correct descriptive terms, but in times of social instability political language lends itself to greater freedom.

Comparing Plato's and Aristotle's records of democracy, it is noteworthy that the former makes no attempt to understand democracy from its inner possibilities. But remembering Plato's program and

---

[1]) Sartori, *IESS*.

[2]) This free and unconcerned way of living together was, it is reported, a striking feature of democratic Athens, the classic home of liberty; there even foreigners, says Glotz, breathed a quickening air, *The Greek City*, p. 128.

[3]) "The Athenian citizens had their defects: they loved the free theatre almost more than the free city; yet the last days of Athenian freedom were not a disgrace, either to the city-state or to the democratic constitution, and the career of Demosthenes was an answer to the strictures of Plato and Aristotle" *CAH*, vol. VI, p. 526.

[4]) Adam writes: "As a representation of actual fact, the picture is doubtless somewhat exaggerated, as usual; but it is extraordinarily vivid and powerful, and shews that the Platonic analogy between the individual and the State may prove in the hands of a master an admirable clue whereby to unravel the workings of the human soul in the individual as well as in the State." vol. II, p. 240.

method of research, we can expect only rough pictures, given as contrasts to the righteous *polis*. All the same important features of historical character can be identified. But as it was Plato's aim to illustrate man's personality by reference to his social situation, the people's way of life also became relevant, a branch of study which the Greeks included in *politike*.[1]) The public behaviour of the people in the open presents just those observable qualities which the *polis-psyche* method demands. Plato's method to detect the typical by means of extremities involves exaggerations and simplifications. But these features are counterbalanced by the sociological out-look: the acute socio-economical analyses, the realistic descriptions of how a personality is formed, and the clear insight into the relation between changing society and changing values. All in all, I think that Plato attained his goal of providing a realistic background for his study of democratic personality.

4. Conclusions and observations

In timocracy and oligarchy the good of the whole is subjected to the happiness of a small minority. Plato considers this a grave fault. Now, if Thrasymachus' realistic theory of politics is true, implying that every ruling body only looks to its own advantage, it could at least be said of the rule of the *demos* that it favours a much larger number of people. Is not this a progress? Plato does not think so.

If one thinks of *polis* as an organism, one cannot measure its well-being by the happiness of some of its parts. Happiness must be predicated the city as a whole. If a city is torn by internal strife, if it is drifting towards anarchy, and is on the road to tyranny, it has a bad constitution. And it is bad even if, on a short-term basis,[2]) it appears good to the masses. Excessive freedom ends in the opposite;[3]) under the ruthless tyrant the *demos* will be worse off than in oligarchy.

The model *polis* is one and simple. Democracy is manifold. This is a radical contrast. Manifoldness is short for a number of weak points in democracy. This side of the contrast must be supposed to be known by Plato's contemporaries. By the use of current anti-democratic labels, Plato stresses or exaggerates the weak sides of democracy. But

---

[1]) Cf. Sinclair, p. 3.

[2]) 558a2, ... ἐν τῷ παραυτίκα, for the moment.

[3]) Prior to Plato there seems to have existed a sophistic *metabole*-speculation. One of its main theses was the idea (founded by Solon) that *anomia* leads to tyranny. Cf. H. Ryffel, p. 79.

at the same time it is essential that these features should be recognized as inherent in the social reality, for if the actual society can be identified with serious defects, the model *polis*, constituted in the opposite way, is simultaneously confirmed as good.[1])

The *polis-psyche* analogy, democratic version, can be put down in this way.

Democratic pattern of polis and psyche.

Polis, 555b3–558c7.	Psyche, 558c8–562a3.
Demos in power, dominated by the great mass of drones.	*Epithymiai* rule, dominated by the bulk of unnecessary appetites.
Direct democracy of the town-meeting type.	Spontaneity.
Liberty and equality.	All appetites on equal footing.
Rulers appointed by lot; ruling in turn.	Adherence, as by lot, to one passion after another.
Polis not one, but many.	Personality broken into many fractions.

What is said of the democratic *polis* in respect to instability, disorder and lack of leadership, is equally applicable to *psyche*, *TABLE* 2, nrs 44–49.

There is, however, a parallel which should be observed in relation to the peculiar Pan-hellenic situation. If a party was defeated in a city and its leaders exiled, they would flee to another city from where they could watch and wait for a successful come-back. In a similar way this holds good for the individual, for if one personally happens to get rid of some unnecessary appetites, one will most likely find them very much alive in other persons from whom one cannot isolate oneself. Victory is only temporary; in a new situation, the exiled passions return.[2]) Self is not a lonely island. Personality must therefore be supported by a good society.

The record of the enormous force of public opinion, and the moulding power of the entire social and cultural environment, is not given in the democratic section of *Bk VIII*, but in *Bk VI*, 487b–497a. The noblest characters, we learn there, are spoiled in the grip of the mass-dominated society.

---

[1]) This is what B. Bosanquet calls the negative verification of the Platonic values, p. 311.

[2]) 559e4–7. Cf. *TABLE 2*, nr 47.

CHAPTER XIII

TYRANNY

(Bks VIII:562a4–IX:576b10)

1. Change to tyranny

562a4-566d4. Plato proceeds with the *polis-psyche* method, cf. *TABLE 2*, nr 50. As oligarchy was wrecked by excessive desire for wealth, democracy is now ruined by excessive freedom, 562a10–c2. The thirst for liberty is unquenchable. Served by bad cup-bearers (κακῶν οἰνοχόων) the *polis* is intoxicated by the strong wine of freedom. When the people want more of it, the rulers must comply, otherwise they are cursed as oligarchs and punished, 562c8–d4. Law-abiding citizens are despised, the others are approved of; inevitably the urge for more liberty spreads to all the people, and finds its way into private houses; finally the anarchic movement even reaches the domestic animals, 562d6–e5.

The old standards of respect are upset. Fathers now fear their sons, and the sons have no respect for their fathers; the classic father-son pattern is totally broken. Citizens, *metoics* and 'foreigners are on the same footing. Teachers fear and flatter their pupils, and the young compete with the elders, who, in turn make themselves agreeable to the young, 562e7–563b2. The full measure of liberty is reached when the slaves are as free as those who bought them. Between men and women also the spirit of *isonomia* and *eleutheria* flourishes, 563b4–9. The whole city is almost bursting with liberty; horses and donkeys walk down the street with the dignity of freemen, bumping into any person who does not get out of their way, 563c3–d1.

With all this liberty, the citizens become hypersensitive to the slightest touch of authority. No laws or masters of any kind are respected, 563d4–e1. And we arrive here at the starting point of tyranny, 563e3–4. Out of excess springs an equally violent anti-force; this is, it seems, a general law, 563e6–564a1. We must then expect, says Socrates, that excessive liberty makes man and society the victims of excessive slavery;[1]) the doctrine of polarity—often found in Greek philosophy—is here clearly exemplified.[2])

The change from democracy to tyranny is explained in 564b4–566d3. The democratic *polis* can, we now learn, truly be divided into three classes. First there are the drones, no less numerous than before. Some of them, Socrates reminds us, are stingers, others non-stingers, 564b4–7. These two groups of spendthrifts create disorder in any society in which they appear; they are the phlegm and bile of the body.[3]) The democratic drones are vigorous ones; in oligarchy they were kept from office, now they are trained and in a ruling position; with few exceptions they provide the leaders. The stingers take the lead in speech and action, while the less enterprising drones settle themselves around, and hum so that the voice of opposition is drowned, 564c9–e2.

Secondly there is the wealthy class, which is prone to develop in a society where everyone is intent on money; the most orderly by nature (οἱ κοσμιώτατοι φύσει) usually become prosperous. The second class provides the honey for the drones, 564e4–14.

The *demos* makes up the third class, comprising all those who work with their hands and are not well-to-do. This class is the largest in number, and, when assembled, its power is supreme. But the members of this class will not come together often, unless they get some share of the honey. And they always get rewarded when the leaders, after helping themselves first, distribute what they have extracted from the wealthy, 565a1–b1.

The plundered rich are now driven to defend themselves before the people. Doing this they are accused of being oligarchs, revolutionaries, who are plotting against the *polis*. Being unjustly treated, the wealthy become oligarchs in earnest by the force of the situation. Impeachments and trials between the two parties follow, 565b2–c8.

A fateful stage is reached when the people in this struggle makes

---

[1]) 564a3–4, Ἡ γὰρ ἄγαν ἐλευθερία ἔοικεν οὐκ εἰς ἄλλο τι ἢ εἰς ἄγαν δουλείαν μεταβάλλειν καὶ ἰδιώτῃ καὶ πόλει.

[2]) 564a7–8, ... ἐξ οἶμαι τῆς ἀκροτάτης ἐλευθερίας δουλεία πλείστη τε καὶ ἀγριωτάτη.

[3]) Plato's language is here (564b9–c4) rich in metaphors; the lawgiver must act as the good physician or the wise bee-master, and try to prevent in advance disorders.

someone their champion, nursing him to greatness. This is the root of tyranny, 565c9–d2.

How does the people's champion change into a tyrant? Finding himself in full control of the masses (λαβὼν σφόδρα πειθόμενον ὄχλον, 565e3–4) there is no crime which he cannot commit in the name of the people. The usual practice is to drag suspicious persons to the court on false accusations and then dispose of them by death or banishment. At the same time the developing tyrant hints to the crowds that debts will be cancelled and land redistributed. In this state of things it is his destiny to be either destroyed by his enemies or to become a tyrant, 565d4–566a4.[1])

The rest of the tyrant's career is also firmly determined. There is civil war, and he leads a party against the land-owners. If he is expelled he may return, in spite of his enemies, as a full-fledged tyrant. Alternatively, if he cannot be banished or put to death by setting the citizens against him, the oligarchs will conspire to assassinate him. This is the great moment for the would-be tyrant. He can ask for a personal bodyguard, a request which cannot be denied the champion of the people, 566a6–b11. To the man of property, under suspicion of being an enemy of the people, there is no alternative to leaving the city or to getting killed, 566c1–9. The power is now in the hands of the complete tyrant, 566c10–d3.

2. *Tyrannic polis*

566d5–569c9. An exposition then follows of tyrannical statesmanship.

The *polis-psyche* parallel is useful, *TABLE 2*, nr 51.

The tyrant starts with a charm- and promise policy. He is friendly and nice, so unlike a despot. Promises are made, debts are cancelled, and land is re-distributed to the people and his supporters, 566d8–e4. But the honeymoon soon comes to an end. When he has disposed of his foreign enemies, he starts fresh wars. He does this in order to make the people continually conscious of the need for a leader, and to keep them suppressed. Loaded with taxes, forced to work, they lack time for political plotting. In time of war one can also conveniently get rid of suspected persons, 566e6–567a9.—War has a highly functional purpose inside a tyranny.

---

[1]) At 565d4–e1 Socrates refers to the fable of the man who had tasted human flesh and was transformed to a wolf. In a like manner the man who spills the blood of the *polis* is destined to become a tyrant-wolf.

But there is no stop to the evil train of events. The new course of policy is naturally unpopular. Supporters fall out. Some even dare to pronounce criticism. The tyrant is again forced to answer with bloodshed, disposing of one citizen after another. Knowing full well that potential danger comes from men of competence, the tyrant is watchful of courageous, high-minded, intelligent and rich people He finally purges the city of such men. This is an inverted sort of purging: the doctor removes what is bad and leaves the healthy elements, the tyrant removes the good and leaves the bad, 567a10–c7. But even here he is left with no alternative, if he wants to survive and remain in power, 567c8–d3.

Living with people most of whom are bad, and who furthermore hate him, the tyrant requires a bodyguard. And the less his popularity, the larger and the more trustworthy must be his bodyguard, 567d5–7. As it cannot be recruited from the ordinary citizens, he must look for recruits in other directions. Some will, no doubt, flock like drones from other cities, if enough pay is offered, 567d9–e1. Only slaves will be enlisted from his own city; robbed from the citizens and set free, the slaves will become his trusted friends, 567e3–568a2.

The tyrant and his supporters first spend the public funds, and when these sources fail, the *demos* has to take over the burdens. If objections are raised, force is used. Being disarmed, the people cannot resist. Symbolically the *polis* stands as a father to the citizens; the tyrant, steeped in vice, does not shrink from parricide,[1] 568e2–569b5. The change from extreme liberty to extreme slavery is thus completed, 569b6–c9.

3. *Polis moulds man*

571a1-576b10. The study of the tyrannical personality begins with *Bk IX*, cf. *TABLE 2*, nr 52. A complementary look at the appetites is first given. Previously the necessary, useful desires were distinguished from the unnecessary ones, i.e. those more or less harmful. Now we are

---

[1] By means of putting the *polis* in the father's place Plato is able to denounce the tyrant in the severest way. About the peculiar horror with which the Greeks viewed offences against a father, see E. R. Dodds, *The Greeks and the Irrational*, Berkeley and Los Angeles, 1951, p. 46.

told that in the main body of the latter some are unlawful.[1]) Everyone seems to have them in a higher or lesser degree, 571b3–c1.

This new kind of desires are aroused in dreams when we are asleep. Then the bestial and wild nature, animated by too much food and drink, ravages in us, 571c2–7. Without any sense of shame or prudence all sorts of depraved instincts are gratified, 571c7–9. Incestuous acts are imagined, and other unnatural acts are conceived with man, beast or god, as well as murder and sacrilege,[2]) 571c9–d4.

In contrast to the internal riot of the tyrannical character, we are offered a picture of the inner harmony of the sound and temperate man, 571d6–572b1. We see the three components of *psyche*, orderly placed and properly nourished, ready for the night's sleep; the *logistikon* is collected in meditation, the *thymoeides* is pacified, and the *epithymetikon* is lulled to rest. Freed from the trammels of the flesh, the reasonable part of the soul can enjoy sleep.

Socrates takes us back to the subject of how the tyrannic man is formed.[3]) Trained first by his oligarchic father, then, as a reaction, coming under the influence of the drones, the democratic man becomes a sort of compromise between the two conflicting ways of life, 572b10–d3. Years have now passed, and the democrat in turn has a son. He is brought up in his father's ways of moderation, indulging—we remember —in a little of everything. But the son is also unavoidably exposed to all those lawless and wild passions which flourish in the society under the name of complete liberty. The father and the family support moderation, while others assist licentious living. A struggle goes on inside him.

---

[1]) The term παράνομοι (571b5) means rather "unnatural" than lawless, comments Adam, vol. II, p. 319.

[2]) Such undisguised Oedipus dreams were, writes Dodds, common in classical and later antiquity, *Op. cit.* p. 47 and n. 105.—The Freudians have of course observed this likeness with the Oedipus complex. There is even in Freud a remarkable parallel to Plato's analogy between the social and personal power structure. The mind, writes Freud, "is no peacefully self-contained unity. It is rather to be compared with a modern State in which a mob, eager for enjoyment and destruction, has to be held down forcibly by a prudent superior class . . .". Quoted by T. Gould, *Platonic Love*, London 1963, p. 15 and n. 30, p. 188. See also Popper, *OSE* vol. I, n. 59, pp. 313–314.

[3]) Going back to the subject Socrates makes clear that everyone of us, even the most respectable or moderate, are exposed to these untamed desires in our dreams, 572b3–8.

To help the riotous appetites to victory, the seducers contrive to kindle a master passion in the young man's heart. And this sort of love—residing in him like a winged, huge drone[1])—takes the lead of his idle and spendthrift lusts, 572d5–573a2. Finally, the erotic passion is intensified to a mania. It becomes lord of the soul, takes madness as captain of his guards, and purges the person of any remnant of *dikaiosyne*, 573a4–b4. Lust, drink, and madness conspire to make the tyrannical character complete, 573b5–c10.

The tyrant's way of life is now told.

First there are feasts and revels and every sort of amusement, for now *Eros tyrannos* wholly dominates the *psyche*.[2]) New and strong desires rapidly arise, demanding to be maintained. But such a life is expensive and money dwindles rapidly. To mitigate the pain of his frustrated desires he is driven in desperation to plunder and robbery, 573d2–574a5; he does not even spare his parents, 574a6–c9. When he has exhausted his resources, he is driven to new crimes, 574d1–5. A change of values occurs in him. The old conventions concerning good and bad, implanted during his democratic youth, are overthrown by the new passions, which now form the bodyguard of his erotic obsession. In the end, he becomes in reality the person he before only momentarily endured in his licentious dreams, 574d5–575a7, cf. *TABLE 2*, nr 53.

If there are only a few tyrannic personalities in a city, they will join some despot in another city or else fight as hired soldiers in any war. In times of peace they engage in crimes of different kinds. When the number of such criminals and their followers increases, they become aware of their strength. Helped by the folly of the people, they will produce a tyrant; the most tyrannical character will be promoted, 575a9–d1.

The tyrannic personality does not know what friendship is; he is wanting in truthfulness. If the earlier established notion of *dikaiosyne* is true, he embodies the extreme of *adikia*, 575e2–576b2.

---

[1]) 573a1–2, . . . ὑπόπτερον καὶ μέγαν κηφῆνά τινα . . .

[2]) Apropos ἀφροδίσια, we may note that already in *Bk I* the lusts of the flesh were spoken of as despotic, 329c1–d1.

4. Some historical notes

The word *tyrannos* means absolute ruler, unlimited by law or constitution, (*LSJ*); it possibly first meant usurper; in its early history it did not necessarily carry any odium.[1]

Aristotle knew three kinds of tyranny. The most typical is when the power is arbitrarily in the hands of one man, who is responsible to no one; it is the counterpart of perfect monarchy; no freeman will, if he can avoid it, live under such a government, *Politics* 1295a17–24. The contrast between the good king and the wicked tyrant was not established until the fourth century.[2]

In the *Republic*, the philosopher-king and the brute self-assertion of the tyrant are of course opposite poles. Adhering to the method of the extreme types, Plato propels the tyrant type to its limit.

No names are mentioned as to the historical foundation of the tyrannic type of *polis*. It is more than a guess that Plato, however, had the history of Syracuse and Dionysian despotism in mind, cf. 577b6–8.[3] Both Barker and Field find close parallels with the life-history of Dionysius I.[4] Adam also thinks that several features are borrowed from this most conspicuous tyrant of Plato's own age.[5] On the other hand we should not forget that Plato is depicting a *type*, not a person. Some of the features fit other tyrants as well.[6] It is evident that Plato has been exaggerating in depicting the tyrant as a monster. Still the picture of despotism is convincing enough. There are those who have lived through the rule of a paranoiac, and can testify to Plato's insight.[7]

5. Conclusions and observations

True to purpose and method, we have been led to the extreme *adikia*. To use the words of Thrasymachus, *adikia* in the grand style, has been

---

[1] S. v. *Tyranny* by Ehrenberg in *OCD*.

[2] Field, p. 129.

[3] J. Luccioni thinks that both Dionysius I and II contributed much to the making of the type of tyranny in *Rep.*; the suggestion that Dionysius II plays a role in this connection presupposes that the section on tyranny was revised after Plato's second visit to Sicily, pp. 78 ff.

[4] Barker, p. 259, Field, *Plato and his Contemporaries*, p. 129. So also Apelt, 567c, n. 54, p. 522.

[5] Adam, vol. II, p. 250.

[6] Wilamowitz, pp. 431 ff.

[7] Cf. Sinclair, p. 165.

demonstrated. And the transit from freedom to slavery in *polis* is more than a philosophical formula.

But the *Republic* is not, as it may seem, primarily a book on politics. It is professedly a book on human character. The picture of the tyrannic personality is the end of a systematic review. It has brought us to the abnormal *psyche*, the region of psycho-pathology, a branch of study which, in its modern form, implies that the examination of the insane can bring light upon the mechanisms governing also normal man.

This is in brief the analogy between tyrannic *polis* and tyrannic man.

Tyrannic pattern of polis and psyche

Polis, 562a4–569c9.	*Psyche, 571a1–576b10.*
The lawless rule of the tyrant, supported by a gang of criminals, liberated slaves and hired soldiers of foreign origin.	The rule of the beastly eros, supported by the criminal (or, in other words, unnatural) appetites.
The *demos* subjected to slavery.	The great bulk of ordinary appetites dominated by the lawless ones.
Polis bereft of noble and capable men.	*Psyche* swept of all noble inclinations.

The illustrative use of *polis* is recorded in *TABLE 2*, nrs. 50–53. In the course of our study of tyranny we have also seen the *polis-makes-man* and the *man-makes-polis* motifs at work.

Looking back at Plato's survey of the disorganized societies, we see the features of a very systematic study. The *polis-psyche* analogy is actively employed. In each case *polis* is first described. In each case man is closely studied in relation to society. The transition from one type of *polis* to another is accompanied by a description of a corresponding relation holding between a father and his son.[1] In *polis* after *polis* we see the social and cultural agencies working upon the individual, moulding his personality in accordance with the prevailing pattern of behaviour. Observing the *polis-makes-man* motif in operation, it also is explained how *polis* can illustrate *psyche*. Both these elements of thought are operative in the main line of reasoning, describing how *polis* both forms and illustrates personality.

---

[1] Cf. K. von Fritz, *The Theory of the Mixed Constitution in Antiquity. A Critical Analysis of Polybius' Political Ideas.* New York 1954, p. 63.

CHAPTER XIV
CONTRAPOSITIONS
(Bk IX:576b11–592b6)

I. A preliminary note

Socrates has argued out *dikaiosyne* against the extreme case of *adikia*. There now remains to arrange the opposites and draw the conclusions. But les us first remind ourselves of the distinction between the established analogy, built up in *Bks II–IV*, and the extended ones of *Bks VIII–IX*. In order to be able to discuss both of these kinds of comparison in a wider scope, the term general analogy was adopted.

The established analogy and the extended analogies present respectively a sequence of construction and a sequence of destruction, a way up and a way down.

The ↑	(4) ἀριστοκρατία	(5) τιμοκρατία	The
way	(3) τρυφῶσα πόλις	(6) ὀλιγαρχία	way
up	(2) ἀληθινὴ πόλις	(7) δημοκρατία	down
	(1) ἀναγκαιοτάτη πόλις	(8) τυραννίς ↓	

There is a rough symmetry between the two ways, but the importance of this should not be over-stressed. The two end stations (4) and (8) constitute the extreme types. According to the request they should be confronted, though, of course, the intermediary stations help to carry out the intentions. But (8), *tyrannis*, manifests "in the utmost conceivable degree" the opposite of (4), *aristokratia*.[1]

---

[1] Plato's description of how the imperfect societies change from one type to another is clearly not a cycle of constitutions, writes K. von Fritz. "What Plato describes is, on the contrary, a continuous downward movement ... But it is interesting to see that Aristotle when discussing this part of Plato's *Republic* blames Plato for not having made it a cycle, or for not having completed the cycle", p. 66.—From our point of view, having traced Plato's use of the method of the opposite extremes, tyranny is an end-station. The elaboration of a cycle would only have blurred the contrast between complete *dikaiosyne* and extreme *adikia*.

2. Need of a competent judge

576b11-577b9. Socrates was in *Bk II* requested not only to illustrate the internal structure of a just person compared to an unjust one, but also to show which of them is the happier of the two. At 576b the time is ripe for answering this question. The double text method is repeatedly mentioned (cf. *TABLE 2*, nrs 54-65), and the technique of contraposing the opposites becomes conspicuous. By the former method the whole of the tyrannical *polis* should be carefully inspected, and then the tyrannical personality should be thoroughly scrutinized.[1] And it is important that judgement is made by a competent judge, who is not dazzled by the outward show of power, but has himself lived under the roof of a despot, and has witnessed both his private life and his political crises, 576e6-577b4. Socrates and Glaucon then assume that they are qualified to make such a judgement 577b6-9.

This invocation of the necessity for personal experience promises extra support to the achievements acquired so far. When the attributes of happiness and unhappiness are now to be distributed, Plato claims for his spokesmen a more thorough knowledge of tyranny.

Three proofs are offered for the thesis that *dikaiosyne* and *eudaimonia* are closely bound up with each other. We will attend to them as they appear.

3. The first proof

577c1-580c8. This demonstration rests on the practice of the double text method,[2] one should bear in mind the similarities between society and man, and compare them point by point,[3] cf. *TABLE 2*, nr 56.

(a:1) In tyranny almost all people, including the best men, are completely enslaved under a despot and a few of his kind, playing masters, 577c5-10;

(a:2) the tyrannical soul is burdened with much slavery, embracing

---

[1] 576d9-e2, ἀλλ' ὡς χρὴ ὅλην τὴν πόλιν εἰσελθόντας θεάσασθαι, καταδύντες εἰς ἅπασαν καὶ ἰδόντες, οὕτω δόξαν ἀποφαινώμεθα.

[2] G. E. R. Lloyd, referring to 577c ff., writes that Plato has earlier mentioned the need to verify in *psyche* what is found in *polis*, but here Plato simply assumes, without further examination, that the conclusions drawn are correct, p. 397.

[3] 577d4-c5, μικρὸν δὲ καὶ τὸ μοχθηρότατον καὶ μανικώτατον δεσπόζειν; cf. *JC*, vol. III, p. 417.

also the better elements, while a small and most corrupted part is dominant, 577d2–9.

(b:1) being enslaved the *polis* cannot do what it likes, 577d10–11;

(b:2) the τυραννουμένη ψυχή like the τυραννουμένη πόλις, understood as a whole, is incapable of doing what it likes, 577e1–3;

(c:1) further, the *polis* is poor, being plundered by the despot, cf. 577e5–7;

(c:2) thus the enslaved soul must necessarily always (ἀνάγκη ἀεὶ εἶναι) be poverty-stricken and insatiable, 578a1–3;

(d:1) the *polis* is also full of pains, tears and grief, 578a4–9;

(d:2) comparing this *polis* (τοιαύτην πόλιν) to this man (τοιοῦτον ἄνδρα) one finds them both alike in this respect, 578a4–13.

The immediate conclusion drawn is that the tyrannical *polis* is unsurpassed in unhappiness, while the tyrannical man is a very unhappy kind of person, 578a10–b6.

If, however, within the species of *aner tyrannikos* you want to see the most miserable of men you must turn to him who "is raised from a private station to despotical power".[1]

As this distinction between tyrannical type of character and an actual tyrant is important, it should be carefully considered and not be left to mere assumptions, 578c5–7. Socrates offers an illustration. It is given in 578d3–580c8.

In one respect a tyrant resembles one of those rich men who owns many slaves. Both rule over many men, though the tyrant's flock is larger. The private slave-owner does not fear his slaves, because he lives in a community where, explicates *JC*, "all the masters unite for mutual protection".[2] Imagine now that such a slave-owner with his family, property and, say, fifty slaves were transported by a god to some lonely land, where he could find no allies. Fearing for the safety of himself and his family, he would be driven to coax and flatter some of his slaves, promising, much against his will, to set them free. The prison of the tyrant is of a similar character.[3] His soul craves for pleasure, but he, of all people, cannot travel abroad to attend the great festivals and see what is worth seeing in foreign lands, but must live buried in

---

[1] *JC*, vol. III, p. 420.

[2] Vol. III, p. 419.

[3] 579b3–4. Ἆρ᾽ οὖν οὐκ ἐν τοιούτῳ μὲν δεσμωτηρίῳ δέδεται ὁ τύραννος, κτλ.

his house like a woman, 579b5–c2.—It is the actual tyrant (by Thrasymachus praised as strong, free and happy, cf. 343b1–344c8) who is now exhibited as the most miserable of all creatures. Surrounded by hostility and dependent on the vicious elements, he is the real slave. If one knows how to study a soul in its entirety[1]), the tyrant is the poorest of the poor. Throughout his life he is haunted by terrors and he resembles in fact the *polis* he governs, *TABLE 2*, nr 63. By his political position the faults of his character are exaggerated to the utmost, 580a1–7.

Glaucon is then allowed to pronounce the judgement that the five types of character should be ranked in the order they were introduced: the kingly, the timocratic, the oligarchic, the democratic and the tyrannic, 580a9–b7. And the kingly type of character is first in goodness, justice, and happiness, while the actual tyrant is the most vicious, unjust, and unhappy person to be found. Referring to what he was requested to do in *Bk II* 366e5–9[2]), Socrates concludes that the demonstration holds true whether the real nature of the agent is revealed to others or not, 580c6–8.

4. The second proof

580c9–583a11. The demonstration (ἀπόδειξις) starts from the concept of the tripartite soul. Each of these three fundamental elements can dominate a soul, 580d3–8. Knowledge is obtained by the first part, ambition is fired by the second. The third part consists of the bulk of appetites. As a characteristic feature the money-loving trait is picked out, money being the principal means for satisfying our different appetites, 580d10–581a8. Thus there are three basic types of men, the truth-loving, the honour-loving and the gain-loving.[3]) As each of these kinds of men sticks to his particular love, there is no agreement between them as to which pleasure is the pleasantest; the money-gainer, for instance, despises learning and fame, if they do not bring him in any money.

How is this dispute to be settled? Are there better foundations for a sound judgement than experience, insight and reason?[4]) The

---

[1]) 579e3, ἐάν τις ὅλην ψυχὴν ἐπίστηται θεάσασθαι, κτλ.

[2]) *JC* notes that "this is one of the threads by which Plato connects the end of the *Republic* with the beginning", vol. III, p. 422.

[3]) 581c3–4. Διὰ ταῦτα δὴ καὶ ἀνθρώπων λέγομεν τὰ πρῶτα τριττὰ γένη εἶναι, φιλόσοφον, φιλόνικον, φιλοκερδές; ... Καὶ ἡδονῶν δὴ τρία εἴδη κτλ.

[4]) 582a5–6. ἆρ' οὐκ ἐμπειρίᾳ τε καὶ φρονήσει καὶ λόγῳ; ἢ τούτων ἔχοι ἄν τις βέλτιον κριτήριον;

philosopher must decide because he has a wider range of experience and is superior in intelligence and reasoning, 582a8–e9. With these qualifications the philosopher sets the pleasure derived from science and knowledge above those pleasures which come from ambition and gain, 583a1–11.

5. The third proof

583b1-588a11. The third demonstration is announced as decisive. The following classifications are basic for the analysis of pleasure and pain.

(a)   pleasure (ἡδονή) is the opposite of (c) pain (λύπη);
(b)   there is an intermediate state (ἐν μέσῳ) or a rest (ἡσυχία) between (a) and (c); (b) is neither (a) nor (c);
(c)   pain is the opposite of (a), 583c3–9.

At the first analysis (b) is perplexing, for the cessation of pain may be pleasant,[1] and the cessation of pleasure may be painful, 583c10–e8. It is odd that (b), being the absence of both pleasure and pain, should appear from time to time sometimes pleasant and sometimes painful, 584a1–5.—The deceptive sensations are, we are told, due to the illusion of contrast, 584a7–10. But all pleasures are not of this pseudo-character. Smell, for instance, being a pure (physical) pleasure, can occur suddenly and with great intensity without leaving a sense of pain behind, 584b1–c2. The pseudo-pleasures, reaching the soul through the body, are still the more numerous, 584c4–7.

The popular predicament is in 584d3–e5 described as a desorientation within a three-plane world: an upper region, a middle region, and a lower one. Going upwards from the lower, and arriving at the middle, people think they are in the upper region. Having no experience of real pleasure they can only compare pain with relief from pain, 584e7–585a5.—But one can also look at the question in this way, says Socrates. As hunger and thirst are states of bodily depletion (κενώσεις), so ignorance and folly are emptiness of the soul, 585a8–b4. The corresponding replenishments are in the former case food, and in the latter understanding, 585b6–7. This latter kind of filling consists of true belief, science and understanding, including all the virtues. As they participate

---

[1] For an analysis of the "sick man's error", cf. Murphy, pp. 213–217.

more in the true existence (οὐσίας μετέχειν), they give more satisfaction, fill up more, than do food and drink, 585b9–e5.[1]

Those who are unacquainted with wisdom and virtue and spend
their time in feasting, are moved at random between the lower and the
middle planes. They never reach the upper region of true pleasures.
Dominated by the sensuous appetites, they feed and breed like cattle.
Greedy for more, they kick and butt and kill one another, in order
to satisfy their unlimited lusts, 586a1–b4.[2] And no less vain is the satisfaction which *thymoeides* is hankering after, if let loose on its own,
586c7–d3.—Both the lower classes of desires should be guided by
knowledge and reason. They thus find their proper place within the well-
functioning soul, conceived as a whole. Each doing its own work, they
find the best satisfaction each for themselves.[3] But if the right order is
changed, inner conflict arises, and the greater the distance of the
dominating element from the rational part, the greater the disorder; the
tyrannical desires are the farthest away, 587a3–b1. Finally we see the
king and the tyrant as representatives of the extreme poles of virtue.

6. Dikaiosyne pays

588b1-592b6. The question next arises as to whether justice is advantageous or not, 588b1–8. We are asked to imagine some sort of
creature like Chimera, Scylla or Cerberus, 588c2–5. First we must mould
the figure of a large and multifarious beast, which is more or less wild,
and can be grown or transformed at will, 588c7–10. Add, secondly, the
form of a lion, and, thirdly, that of a man. Let the three grow together
into one and be given the shape of a human being, 588d3–e1.

If one thinks that *adikia* pays, then this means that it is profitable
to feed and strengthen the many-headed beast and the lion, and to
starve and enfeeble the inner man, 588e3–589a4. The contrary position
is that justice pays, requiring that the inward man has control over the

---

[1] 585c1–5. As for the difficulties of this passage, see Adam, vol. II, p. 354.

[2] The passage καὶ ἕνεκα τῆς τούτων πλεονεξίας, 586b1, reminds of the ἐπὶ χρημάτων
κτῆσιν ἄπειρον, ὑπερβάντες τὸν τῶν ἀναγκαίων ὅρον, 373d9–10. Cf. JC, vol. III, p. 430.
Luxury and the cause of war.

[3] 586e4–587a1. Τῷ φιλοσόφῳ ἄρα ἑπομένης ἁπάσης τῆς ψυχῆς καὶ μὴ στασιαζούσης
ἑκάστῳ τῷ μέρει ὑπάρχει εἴς τε τἆλλα τὰ ἑαυτοῦ πράττειν καὶ δικαίῳ εἶναι, καὶ δὴ καὶ τὰς
ἡδονὰς τὰς ἑαυτοῦ ἕκαστον καὶ τὰς βελτίστας καὶ εἰς τὸ δυνατὸν τὰς ἀληθεστάτας καρποῦσθαι.

entire person.[1]) Rational man integrates the personality in a friendly way.[2])—From every point of view, whether of pleasure, reputation or advantage, the panegyrist of justice is right and his opponent wrong, 589b8–c4. This fits in with common experience: licentiousness has always been censured because it allows the monster in us to grow, 590a5–7; self-will and ill-temper are reproved likewise for strengthening disproportionally the lion in us, 590a9–b1; whereas luxury is blamed, because it makes the lion-like nature weak or monkey-like, 590b3–9; and, finally, manual work is despised, because it indicates a weakness, making man unable to rule himself properly, 590c2–6.

People of this weaker kind should therefore be placed under the rule of the highest type of man, who himself is controlled by his internal and divine element. Then these people are not, as Thrasymachus thought, dominated to their disadvantage, but are ruled under the law which aims at the common good of the whole *polis*, 590c8–d6.

What of those who appear to be just, but in reality are unjust? The undetected wrong-doer deprives himself of the correction implied in the punishment, which aims at restoring his internal order; this is a prize more precious than the strength and beauty that health brings to the body, 591a10–b7. To the man of understanding, physical health is instrumental to the ultimate end of the harmonious soul, 591c1–d3. The acquisition of wealth is no goal for this kind of man, 591d6–9. He will contemplate his inner constitution (τὴν ἐν αὐτῷ πολιτείαν) and rule himself accordingly, steering between wealth and poverty, and accepting such honours as are likely to make him a better man, 591e1–592a4.—What is his stand in politics?—Surely he will take part in the politics of his own inner *polis* (ἔν γε τῇ ἑαυτοῦ πόλει), which should not be confused with the politics of his native city (ἔν γε τῇ πατρίδι); for engagement in the latter, some sign from heaven is needed, 592a5–9. "I understand", says Glaucon, "you mean the *polis* we have discussed and founded, existing in theory, for on earth, I think, it will never be found".[3])

---

[1]) 589a7–b1, . . . ὅθεν τοῦ ἀνθρώπου ὁ ἐντὸς ἄνθρωπος ἔσται ἐγκρατέστατος, κτλ. Cf. 589c8–d3. τὰ μὲν καλὰ τὰ ὑπὸ τῷ ἀνθρώπῳ, μᾶλλον δὲ ἴσως τὰ ὑπὸ τῷ θείῳ τὰ θηριώδη ποιοῦντα τῆς φύσεως, αἰσχρὰ δὲ τὰ ὑπὸ τῷ ἀγρίῳ τὸ ἥμερον δουλούμενα;

[2]) 589b3–6, . . . σύμμαχον ποιησάμενος τὴν τοῦ λέοντος φύσιν, καὶ κοινῇ πάντων κηδόμενος, φίλα ποιησάμενος ἀλλήλοις τε καὶ αὐτῷ, οὕτω θρέψει;

[3]) 592a10–b1. Μανθάνω, ἔφη· ἐν ᾗ νῦν διήλθομεν οἰκίζοντες πόλει λέγεις, τῇ ἐν λόγοις κειμένῃ, ἐπεὶ γῆς γε οὐδαμοῦ οἶμαι αὐτὴν εἶναι.

These words seem apt to round off the long discussion about the model *polis*. But *Bk IX* ends with some of the most famous words of the whole *Republic*. Perhaps there is laid up in heaven an example of the *polis* for him who desires to see it, and, seeing it, to found one in himself.[1]) Whether such a city exists anywhere or not, or ever will exist, is of no importance, for he will stick to this one and no other, 592b2–5.

7. A retrospective view

Having reached the end of *Bk IX* we return to the three proofs in order to see how they stand in relation to the general ground of the *Republic*.

The first one consists of an analogical argument (577c5–578c7) supplemented by an illustration (578d3–580c8). It is stipulated, further, that the judge must now have a first hand acquaintance of tyranny. At page 184 above, we have observed that it is essential for the negative verification of the model *polis* that its counter cases are identified, at least roughly, as being realistic. This demand of identification grows in importance when the worth of tyranny is now finally to be decided, because tyranny is the very opposite pole of the model *polis*. It must, however, be confessed that Plato's reference to matters of fact is veiled, and does not satisfy the empiric request for specification and verifiability. We are left with guesses as to which particular and actual states are selected as being decisive for the type-construction.

But let us now consider the first part of the proof, see p. 195 above. It may seem rhetorical or uninteresting;[2]) having earlier depicted the tyrant as an advanced psychopath with a record of the greatest crimes, this array of parallels carries little weight. But if one takes this portion of the text partly as a summing-up, and partly as an extraction of what can be learnt from the extended analogy about unhappiness, it certainly deserves its place.

With the additional simile of the slave-master, who is transported with all his household to some deserted spot, Plato ends the double text reading. The picture of "the tyrant's splendid but awful isolation"[3])

---

[1]) 592b2–3. 'Αλλ', ἦν δ'ἐγώ, ἐν οὐρανῷ ἴσως παράδειγμα ἀνάκειται τῷ βουλομένῳ ὁρᾶν καὶ ὁρῶντι ἑαυτὸν κατοικίζειν.

[2]) This demonstration is simple, says Crombie, vol. I, p. 136. And Cross and Woozley hold it philosophically unimportant, but it "merits attention as a remarkably graphic and penetrating picture of morbid psychology", p. 264.

[3]) Adam, vol. II, p. 338.

well illustrates the anti-Thrasymachian thesis that *adikia*, practised in the grand style, drives the agent out from humanity and from the friendly, trustful, co-operative, and communal living that alone deserves to be called a *polis*. In a sense the full-fledged tyrant is expelled from the city over which he reigns.—As a personality the tyrant is out of himself.

The ceremonial at 580a9–c4 marks the successful completion of the effort to illustrate *psyche* by the help of *polis*. Remembering, however, Plato's own doubts on the double text method, expressed in 435c9–d5 (cf. p. 104 above), the triumphant conclusions may sound somewhat high-pitched. But the matter is not left there. Two more arguments, we know, are adduced. They bear witness to Plato's restricted confidence in the analogy; *eudaimonia* is after all experienced as a very personal matter, therefore an analysis in terms of pleasure may help to produce a stronger conviction.

The doctrine of the tripartite soul, carefully out-argued in *Bk IV*, 435e1–441c7, proves a suitable basis for the failing analysis. So far we have associated the appetites ($\dot\epsilon\pi\iota\vartheta\upsilon\mu\dot\iota\alpha\iota$) wholly with the third part of the soul.[1] Now we learn (580d3–8) that each of its fundamental parts has a characteristic desire, whose satisfaction generates a sort of pleasure. What is essentially new is the intellectual pleasure, which prevails in the philosopher.[2] Thus the second proof connects with the earlier established theory of the tripartite soul. And as the first proof exhibits the great unhappiness and distress of the tyrant, the second proof describes the bliss of the philosopher.

But there is still place for an argument of a more general nature. From the third proof (which is indeed complicated and inclusive) one can deduce among other things that the righteous man, whoever he is, has chosen the better life, because his pleasure derives from things more real than those sensual satisfactions which dominate the common crowd. In the *psyche* of the just man there is order. There you find enlightened leadership, division of work and co-operation for the well-

---

[1]) Adam, vol. II, p. 342.

[2]) There is as a matter of fact no explicit reference to the philosophers of the ideal city, observes Murphy, "but it seems natural to take them as a test case", p. 208. See also Adam's note on the term $\tau\hat\eta\varsigma$ $\tau o\hat\upsilon$ $\check o\nu\tau o\varsigma$ (582c7–8), indicating the discussions of *Bk VII*, and Crombie, vol. I, p. 136.

being of the whole. The description is, we note, sociomorph in character, cf. 586d4–587a1.

The examination of pleasure is an important topic in the dialogue. We are not prompted to delve into it. But the addition of the pleasure-argument, as a complement to the double text, helps us to see the *polis-psyche* motif in a wider perspective.

Finally we cannot avoid asking if the three proofs are convincing. Surveying the commentaries of Nettleship, Bosanquet, Murphy, Crombie and Cross-Woozley a number of unsatisfactory points are enumerated.[1])

8. Conclusions and observations

Coming to the end of *Bk IX* we see the wide range of the general analogy between *polis* and *psyche*. It is extensive in the text and it offers a circumspective study of the total field of society and man. As a prerequisite for this mode of analogical research, we may think of the pre-Socratic *kosmos* speculation with its belief in rational explanation and its propensity for finding the same pattern repeated in different levels of nature. There are also the conceptions of balance and harmony in ancient medicine to which the Platonic notion of *sophrosyne*—a keyword for social and personal harmony—bears significant marks of kinship.[2]) With this ancestry, *sophrosyne* evokes a disposition to treat *polis* and *psyche* in terms of organism and health. A number of equations witness to this attitude: health/body$=dikaiosyne/polis$ and doctor/patient$=$philosopher/society. To elicit the Platonic version of harmony as instigated and upheld by competent ruling we meet the complementary equations of captain/crew$=$shepherd/sheep$=$philosopher/people; and as a rough indication of the internal social order in the model *polis* there are the comparisons rulers/auxiliaries$=$shepherds/dogs. Seeing, furthermore, that the *Republic* is suspended between the functional opposites of *dikaiosyne* and *adikia*, we are introduced to a number of important and well-established contrarieties: The One/the many, the whole/the divided, order/disorder, health/disease, co-operation/contest. To this table of opposites we may add as functional requisites,

---

[1]) Cf. Nettleship, p. 316; Murphy, p. 207, and his assessment, pp. 222–223; Crombie thinks that the discussion on pleasure is worth serious attention, if it is stripped of its proof-aspirations and made more tentative, pp. 139–142; Cross and Woozley, pp. 265 ff.

[2]) Cf. pp. 78–79 above, and 444d3–6, Ἔστι δὲ τὸ μὲν ὑγίειαν κτλ.

on the one hand, the whole body of cardinal virtues, and, on the other hand, the disintegrative powers of the cardinal vices. In the light of the *polis-psyche* motif, we see clearly that all these equations and contrapositions have a doubly illustrative function, elucidating not only *polis* but ultimately also *psyche*.

In spite of a supposed contemporary disposition to reason by analogy,[1] and Plato's own execution of the general comparison between *polis* and *psyche*, he is not unrestricted in his use of analogy. Both these components should be inspected, and even so he is markedly cautious. His doubt does not, it should be observed, initiate an empirical orientation, but rather a movement to a higher level of speculation.

Thrasymachus had, we remember, quite a program for the study of political power. Basically this approach is empirical. But when Glaucon and Adeimantus restate Thrasymachus' opinions, they do not develop the empirical possibilities. Asking for genuine and intrinsic realities, they frame the problem instead in such a way that no significant reference to appearances is possible; Socrates is asked to do what nobody had ever done before (366e7–9), that is to demonstrate by rational argument[2] what *dikaiosyne* and *adikia* each of them really is in the *psyche*. When, under such conditions, Socrates accepts to investigate the matter without reservations (except for the usual Socratic understatements about his own capacity), then the course is destined to be speculative. The reasoning contained in *Bks II–IV* and *VIII–IX* we have characterized as a thought experiment. Its logical bases are analogy and polarity. Both are risky tools to use.

The fruitfulness of Plato's analogical operations is due to the functional approach. The scheme of organic function dominates as a norm *Bk II*, where the construction of the *polis* is begun under the auspices of cooperation and division of work. A modern test of the plausibility of this approach is that the social anthropologists have "almost to a man,

---

[1] Cf. G. P. Conger, *Theories of Macrocosms and Microcosms in the History of Philosophy*, New York 1922, pp. 7–8, and G. E. R. Lloyd, *op. cit.*, pp. 210 ff. See also W. H. Greenleaf, who warns us to simply reject analogies and similitudes of this kind as merely fantastic; often they are not simply a method of arguments" but a whole style of political thoughts". *Order, Empiricism and Politics. Two Traditions of English Political Thought 1500–1700.* London 1964, p. 6.

[2] 367b3, e2, ἐνδείξῃ τῷ λόγῳ.—This challenge to isolate rightness dominates the whole work, writes Havelock, *Preface to Plato*, pp. 12 and 231, n. 13.

embraced the functionalist principle of explanation which is essentially part and parcel of the wider tradition of organicism".[1]) A cue to the analysis of unjust agents in terms of functional disturbances is found already in *Bk I*. This preparatory view of the disfunctional effect of *adikia* is systematically carried out in *Bks VIII–IX*. The model *polis* is thus created and the actual societies are criticized by means of the same test, namely that of function. In this way Plato can reconcile a vast amount of theoretical speculation and empirical findings within the spans of *dikaiosyne-adikia* and *polis-psyche*.

Now to another question. In his exposition of the swollen *polis* (*Bk. II*, 372e2 ff) Plato hints that the study of excess may have a heuristic value, just as, we conjectured, the observation of physiological hypertrophy may contribute to our knowledge of health. Is perhaps Plato's model city a reconstruction springing from his analysis of social disease? There are two arguments by which this view is at least formally denied: (a) we are compelled to read about the model *polis* before we arrive to the systematic treatment of the diseased societies in *Bks VIII–IX*; (b) theoretically, it is shown in the middle books that *dikaiosyne* is not posited as merely the opposite of *adikia*, but must be deduced in the dialectical way from the Idea of Goodness. By (a) and (b) a canon is provided for a critical study of constitutions. On the other hand we saw in the introductory dispute with Thrasymachus in *Bk I*, that the analysis of *adikia* preceded that of *dikaiosyne*. And, furthermore, towards the end of *Bk I*, we found the fundamental proposition about functional opposites pronounced. *Adikia* creates divisions, hate and fighting, whereas *dikaiosyne* brings men together in unity and friendship.[2]) This proposition we can now see as a cardinal proposition in the *Republic*. In this passage *Bks II–IV* and *VIII–IX* are reduced to their barest meaning.

The method of polarity is a recurrent feature in early Greek thought. To some extent our examination of the *polis-psyche* motif has turned

---

[1]) W. Stark, *The Fundamental Forms of Social Thought*, p. 91, London 1962.—We may also compare the case of Plato with that of Comte, the father of positivism, whose insistence on the validity of the organic pattern reflected, not the alleged "anarchy" of his own times, but his yearning for a more ordered and pacified social life, p. 99.

[2]) 351d4–6. Στάσεις γάρ που ... ἤ γε ἀδικία καὶ μίση καὶ μάχας ἐν ἀλλήλοις παρέχει, ἡ δὲ δικαιοσύνη ὁμόνοιαν καὶ φιλίαν.

out to be a study of extreme opposites and significant similarities in the *Republic*.[1])

We have dwelt with the positive effects of the method of the extreme types, but disadvantages can also be noted. The appeal to pairs of opposites is closely bound up with the practice of dichotomous classifications.[2]) Rigidly operating with pros and cons, idealizing the one pole and (to some extent) caricaturing the other, makes the investigator less able to consider rival ways of classification and alternative patterns.[3]) Gradually the constructed *polis* rises from illustrative mean to absolute standard. Plausibility and references to general experiences do not suffice: the matter must be rationally proved. It has already been hinted that this over-ambition is inherent in what Socrates is requested to do by Glaucon and Adeimantus.

---

[1]) In a sense the use of polarity and analogy in the *Republic* seems to spring from the same practice of vigorous comparison within pairs. The passage 434d2–435a3 is in this respect interesting, cf. 104 above.

[2]) Lloyd, pp. 15 ff.

[3]) Cf. R. K. Merton, *op. cit.* Modern functional theory is, according to Merton, neutral to ideological systems. If we test Merton's paradigm for functional analysis on the *Republic*, we find that the institutions of family and private ownership disturb function, if they occur in the two higher classes, but not if they exist in the third class. From this we may conclude that the third class is so controlled by the two higher classes that the disfunctional effects of family and private ownership are quite insignificant for the whole society, if they occur only in the lower social strata. —Whereas modern functional theory propounds to be neutral to ideological systems, Plato reckons only with one (and true) functional system.

PART SIX
EPILOGUE

CHAPTER XV

NATURE OF ART AND IMMORTALITY OF THE SOUL

(Bk X:595a1–621d3)

1. Art and illusion

595a1-602b11. Looking back at the model *polis* Socrates is satisfied. He is particularly pleased with the resolutions concerning literature; poetry and the whole branch of imitative literature is harmful to minds, which have no knowledge of the true nature of reality, 595a1–b7. But what is imitation?[1] What position has the imitator in relation to the creative activities?

We may assume that there is one single idea corresponding to each class of particulars with the same name.[2] There is thus, for instance, (a) the idea of the bed produced by god. Corresponding to (a) one has, on a lower level of reality, (b) the particular beds made by a carpenter, who, in a way, looks at (a) as a model.[3] Finally, there is (c) the picture of the bed painted by the artist from some particular specimen of (b). Then (a) is original and real, (b) exists in the world of our senses and is in a pragmatic way real; and (c) is appearance only.—The tragic poet belongs to the class of imitators, and he is third in succession from king and truth.[4] An imitator, painter or poet, is in fact only operating with appearances and illusions.

To the protagonists of poetry knowledge of technical, human, ethical, and divine matters was a necessary precondition for a really good poet. Go to Homer himself, the leader of the tragic poets, and ask for his contribution to the branches of human knowledge and ability.

---

[1]) The term μίμησις occurred first at 392d5, see p. 89 above.

[2]) 596a6–7, εἶδος γάρ πού τι ἐν ἕκαστον εἰώθαμεν τίθεσθαι περὶ ἕκαστα τὸ πολλά, οἷς ταὐτὸν ὄνομα ἐπιφέρομεν.

[3]) "i.e. thinking of the function which a bed has to serve," Murphy, p. 225.

[4]) 597e6–8. Τοῦτ' ἄρα ἔσται καὶ ὁ τραγῳδοποιός, εἴπερ μιμητής ἐστι, τρίτος τις ἀπὸ βασιλέως καὶ τῆς ἀληθείας πεφυκώς, καὶ πάντες οἱ ἄλλοι μιμηταί. Cf. 598e5–599a4.

In vain, Socrates goes on, we look for any reminiscences of him as a statesman, or as a *strategus*, or as a technical inventor, or as a private teacher leaving after himself admiring pupils and followers, 599b9–600d4.—It is improbable that the contemporaries of Homer and Hesiod would have let capable teachers in human excellences go from place to place as mere rhapsodists, 600d5–e2. Strip poetry of its poetic colouring and we find that there is no knowledge of the proper function of things; unlike, for instance, the flute-maker, who has to take note of the instructions of the flute-player, the poet labours uncorrected by the impact of knowledge and experience[1]) and does not know whether his representations are really good or bad, 600e4–602b10.

2. Art appeals to the lower levels of psyche

602c1-608b10. The doctrine of imitative art is next related to the theory of the structured self.—What part of human nature does poetry affect, 602c4–5?

Our senses present us with confusing collections of appearances, which *logistikon* can only reduce to conformity by measuring, counting, and weighing. By such operations reason represents a higher state of judgement, and impression a more careless one. Impressions working on an inferior level, produce inferior offspring.[2]) This holds true not only for the visual arts, but also for poetry, which is engaged in reproducing, for good or for bad the incidental fortunes of men involved in various actions, 603b6–c8. As painting plays upon certain illusions of sight, so poetry affects the feelings of the moment,[3]) and there is in man a myriad of conflicting tendencies, 603d3–7. But a man of good character does not give way in public to his emotions— whatever is his behaviour in secret. He tries to control himself and listens to the advice of reason. By such experiences we arrive (without analogical reasoning from painting, 603b9–c2) to the conclusion

---

[1]) "The user alone has knowledge of the object; the maker, when the user instructs him, has correct opinion", comments Adam. The positive relation between ἐμπειρία and ἐπιστήμη in 601d8–602a1 is, it has been observed, not easy to reconcile with the dialectic theory of knowledge earlier expressed. Cf. Adam, vol. II, pp. 403–404.

[2]) 603b4. Φαύλη ἄρα φαύλῳ συγγιγνομένη φαῦλα γεννᾷ ἡ μιμητική.

[3]) Cf. Nettleship, p. 350.

about the structured self and its two opposed forces of rationality and irrationality, 603e3–604d2, cf. 439d4–8.

On the emotional field, great opportunities are provided for dramatic poetry, the aim of which is not to calm, but to excite feelings to which the popular audience can respond, 604d8–605a6. The poet and the painter may then fairly be placed side by side: with inferior products they do not address themselves to the best part of the soul, 605a8–b2. The poet is therefore to be banished from the well-ordered *polis*; poetry strengthens the wrong part of *psyche*, 605b2–5. Poetry sets up an evil constitution in the individual soul; using a political metaphor, Socrates says it is like transporting power from the better to the worse citizens.[1]

The greatest charge, however, against poetry is its corruptive power on the best characters;[2] cf. the discourse at 487e7–495c6. Now, at 606a3–b4, we are told, as Shorey sums it up, that poetry "subtly corrupts even the best of us by stimulating the lust for tears and excitement in fictitious sorrows where we think it no shame to indulge them, forgetting that we shall thus be led to abandon ourselves to them in reality".[3] This holds good not only for grief, but also for lust, anger, the comic, etc. We must keep to the rules laid down for our *polis*, which permit only hymns to the gods and praise in honour of good men,[4] 606e1–607a8.

3. Explications

Plato's treatment of art belongs of course to the great and ever-discussed topics of his philosophy; "Platons Homerkritik ist der Gipfel-

---

[1] 605b5–8, ὥσπερ ἐν πόλει κτλ. cf. *TABLE 2*, nr 66.

[2] This susceptibility of the best natures is regrettable because from this class of men, if properly educated, society can expect the greatest good—σμικρὰ δὲ φύσις οὐδὲν μέγα οὐδέποτε οὐδένα οὔτε ἰδιώτην οὔτε πόλιν δρᾷ, 495b5–6, cf. 491e1–6.

[3] *What Plato Said*, p. 249.

[4] This conclusion is, writes G. Sörbom, compatible with the views advanced in *Bk III*. "The most obvious divergence between the two discourses on mimetic art in the *Republic* is, then, the greater severity of tone in the tenth book compared to the tone of the second and third books. This, too, is readily accounted for with regard to the greater values at stake (real knowledge which is most essential to the governance of the "ideal city", not the education of the lower classes of guardians) and the dazzling contrast to the world of Platonic ideas," *Mimesis and Art. Studies in the Origin and Early Development of an Aesthetic Vocabulary.* Stockholm 1966, pp. 150–151.

punkt des Streites zwischen Philosophie und Poesie, der zu Platons Zeit schon 'alt' war (607c)".[1]—Here are a few notes appropriate to the *polis-psyche* motif.

We must first realize the importance of the constellation *poetry and polis*. "To understand Plato's attitude", writes G. M. A. Grube, "it is essential to keep in mind that it springs from a profound belief in the power of poetry and the fine arts to mould character and to influence the moral attitudes of the community; . . .".[2] To preserve your inner *politeia*, you do right to distrust poetry, 608a6–b2, cf. *TABLE I*, p. 242. Much is at stake in the choice between good and bad; poetry, no less than wealth, power and honour, should tempt us to be careless of justice and the other virtues, 608b4–8. In the earlier books we have seen how Plato radically reforms economy, religion, family life, education and politics. The canons of simplicity and unity, and the notion of *psyche* as something tender and mouldable are factors which conspire against the freedom of the artist to create *his* visions spontaneously.

Nettleship maintains that the first half of *Bk X*, which gives the final views on art and poetry, is disconnected, sudden and unnatural.[3] To Cornford it "has the air of an appendix, only superficially linked with the preceding and following context".[4] But if, on the other hand, Plato challenged the principles of literary composition, he must have had his reasons. "An author possessing Plato's skill in composition is not likely to blunt the edge of what he is saying by allowing his thoughts to stray away from it at the end", writes Havelock.[5]

The explicit excuse for returning to the topic of poetry is that, after having distinguished the parts of *psyche* (*Bks IV, VIII, IX*), the reason for not admitting poetry in the *polis* seems clearer, 595a5–b1. Poetry is a poor educational instrument, because it affects the wrong part of the soul, 605a8–b2. This holds good not only for most men, but with few exceptions, also for the best characters, 605c6–d5. A relation between mass psychology and poetic performance is now indicated. Plato does not expound the point, but it is natural, I think, to associate with the

---

[1] E. R. Curtius, *Europäische Literatur und Lateinisches Mittelalter*, Bern 1954, p. 211.

[2] *The Greek and Roman Critics*, London 1968, p. 46.

[3] Nettleship, p. 340.

[4] Cornford, *Rep.*, p. 314.

[5] *Preface to Plato*, p. 3.

vivid picture of a mass meeting (a law-court, a theatre, or a camp) given in 492b5–c8. What is recited on the stage, we may conjecture, is reinforced by the public and sweeps the individual away in an emotional storm. It is a sad fact that this powerful instrument of influence does not lend itself to the goals of the model *polis*. The difficulties are two: (1) it would not be easy to create on stage such a type of wisdom and calmness; (2) the public, dominated by the lower instincts, would not be able to respond to it, 604e1–6.—We have not yet mentioned the most important contribution that lies between *Bks III* and *X*.This is Plato's theory of knowledge and truth together with his teaching about the precious instrument (the eye of the soul) which everyone possesses, 527d6–e2; this higher capacity of the *psyche* must be trained, and we must liberate ourselves from the bondage of the senses. Poetry simply does not fit into this program of education;[1] poetry says the wrong thing, and says it too vividly. Unlike the institutions of private ownership and private family, poetry can hardly be isolated for the use and enjoyment of a certain class of people. Poetry charms the whole society, alluring even the best characters, those who are meant to be the safeguards of the *polis*.

4. Immortal soul

608c1-612a7. The second division of *Bk X* reaches from 608c1 to the very end of the dialogue. *Psyche* is not only the nucleus of man's personality, but also something immortal and imperishable, 608d3–4.

There is a law of decay in nature. By some internal defect (rust, putrefaction, disease) things and organisms are subject to destruction. Dissolution is an evil; the good, contrariwise, preserves nature, 608e3–609b2.

Psyche also has its diseases; there are the disfunctional forces of *adikia, akolasia, deilia* and *amathia*, (the opposites of the four cardinal virtues, 609b11–c1, cf. 444b6–8). But whereas the body dies of its internal afflictions, the soul does not, 609c2–d8. It is absurd to think

---

[1] In contemporary society poetry was central in the educational theory, providing "a sort of encyclopedia of ethics, politics, history and technology which the effective citizen was required to learn as the core of his educational equipment", Havelock, *Preface*, p. 27. "Allgemeinste *Bildung*, ethische *Erziehung* durch heldenhaftes Vorbild, sachlichen *Unterricht*, alles dies konnte die alte griechische Erziehung des freien Mannes durch Homer leisten", J. Stenzel, *Platon der Erzieher*, p. 12.

that *adikia* causes the death of *psyche*, for then the vicious man would die simply from his own wickedness. If then internal vice is unable to kill the soul, it is improbable that external causes would have the power to do so, 610e5–9. And if *psyche* cannot perish, it must be immortal. Further we gather that the souls preserve their essential identity through eternity, and that their number is fixed once and for all, 609e10–611a9.

The time is now ripe for a distinction between (1) the tripartite *psyche* of *Bks II–IV, VIII–IX*, in which the soul was treated as a composite full of diversity and contradictions, and (2) the essential *psyche* in its true and simple identity,[1]) 611a10–b7. To contemplate her original beauty we must abstract from the repulsive overgrowth which clings to her because of the communion with the body and the lower elements of the soul.[2]) We must fix our attention to the soul's love of wisdom and her aspiration to reach the divine sphere.[3])

5. Rewards of dikaiosyne

612a8-621d3. Socrates was requested to defend *dikaiosyne* without the introduction of rewards and glories. So far, he says, this stipulation has been respected. We have found that justice by itself is best for the soul itself. The given stipulation was respected for the sake of argument, but now it is only fair to take into consideration also the rewards, 612a8–d9.

The characters of men are not hidden from the sight of the gods. True to their nature, the gods embrace the just with friendship. The righteous man, whatever his present conditions, can rest in the conviction that he will not be neglected by the gods, 612e2–613b8. *Adikia* brings no lasting satisfaction; the clever rogue is like the runner who is quick off the mark, and runs well first, but collapses before the end of the course, 613b9–c6.

---

[1]) In the light of 611 b–c, writes Adam, ''we may suppose that when the soul altogether follows after the divine it shakes itself clear of the body and the lower parts of soul associated therewith, and appears in its true unity as pure *logistikon*'', vol. II, p. 428. Cf., however, A. Graeser, who propounds ''die Unsterblichkeit der ganzen dreigeteilten Seele'', pp. 27 ff. See also *Soul and Immortality in Republic X*, by T. M. Robinson, *Phron.*, vol. XII. 1967, pp. 147 ff.

[2]) Cf. 611c7–d8, the comparison with Glaucus, the sea-god.

[3]) 611e1–3. Εἰς τὴν φιλοσοφίαν αὐτῆς, καὶ ἐννοεῖν ὧν ἅπτεται καὶ οἵων ἐφίεται ὁμιλιῶν, ὡς συγγενὴς οὖσα τῷ τε θείῳ καὶ ἀθανάτῳ καὶ τῷ ἀεὶ ὄντι, κτλ.

Glaucon and Adeimantus had in *Bk II* distributed respectively external success and external failure: the one to the unjust, the other to the just. Socrates now redistributes them so that happiness goes with virtue, and unhappiness with vice, 613c8–e4.

The *Republic* ends with the eschatological myth of Er, 614b2–621d3. It does not need be retold here. A few notes are, however, justified.

The individual is in *Bks II–IV, VIII–IX* not only illustrated by means of the model *polis*, but is also very much discussed as a social being. He is educated under the super-individual aims of the *polis* as a whole; the cardinal virtues, we have seen, are state-supporting excellences. Even in the middle books, where higher education and the theory of ideas are expounded, the relevant connection is not the philosopher as such, but the requirements of able rulers. We have repeatedly been told that the aims of constructing a *polis* is not to establish extraordinary happiness for a few, but to promote the long-term interest of the total society. It may then be asked if there is, beside the social motivation for virtue, also an individual motivation for upholding the established table of virtues.

One affirmative answer lies in the fact, that, in a highly integrated society, a balance must be struck between the interests of society and man; within the functional society, properly run and governed, one finds the best conditions for individual happiness, cf. 590c8–d6. Another answer Plato sought to provide in his analysis of pleasure, *Bk IX*. A third answer is given at 609d4–611a8, where Plato briefly demonstrates the immortality of the soul. This answer, which seems to be seriously meant, is supplemented with the myth of Er. The myth asserts that our present life is ephemeral. It is therefore of superior importance to use the opportunities of one's present life to prepare oneself for a future life. If, in believing that the soul is immortal, we stick to *dikaiosyne* with the aid of wisdom, we shall live in friendship with ourselves and with the gods; ἵνα καὶ ἡμῖν αὐτοῖς φίλοι ὦμεν καὶ τοῖς θεοῖς, 621c3–d3.

To live in friendship with oneself and the gods, and with good prospects of a better sort of happiness, provides a private motivation for virtuous living. Thus ends and means are reversed in the very last pages of the *Republic*. It is true that the citizens of the good city must subordinate their happiness to the ends of the *polis* as a whole, but this end becomes, in the light of *Bk X*, the means and precondition for the individual to promote his own goal.

6. Conclusions and observations

From the point of view of the *polis-psyche* motif we are not concerned with Plato's philosophy of art, but with his general thought on education and culture.[1] Art, experience tells, has a fascinating power. Art sets up examples, prepares our dispositions and moulds our habits.[2] Such an instrument, rightly handled, could have a great educational value. Unfortunately, in the hands of uninstructed or irresponsible artists, art lends itself to unworthy subjects. In the model *polis* such careless and misguided artistic creativity cannot be accepted. Therefore art, taken in the broad sense, must be supervized and integrated with the ends and means of the establishment as a whole. When now Plato in *Bk X* returns to the subject of mimetic art from *Bk III*, he has laid behind himself a long and profound stretch of reasoning about the structure of personality, the mechanisms of social dynamics, and the absolute standards of knowledge. In the retrospective light of these discussions the precautions of *Bks II–III* seem better supported and well-advised.—The lower levels of man's personality are extremely susceptible to the influences of mimetic art. Take dramatic art, for instance, which carries the individual away with all the force of a mass-meeting; and what can be staged is mostly below the standard of what the higher nature of man can accept. By reason of these complementary arguments, Plato made sure that what was uttered in the early books deserved attention, and even grew in importance seen in the light of the total argument.

There is also in *Bk X* another, and most important, discourse to observe. With the second part of this book, *psyche* becomes not merely short for the structured self, including the most valuable intellectual centre of an otherwise mouldable and weak social animal, but some-

---

[1] "One hears a good deal about Plato's philosophy of art. It is not clear to me that he had anything that deserves to be called a philosophy of art. He had a philosophy of culture, as we have seen, and this had repercussions on the liberty that he thought artists should enjoy; but that is a rather different matter." Crombie, *Plato. The Midwife's Apprentice*, London 1964, p. 163.—See also Havelock, p. 29 and his survey of the discussion, n. 37, pp. 33 ff.

[2] Sörbom, p. 124.

thing unmeasurably more: man is the owner of an immortal soul. Here, in the very end of the dialogue, Plato sheds new light on the question of man's character. We might have formed the opinion that, when man is educated under the ultimate goal of making the *polis* good and well-functioning, there is no more to add. Now we are told that in the longer perspective this submission of the individual under the goals of the *polis* is only preconditional for man's inmost life and future destination and happiness. Ultimately the precautions taken (social, cultural) are for the best of the individual.[1])

Coming to the end of the *Republic*, we discern in *polis* three functional dimensions: it is well-advised as an illustrative instrument; it is all-important in moulding man; and it is, if good, a necessary pre-condition for long-term happiness.

---

[1]) "It is only the *polis* which can bring about the just individual who meets Plato's requirement for the right kind of society. In this sense, it is plausible to say that the state is *for* the individual, that its most significant purpose is to help man with what is of the greatest importance to him—the moral well being and tendance of his soul", R. W. Hall, *Justice and the Individual in the Republic, Phron.* 4/1959, p. 158.

PART SEVEN

A SUMMARY

CHAPTER XVI

1. PSYCHE INSPECTED

1. Socrates' answer

Socrates was requested to:

(1) tell us what *dikaiosyne* and *adikia* each is, what power each has in the soul, 358b4–7; or, in other words, explain not only that the former is stronger, but demonstrate also what good or harm each itself does to the soul, 366e5–9, 367b2–5, e1–5;

(2) leave all gain-aspects out of account, 361c3–4, 367b5–6;

(3) use the method of the extreme types, 358d3–6, 360e1–3; and

(4) show by contrast who is the happier (εὐδαιμονέστερος) of the two persons,[1]) 361d1–3.

Then the analogy between the model *polis* and the righteous man is established. The tripartite nature of the soul is found. *Logistikon*, *thymoeides* and *epithymiai* are its fundamental parts with *sophia*, *andreia*, *sophrosyne* and *dikaiosyne* as functional requisites. Within the pattern of organic interaction the formal definition of *dikaiosyne*, τὸ τὰ αὑτοῦ πράττειν, gets its meaning. The righteous man is internally a well-ordered and unified man. Towards the end of *Bk IV* there is a summing up as follows.

The division of work we see in society presents an image of justice, 443c4–7. Essentially, however, *dikaiosyne* is not a matter of external affairs, but has properly to do with man's inward self. The righteous man does not allow the parts of his soul to meddle with each other's work; he keeps his internal household in good order; by self-mastery he is at peace with himself, bringing the component parts together in harmony like the notes of a musical scale. And when he has made himself one man instead of many, he is ready for practical action, private or public, whatever it may be. But his course of action is always such

---

[1]) The content of the request has been summed up by J. D. Mabbott, *Is Plato's Republic Utilitarian? Mind* N.S., vol. XLVI 1937, pp. 469–470.

that it preserves and assists his acquired habit of mind, well knowing that the knowledge which presides over this conduct is *sophia*, 443c9–444a2.[1]) Justice is like a healthy body: to produce health, the component parts must be established in a natural order, 444d3–e2.—This is a substantial part of the answer to point (1) of the request.

In Bks *VIII–IX* the answer is supplemented with an explanation of *adikia*. The aim is set on the ultimate extreme, namely the actual tyrant. To understand this type, the appetitive part is further differentiated, 571a7–572b8.—In brief, when a man has lost his inner balance, the beast in his nature comes to the surface. New desires arise demanding to be nourished. To satisfy his obsessions he is finally driven to crime. By this evil course, the internal beast grows still more dominating, until the entire person is subjugated to the severest slavery.

Extreme *adikia* means to allow one's lowest part to set itself up as a despot. It is essential to see the harm that unjust acts do to the agent himself: they boomerang back on him and originate or hasten, as the case may be, the process of destruction.—With this exposition Socrates has completed, I think, the answer to point (1) of the request.

And as all gain-aspects are so far left out, which agrees with point (2), and the method of the extreme types has been employed (3), the three first points of the request are respected. The remaining question (4) asks whether the righteous man is really happier than the unrighteous.

At 576b11 *Bk IX* Socrates takes up the question of how *dikaiosyne* is related to *eudaimonia*, happiness. Three proofs are offered.

In *the first proof* (577c1–580c8) the double text method is used. And by analogical conclusions Socrates passes from the unhappy state of the tyrannical *polis* to the corresponding condition of the tyrannical man. *The second proof* (580c9–583a11) asserts that the pleasure derived from the exercise of the rational part is superior to those pleasures which come from ambition and gain. And *the third proof* (583b1–588a11) says in short that, if one obeys *dikaiosyne* and lets reason rule, one gets the highest satisfaction because knowledge participates in true existence.

Thus *Bk IX* is marked by the effort to prove that the righteous man

---

[1]) The passage 443c9–444a2 constitutes what has been called the long definition of *dikaiosyne*, see p. 108 above.

is happier and more rich in pleasure than the unrighteous.[1]) We have also seen that just acts (all rewards ignored) are inner-directed, in the sense that they help the agent to preserve his proper hierarchical structure.[2]) But if just acts (a) aim at one's own advantage (*Bk IV*), and (b) give more satisfaction in terms of happiness and pleasure (*Bk IX*), then one arrives at egocentricity and hedonism.[3]) One is alienated from the inter-personal field of action where the need of justice is most intensely felt.[4])

To balance this self-regarding view of *dikaiosyne*, there is the social-directed view of *Bk V*. One may indeed wonder, reading this part, if the individual is not totally extinguished in the cause of the common interest.[5]) Let us also remember the theory of the Form-integrated justice of *Bk VI*. Virtue is not merely to be well integrated.[6]) The

---

[1]) Does Socrates in fact only praise justice as a natural way to happiness? Cf. the discussion by M. B. Foster and J. D. Mabbott in *Mind*, 1937–1938. Later C. Kirwan has revived the discussion, *Glaucon's Challenge, Phron* X, 1965, pp. 162–173.

[2]) This has been explicated by J. Schiller, *Just Men and Just Acts in Plato's Republic, JHPh*, vol. VI 1968, pp. 1 ff. The soul is an organ for living. To prevent the atrophy of an organ designed for life, acton is needed. But it must be action generated by the proper use of the soul.

[3]) This view is opposed by C. R. Morris. "The philosopher is moved by the knowledge of the Idea of the Good, not by the desire for his own good." The philosopher does not *desire* the idea of the good in the same egoistic sense that the timocratic or the oligarchic man desires honour and welth for himself. *Plato's Theory of the Good Man's Motive, PAS*, N.S. vol. XXXIV 1933–1934, p. 142.

[4]) Cf. G. Grote, "A single man, considered without any reference to others, cannot be either just or unjust." vol. III, pp. 147–148.

[5]) The feature of subjugating the individual under the interest of the *polis* is of course conspicuous also in *Bks II–IV*. But as we have stressed the illustrative aim of these books, we may now refer to *Bk V*, which describes *polis, qua polis*.

[6]) "Perfect goodness", writes R. S. Bluck, "is not simply a matter of having each 'part' of the soul performing an appropriate function, but the result of the apprehension of the Good;... and this will explain why the defining of justice in Book 4 does not put an end to the discussion." *Plato's 'Ideal' State, CQ*, N.S., vol. IX 1959, 166. Provoked by an article by D. Sachs (*PhR*, vol. LXXII 1963, 141–158) R. Demos has discussed the question how self-regarding justice possibly can imply a concern for other people. To bridge the gap between internal and external justice there is the theory of Forms; to aim at justice includes that justice should be embodied in human beings in general. *A Fallacy in Plato's Republic? PhR*, vol. LXXIII 1964, 395–398. Later W. S. Cobb has maintained in a diss. that there are several passages in the *Rep.* which suggest a sort of causal explanation between

cardinal virtues derive their usefulness from the Form of the Good, 505a2–4. This is far more than simply enlightened self-interest. To fashion oneself after the Good is also, we may take it, to help to provide for a social kosmos. The righteous self is a centre from which just acts flow.

In *Bks IX–X* Socrates tells what *personal motives* there are for practising *dikaiosyne*; there are the three proofs and the eschatalogical myth. To bind together the inner-directed and the social-directed aspects of just acts, we are given the theory of Form-directed men, or philosopher-kings. They mould the *polis*. In preparing for the good society they assist both their own souls and those of their fellow-citizens.—Seen in this way, it seems that Socrates has answered the request generously and according to the four mentioned points.

2. Representative personalities

If we admit that the philosopher-kings are perfectly just, we may still wonder about the ethical status of the ordinary people, the many, who lack the necessary knowledge. Can they really be just? And what is the illustrative worth of the model *polis* if it can only represent a few extremely rare personalities?

Let us take the last question first. And for reasons of convenience we may begin with the perspective, offered by *the extended analogies*, covering the main types of disordered agents.

That the timocratic *polis* illustrates above all its soldier-minded rulers seems fairly clear. It is equally obvious, I think, that the oligarchic *polis* concentrates its illustrative capacity on the members of the small and wealthy class.[1]) So far *polis* pictures the personality of those who are politically and economically superior, i.e. those who give society its peculiar structure and character. Though the timocrats and the oligarchs are minorities, they express most fully the spirit or ethos, dominant in their respective societies. To distinguish such expressive types of men from the average citizen, we may, for our special aims, adopt the term

---

personal and social justice. *The Relationship Between Internal and Social Justice in Plato's Republic*, Vanderbilt Univ. 1966. (The work is only known to me from *Dissertation Abstracts. The Humanities and Social Sciences*. Sept. 1966, vol. 27/3.) See also the article by R. W. Hall in *JHPh*, vol. IX 1971, pp. 147 ff.

[1]) Cf. R. G. Mulgan, *Individual and Collective Virtues in the Republic*, *Phron*. vol. XIII 1968, p. 87.

representative personality type.[1]) This meaning goes well with the basic idea of the antimotif, which stresses that it is from the small number of really capable individuals that society, for good or bad, receives its characteristic stamp, 495a10–b6.

In coming to democracy, we find that the governing class nominally consists of the majority of the citizens. One is therefore inclined to think that the features of the representative personality type are here lost in those of the average type. But democracy, we are reminded, also has its conspicuous men, i.e. the more aggressive of the so called drones. This relatively small class furnishes most of the leaders. In speech and action they dominate public life, cf. 564d6–e2; the majority of the people (having few possessions and no interest in politics) meet seldom— unless they get some share of the honey, 565a1–5. Thus even in democracy the concept of the representative personality type serves its purpose.[2]) Passing over to tyranny, it is evident without lengthy explanation that the light is here focussed on the actual tyrant and his kind of exceptional men, cf. 577c5–d5.

The conclusion to be drawn is that the extended analogies picture primarily representative characters. This does not mean that the illustrative domain of *polis* is restricted exclusively to the governing class, but that the characteristic features of the society are manifest and most genuine in the leading class. Thus one need not deny that the representative pattern of behaviour has a wider field of application; it seems plausible to assume that the great majority of people tend to imitate

---

[1]) Cf. L. Broom & P. Selznick, *Sociology*, New York 1955, pp. 113–114.—I am of course not propounding that Plato was aware of our modern concept of representative personality type. That would be grossly unhistorical. The term may, however, help us to speak about a layer of thought in his social philosophy.

[2]) R. Demos, starting from the formula "like state, like man", thinks that it is the *general citizen* that is pictured in democracy. *Paradoxes in Plato's Doctrine of the Ideal State*, CQ N.S., vol. VII 1957, pp. 168–169. And J. B. Skemp writes that "the 'small letters' are descriptive of the whole citizenry" of timocracy, oligarchy and democracy, slaves only excluded. *Comment on Communal and Individual Justice in the Republic. Phron.* V 1960, 37. Discussing the views of Demos and Skemp it has been maintained by R. G. Mulgan that at least in timocracy, oligarchy and tyranny the individual characters seem in fact to fit the rulers better than the average member of the citizen body, cf. p. 224, n. 1. In a rejoinder Skemp has conceded "that in the case of the timocratic and the oligarchic man it is a member of the dominant class who is selected as the typical ἰδιώτης. *Phron.* XIV 1969, p. 109.

the examples set up by the upper class. Morever, living in society they cannot avoid being fashioned by the conditions created by the governing class.

Even in *the established analogy* between the model *polis* and the righteous man, I think the concept of the representative personality type is applicable. Through discourses on education and social planning we are in the course of *Bks II–IV* brought step by step to that qualified minority which understands what is best for the whole of society. This concentration on the very élite is confirmed in *Bk IX*, where the kingly type of man is confronted with the radically unjust type.[1]) With this comparative estimation of *dikaiosyne* and *adikia* culminates the ethical argument of the *Republic*.

Looking back now on *the general analogy* between *polis* and *psyche* (such as embodied in both the established and the extended analogies) we find that the representative personality types are consistently put in the foreground. In this perspective, I think, the *Republic* stands out a great deal more systematic in its argumentation than is usually realized.

We may now ask if this sort of answer corresponds to the request. I think it does. Socrates was told to explain the matter by use of extremes and polarization; by taking extremes one does not aim to catch the features of the man in the street. Glaucon prepared the request as an imaginary experiment concerning two extreme types of character, and Socrates was virtually asked to carry out a similar experiment. This he did.

The two extremes are extremes of ethics. They are fashioned to persuade, not to predict or generalize as in empirical science. The one extreme is recommended as a model, the other as a warning. In between, as intermediary forms, are the typified personalities of the timocrat, the oligarch and the democrat, cf. 580a9–b4. Such reasoned ethical standards, out-argued in a social context, are of interest not only to a few, but to everyone concerned in theory or practice with the meaning of *dikaiosyne* and *adikia*. Through exaggeration and personification the types gain in clearness and persuasive power.

---

[1]) In the dialogues of his middle period, Plato was preoccupied with exceptional natures and their exceptional possibilities, and he shows scant interest in the psychology of the ordinary man, writes E. R. Dodds, *The Greeks and the Irrational*, p. 211.

3. Illustrative function of polis

Now back to the other question raised. Is the general citizen in the *Republic* sufficiently equipped for grasping the Platonic conception of *dikaiosyne?* Strictly speaking, can the average man be really just? This is equivalent to asking whether, and in what degree, *logistikon*, one of the fundamental parts of tripartite *psyche*, is distributed also to the people at large and not only to the philosopher-kings.[1]) I think we may take it that every normal person is endowed with *logistikon*, a distinct rational capacity; this power can however, because of constitutional[2]) and educational differences, vary considerably from man to man.—The decisive reason, we may add, for thinking that the tripartite analysis of *psyche* implies that everyone is equipped with *logistikon*, is found in 435b1–441c7; by various arguments (cf. pp. 105–107 above) man's soul is here examined on its own. We also must see that the third class of the model *polis* is heterogeneous.[3]) It includes a relatively large number of trades, skilled and unskilled; and there are professions such as teacher, doctor and judge. Specialization need not reduce the citizens to automatons. Nor can I see why we should think of them as intellectually and ethically maimed men. Since, however, they have no authentic acquaintance with the Forms, they are confined to the scope of *right opinion*. Thus, at the utmost, they might perceive the features of

---

[1]) According to M. B. Foster each class is an exclusive bearer of one essential element of the soul; *logistikon* rests entirely with the ruling class. *The Political Philosophies of Plato and Hegel.* Oxford 1935, pp. 59 ff. The awkward conclusion, implying that in the model *polis* most citizens are not fully human, R. Demos tried to overcome in *CQ*, VII 1957, *op.cit.* In *Phron.* V 1960 J. B. Skemp joined in with a less complicated interpretation. Holding that *logistikon* and *thymoeides* are present in each individual Skemp drew attention to three passages, pp. 441c4 ff, 518c2 ff, and 608d2 ff. "There is only one set of *aretai*", writes Skemp, "but their civic effect varies as between the classes." *Phron.* 5/1960. See also F. M. Cornford, *Plato's Commonwealth*, in *The Unwritten Philosophy and Other Essays*, Cambridge 1950. "Socrates believed that in every human soul there is a faculty of insight, which . . . is capable of discerning where its own true happiness is to be found." p. 59.

[2]) 370a8–b2, . . . φύεται ἕκαστος οὐ πάνυ ὅμοιος ἑκάστῳ, ἀλλὰ διαφέρων τὴν φύσιν, ἄλλος ἐπ' ἄλλου ἔργου πράξει.

[3]) From the point of view of social stratification it is not very illuminating to pick out two small parts of the society and make a third class of the remaining large bulk of people. But as Plato was mainly interested in the steering function, executed by the smallest class, he was justified to do the division which suited his illustrative purpose.

functional dikaiosyne, once the model *polis* is established. The many, says Socrates, have never experienced such an example before, 498d6–499a2. Seeing the same ground-pattern consistently repeated, they may find *dikaiosyne* to be something much more than a honorary term. Thus they surely can practise and admire external *dikaiosyne*, but can they apply it internally?[1] Here it is our business to project that answer which belongs to the *polis-psyche* directed line of thought: the philosopher-kings should mould the *polis* according to the paradigm of the Forms;[2] doing this, they set up *dikaiosyne* in large letters for everyone to read; given suitable social and cultural environment, the general citizen is helped to understand the text and its significance for himself both as a citizen and a person.

Thus we come in the end back to the importance of *polis* as an illustrative instrument.

4. Psyche inspected

Early in the dialogue we are told that *psyche* performs a unique function. Its task is to rule man. Above all, *living*[3] is the function (ἔργον) of the soul. And in order to live well, *dikaiosyne* is needed.

In *Bk II psyche* is mentioned as the most vital part of man's self.[4] There is also in *Bks II–III* a discussion on education, which contains important information about the basic nature of the self, 376e2–412b7. Here we learn that the self of a person is a delicate, unstable and mouldable thing, which is charged with conflicting inclinations and is utterly dependant on the social and cultural environment. An understanding of Plato's thoughts, as propounded here, on the complexity, plasticity and variability of man's personality is, I think, a prerequisite for an

---

[1] I am of course aware that this is a controversial question. Here it is perhaps the best policy to pronounce the problem as clearly as possible and leave the solution to the exegetical imagination of the reader.

[2] Cf. 500d4–501b7. See also p. 140 above.

[3] In one distinct aspect, Plato's concept of the soul "is related to the common idea of a living being as something self-mobile and active, as distinct from inert, passive things without life. This is a concept of soul in which the soul is thought to be an initiating force, a creative faculty, a source of productivity." H. Regnéll, *Ancient Views on the Nature of Life*, Library of Theoria no 10, Lund 1967, p. 122.

[4] 382a7. τῷ κυριωτάτῳ που ἑαυτῶν...

approach to his theory of the tripartite soul. If we fail to consider this, we may find his systematic psychology rather arbitrary or dogmatic. Let us therefore call section 376e2–412b7 *the preconditional view of psyche.*

Plato's approach to systematic psychology is contained in 434d2–444a9. This discourse[1]) is actually in many vital aspects related to the preconditional view. Reverting to the bewildering aspect of how the personalities of men differ, Plato is now looking for a common denominator which may help to provide a systematic explanation of man.[2]) Supported by various arguments (theory of causation, ethnological observations and introspection) a realistic examination of *psyche* on its own grounds is provided. In the first place a fundamental division is pointed out, i.e. the distinction between the rational and the irrational forces in man's self.[3]) But the division is too crude to allow the construction of an operative typology. In this stage of the examination of *psyche* the study of how *polis* is built up in theory becomes helpful.

The fundamental conception behind the model *polis* is of a biomorphic character. The community is a differentiated unity. The best example of such an agent is man himself, conceived as a psycho-somatic unity. And the easiest way to illustrate how such a unit works, is by rational consideration of how a model *polis* functions. Roughly speaking, every *polis* must be ruled, defended, and nurtured. This division does not perhaps in itself enrich sociology, but it serves to elucidate *psyche*. The function of the soldier class offers a clue to a further analysis of the soul. Plato's previous discussion about the unstable soul has made it evident that reason needs support from some allied power. The addition of *thymoeides* to the two other fundamental parts of *psyche*, marks Plato's special contribution to the ancient discussion on the nature of man's self. To support the introduction of *thymoeides*, Plato refers to the behaviour of children and animals; to indicate agreement

---

[1]) I.e. "die phänomenologische Betrachtung", A. Graeser, p. 15.

[2]) J. Stenzel thinks of the *polis-psyche* parallel rather as a fruitful Schema than as a fixed and absolute division. "Der Ansatzpunkt der ganzen Lehre von den Seelenteilen ist vielmehr die Frage, wie der doch selbstverständlich einheitliche Mensch in inneren Widerstreit geraten, wie er sich Vorwürfe machen, wie in ihm Besseres dem Schlechteren unterliegen könne . . .". *Platon der Erzieher*, Darmstadt 1961, p. 111.

[3]) 439d4–d8, λογιστικὸν—ἀλόγιστόν. . .

with earlier observations, Homer and the story of Leontius are called in. And it becomes a main object of *paideia* to integrate *thymoeides* with the personality of an able and community-minded type of men.[1]) By employing the three parts of the soul, Plato can explain personality in terms of rest and change. With these means Plato can also construct the typology of personalities with which we are acquainted from the general analogy embracing *Bks II–IV* and *VIII–IX*. The theory of the tripartite *psyche* seems thus to be fully generated from the internal reasoning of the *Republic* and is well suited to the purpose of describing and explaining the varying patterns of personality.[2])

Logistikon, thymoeides and *epithymetikon* constitute the Platonic denominator of the soul. In order, however, to continue the analysis and undertake a thoroughgoing examination of the irrational powers, found in the depth of the soul, Plato makes an auxiliary division of *epithymetikon*. At 558d4–559d2 the distinction between necessary and unnecessary desires is made. And at 571b3–c1 this latter category is found to contain a layer of utterly harmful drives, which are called unlawful. By means of these extra divisions, and all the time observing man as a social being, Plato descends to the lowest regions of *psyche*. This destination to the opposite pole of rationality was, we have seen, set by the request to use the method of the extremes. But behind this

---

[1]) "Die Ansätze zu einem Berufssoldatentum lagen vor, wie ein Blick auf Xenophon und seinen Kreis lehrt—dies ist also nichts eigentlich Neues. Viel wesentlicher ist das andere, der überaus kühne Gedanke, die gesamte Erziehung dieser Wächter so zu gestalten, dass in diesen Berufskriegern die Idee des Staates lebendig und bewusst ist, dass sie ihre äussere Macht nicht missbrauchen und nicht, wie Platon sagt, diese Wachthunde die eigenen Freunde anfallen." J. Stenzel, *Wissenschaft und Staatsgesinnung, (Das Platonbild)* p. 99.

[2]) For contrary views, probably generated from external and topic-directed approaches, I refer to n. 2, p. 51 above. But in addition to Hippodamus the Pythagorean doctrine of the three types of life open to men should now be mentioned. Those, however, who interpret this doctrine as 'implying' the tripartite division of the soul miss the whole point, writes Grube. "The difference is that whereas the *Phaedo* (and the Pythagoreans) speaks of three different types of *men*, in the *Republic* and the *Phaedrus* these become three *parts of the same soul*." *Plato's Thought*, p. 133.—When Plato in 581c3–4 speaks of three kinds of men (φιλόσοφον, φιλόνικον, φιλοκερδές) this may be interpreted as meaning: though each soul has three parts, our souls can be dominated in a particular way by one or other of these parts. Personality-type is generated by the prevailing power in us, cf. 435e1–436a3.

programme we see all the time a fear of the irrational powers in man,[1]) that has attracted attention in our own Freudian times. Plato articulates the concept of the irrational soul in terms of conflict. This is far from a primitive view, writes G. M. A. Grube. On the contrary it is "one of the most startingly modern things in Platonic philosophy".[2])

Up to 580c9 in *Bk IX* the illustrative and explicative power of *polis* is fully utilized. But frequently Plato has dispensed himself from his reading-glass-*polis* and examined *psyche* either directly by introspection or by the help of other means. In the second half of *Bk IX* pleasure is analysed without the use of *polis*. In each of the three fundamental parts of the soul Plato recognizes a particular kind of pleasure and drive. That *epithymetikon* is pleasure-motivated need not surprise us, nor does the statement that *thymoeides* is fired by the urge for power and prestige. Now we learn that *logistikon* is also endowed with a kind of lust and that this pleasure, judged by the competent arbiter, out-pleasures all other lusts and provides for superior happiness.

If we cannot accept this conclusion as a proof, we can admire Plato's resourcefulness and his attempt to illumine man's self from the most different aspects of theory and experience. If we look back at the long dialogue as a totality, the *Republic* can in itself be taken as a demonstration of Plato's genuine belief in the superiority of intellectual pleasure. This joy is manifested in many ways. By means of the motif and the anti-motif we have observed the thought-experiment and the constructive imagination, dominating five of the ten books of the *Republic*. In the middle books we have also caught a glimpse of the happiness that goes with building a metaphysical system.

---

[1]) Reading the middle books in the light of *Bks VIII–IX*, we have seen the reasons behind Plato's most energetic emphasis on the necessity of creating a unified man and a unified city.—Dodds discusses in *The Greeks and the Irrational* what concessions Plato prepared, in order to make the irrationalism of popular belief work for the stabilization and reform of the 'inherited conglomerate', cf. pp. 217 ff.

[2]) Grube, p. 133.

PART EIGHT

TABLES

TABLE 1. Review of keywords Bks I–X

1	2	3	4
Steph. pag.	Frequencies of $\pi\acute{o}\lambda\iota\varsigma$	$\psi\upsilon\chi\acute{\eta}$	Notes, examples
			Bk I. First main part, serving as introduction.
327	—	—	
328	—	—	328c5–331d9, conversation with Cephalus.
329	—	—	
330	1	1	
331	—	—	331e1–336a10, discussion with Polemarchus.
332	—	—	
333	—	—	
334	—	—	
335	—	—	
336	—	—	336b1–347e7, encounter with Thrasymachus.
337	—	—	
338	2	—	
339	2	—	
340	—	—	
341	—	—	
342	—	—	
343	2	—	
344	—	—	
345	1	1	
346	—	—	
347	1	—	
348	1	—	348a1–354a11, Socrates' preliminary view.
349	—	—	
350	—	—	
351	6	—	
352	—	—	
353	—	8	
354	—	—	
	(16)	(10)	
			Bk II. Second main part.
357	—	—	357a1–358e2, classification of goodness.
358	—	1	358e3–362c8, Glaucon's speech on adika.
359	—	—	
360	—	—	
361	—	—	

TABLE 1. Review of keywords Bks I–X

1	2	3	4
Steph. pag.	Frequencies of πόλις	ψυχή	Notes, examples
362	1	—	362e1–367e5, Adeimantus' speech.
363	—	—	
364	1	—	
365	—	1	
366	1	3	
367	—	—	
368	2	—	368c4–369b4, Polis—an illustrative device.
369	8	—	cf. TABLE 2, nr 7.
370	4	—	Third main part.
371	8	—	Some noteworthy uses of the word polis:
372	6	—	γιγνομένη πόλις, 369a5.—ταύτῃ τῇ συνοικίᾳ ἐθέμεθα
373	5	—	πόλιν ὄνομα, 369c3–4.—τῷ λόγῳ ἐξ ἀρχῆς ποιῶμεν
374	2	—	πόλιν, 369c9.—ἀναγκαιοτάτη πόλις, 369d11. πολίχνιον,
375	—	2	370d6.—ὑῶν πόλις, 372d4.—τρυφῶσα πόλις, 372e3.—
376	2	1	φλεγμαίνουσα πόλις, 372e8.—ἀληθινὴ πόλις, . . . ὥσπερ
377	—	2	ὑγιής τις, 372e6–7.—ἐπλάττομεν τὴν πόλιν, 374a5.
378	3	—	373e9, professional soldier class introduced.
379	1	—	376e2, criticism of culture, reform of education.
380	1	—	
381	1	1	
382	—	3	
383	—	—	
	(46)	(14)	
			Bk III (belongs to the third main part).
386	—	2	
387	—	1	
388	—	—	
389	4	—	
390	—	—	
391	—	—	
392	—	—	392c6 ff. formal aspects of culture.
393	—	—	
394	1	—	Psyche is often replaced by other expressions:
395	1	—	πρὸς ἐγκράτειαν ἑαυτοῦ, 390b3.
396	—	—	ὥστ' ἔχειν ἐν αὑτῷ νοσήματε δύο ἐναντίω ἀλλήλοιν,
397	2	—	391c4.

TABLE 1. Review of keywords Bks I–X

1	2	3	4
Steph. pag.	Frequencies of πόλις	ψυχή	Notes, examples
398	3	—	σμικρότερα κατακεκερματίσθαι ἡ τοῦ ἀνθρώπου φύσις,
399	3	—	395b4.
400	—	1	αὐτὸν ἐκμάττειν, 396d7.—ἁμαρτάνουσιν εἰς αὐτούς,
401	—	3	396a2.—διπλοῦς ἀνήρ, 397e1, cf. pp. 92–93 above.
402	—	2	τούτων ἕνεκα κυριωτάτη ἐν μουσικῇ τροφή ὅτι μάλιστα
403	1	2	καταδύεται ,εἰς τὸ ἐντὸς τῆς ψυχῆς, 401d5-7.
404	—	1	
405	2	—	
406	1	—	
407	2	—	
408	1	1	
409	1	5	
410	1	4	
411	—	5	
412	5	1	412b8–415d2, fundamental classes of polis.
413	2	—	
414	3	—	
415	4	1	415d3–427c5, features of a unified polis.
416	—	1	
417	3	—	
	(40)	(30)	
			Bk IV (belongs to the third main part).
419	2	—	ἵνα δὴ ὅλη ἡ πόλις εὐδαιμονῇ, 420e7. ἑκάστη γὰρ αὐτῶν
420	4	—	πόλεις εἰσὶ πάμπολλαι ἀλλ' οὐ πόλις, 422e8 (belongs
421	10	—	to the stock ex. of polis, s.v. Steph. Hase, Astius,
422	6	—	LSJ, Bailly)
423	5	—	
424	1	—	
425	1	—	
426	4	—	
427	4	—	427c6–434d1, cardinal virtues of polis.
428	9	—	
429	5	—	
430	1	—	
431	4	1	
432	4	—	
433	7	—	

TABLE 1. Review of keywords Bks I–X

1	2	3	4
Steph. pag.	Frequencies of πόλις	ψυχή	Notes, examples
434	8	—	434d2–441c3, fundamental parts of *psyche*.
435	5	2	In the section 427c–445c the *polis-psyche* method
436	—	1	is frequently employed, cf. *TABLE 2*, nrs. 9–25.
437	—	2	
438	—	—	
439	—	4	
440	3	2	
441	4	3	441c4–444a9, cardinal virtues of *psyche*.
442	3	3	
443	3	1	
444	1	4	444a10, transfer to *adikia*.
445	1	2	πέντε ... πολιτειῶν, πέντε δὲ ψυχῆς, 445d1.
	(95)	(25)	

Bk V. Fourth main part.

449	2	1	
450	—	—	
451	—	—	451c4–461e4, social reconsiderations.
452	—	—	
453	1	—	
454	—	1	
455	3	—	
456	3	—	
457	2	—	
458	2	1	
459	—	—	
460	4	—	
461	4	—	461e5–471c2, stress on unity.
462	9	1	ἔχομεν οὖν τι μεῖζον κακὸν πόλει ἢ ἐκεῖνο ὃ ἂν αὐτὴν
463	3	—	διασπᾷ καὶ ποιῇ πολλὰς ἀντὶ μιᾶς, 462a9–b1; ἡ ἄριστα
464	4	—	πολιτευομένη πόλις, 462d7.
465	3	—	
466	3	—	
467	1	—	
468	—	—	
469	1	—	
470	2	—	

TABLE 1. Review of keywords Bks I–X

1	2	3	4
Steph. pag.	Frequencies of πόλις	ψυχή	Notes, examples
471	2	—	471c4 ff. *Fifth main part.*
472	2	—	
473	5	—	473b4–487a8, philosopher-kings.
474	1	—	οἱ φιλόσοφοι βασιλεύσωσιν ἐν ταῖς πόλεσιν, 473c11–d1.
475	1	—	
476	—	—	
477	—	—	
478	—	—	
479	—	—	
480	—	—	
	(58)	(4)	
			Bk VI. *(belongs to the fifth main part)*
484	2	1	
485	1	1	
486	—	4	
487	2	—	487b1–502c8, how *polis* moulds man.
488	1	—	
489	2	—	
490	—	1	
491	1	3	
492	—	—	
493	1	—	
494	1	1	
495	2	1	
496	4	1	ὅτι οὔτε πόλις οὔτε πολιτεία οὐδέ γ᾽ ἀνὴρ ὁμοίως μή
497	5	—	ποτε γένηται τέλεος πρὶν ἂν τοῖς φιλοσόφοις κτλ, 499b2–3.
498	—	1	ἑαυτὸν πλάττειν, 500d6.
499	6	—	λαβόντες ... ὥσπερ πίνικα πόλιν τε καὶ ἤθη ἀνθρώπων
500	1	—	πρῶτον μὲν καθαρὰν ποιήσειαν ἄν, 501a2–3.
501	5	—	
502	1	—	
503	—	—	502c9 ff., knowledge of the Good.
504	1	1	
505	—	1	505b5–509b10, Sun-Good analogy.
506	1	—	
507	—	—	
508	—	1	ἐν τῷ νοητῷ τόπῳ, 508c1.

TABLE 1. Review of keywords Bks I–X

1	2	3	4
Steph. pag.	Frequencies of πόλις	ψυχή	Notes, examples
509	—	—	509c1 ff. nature of dialectic thought.
510	—	1	
511	—	2	
	(37)	(20)	
			Bk VII (belongs to the fifth main part)
514	—	—	514a1–521b11, science and social duty.
515	—	—	
516	—	—	εἰς τὸν νοητὸν τόπον τῆς ψυχῆς, 517b4–5.
517	—	2	οὕτω σὺν ὅλῃ τῇ ψυχῇ ἐκ τοῦ γιγνομένου, περιακτέον
518	—	5	εἶναι, 518c8–9.
519	3	1	
520	8	—	
521	4	2	521c1–530c5, ideal of science.
522	—	—	
523	—	1	
524	—	5	ἀλλὰ ψυχῆς περιαγωγὴ ἐκ νυκτερινῆς τινος ἡμέρας
525	1	2	εἰς ἀληθινήν, 521c6–7.
526	—	2	
527	1	2	καλλιπόλις, 527c2.
528	3	—	
529	—	3	
530	—	1	530c5–535a2, route of pure thought.
531	—	—	
532	—	1	
533	—	2	τὸ τῆς ψυχῆς ὄμμα, 533d2.
534	1	—	
535	—	2	535a3–541b5, education for dialectics.
536	2	1	
537	—	—	
538	—	1	
539	—	—	
540	7	1	τὴν τῆς ψυχῆς αὐγὴν, 540a7.
541	3	—	
	(33)	(34)	

TABLE 1. Review of keywords Bks I–X

1	2	3	4
Steph. pag.	Frequencies of πόλις	ψυχή	Notes, examples
			Bk VIII Sixth main part. Double text study
543	4	—	continued.
544	4	1	543a1–545c7, types of disorganization.
545	2	1	545c8–547b1, fall of the ideal polis.
546	2	1	
547	—	1	547b2–548d5, timocratic polis.
548	—	—	548d6–550c3, polis moulds man.
549	2	—	φιλότιμος ἀνήρ, 550b7.
550	3	1	550c4–552e11, oligarchic polis
551	4	—	τὸ μὴ μίαν ἀλλὰ δύο ἀνάγκη εἶναι τὴν τοιαύτην πόλιν,
552	6	—	551d5.
553	1	1	553a1–555b2, polis moulds man.
554	1	1	
555	3	—	555b3–558c7, democratic polis
556	5	1	
557	4	—	ἀνὴρ δημοκρατικός, 557b1–2.
558	1	—	558c8–562a3, polis moulds man
559	1	1	κατέλαβον τὴν τοῦ νέου τῆς ψυχῆς ἀκρόπολιν, 560b7–8.
560	—	4	στάσις δὴ καὶ ἀντίστασις καὶ μάχη ἐν αὐτῷ πρὸς αὑτὸν . . .,
561	1	—	560a1–2.
562	3	—	562a4–569c9, tyrannic polis
563	1	1	
564	3	—	Ἡ γὰρ ἄγαν ἐλευθερία . . . εἰς ἄγαν δουλείαν μεταβάλλειν
565	—	—	καὶ ἰδιώτῃ καὶ πόλει, 564a3–4.
566	3	—	καὶ λύκῳ ἐξ ἀνθρώπου γενέσθαι, 566a3–4.
567	1	—	
568	2	—	
569	2	—	
	(59)	(14)	
			Bk IX (belongs to the sixth main part).
571	—	1	571a1–576b10, polis moulds man
572	—	—	
573	—	2	Ἔρως τύραννος ἔνδον οἰκῶν διακυβερνᾷ τὰ τῆς ψυχῆς
574	—	—	ἅπαντα, 573d4–5.
575	6	1	ἐν αὐτῷ ᾗ τὸ τῶν ἡδονῶν σμῆνος, 574d2–3.
576	5	—	576b11 ff, Socrates proceeds to prove his case.
577	5	4	577c1, first proof.

242

TABLE 1. Review of keywords Bks I–X

1	2	3	4
Steph. pag.	Frequencies of πόλις	ψυχή	Notes, examples
578	5	1	
579	2	2	ἀνὴρ ὃς ἂν κακῶς ἐν ἑαυτῷ πολιτευόμενος, 579c4–5.
580	2	1	τὸν βασιλικώτατον καὶ βασιλεύοντα αὑτοῦ, 580c1–2.
581	—	2	580c9, second proof.
582	—	—	ἄρχει ἐν ταῖς ψυχαῖς, 581b12.
583	—	3	583b1, third proof.
584	—	1	
585	—	3	
586	—	1	εἰκόνα πλάσαντες τῆς ψυχῆς λόγῳ, 588b10.
587	—	—	
588	—	1	588b1, dikaiosyne pays.
589	—	—	
590	2	1	ἕως ἂν ἐν αὑτοῖς ὥσπερ ἐν πόλει πολιτείαν, 590e3–4.
591	—	4	πρὸς τὴν ἐν αὑτῷ πολιτείαν, 591e1.
592	2	—	
	(29)	(28)	

Bk X. Seventh main part.

595	1	1	595a1–602b11, art and illusion.
596	—	—	
597	—	—	
598	—	—	
599	3	—	
600	1	—	
601	—	—	
602	—	2	602c1–608b10, art appeals to the lower levels of
603	—	3	psyche,
604	—	1	
605	3	4	cf. TABLE 2, nr. 66.
606	—	1	
607	4	—	
608	—	1	608c1–612a7, immortal soul.
609	—	3	περὶ τῆς ἐν αὑτῷ πολιτείας δεδιότι, 608b1.
610	—	9	ὅτι ἀθάνατος ἡμῶν ἡ ψυχὴ, 608d3.
611	—	4	
612	—	2	612a8ff. rewards of dikaiosyne.

TABLE 1. Review of keywords Bks I–X

1	2	3	4
Steph. pag.	Frequencies of πόλις	ψυχή	Notes, examples

			ἀλλ' αὐτὸ δικαιοσύνην αὐτῇ ψυχῇ ἄριστον ηὕρομεν,
613	1	—	612b2–3.
614	—	2	περὶ τοῦ δικαίου ἀνδρός, 613a4.
615	1	—	
616	—	—	
617	—	1	ψυχαὶ ἐφήμεροι, ἀρχὴ ἄλλης περιόδου θνητοῦ γένους
618	—	4	θανατηφόρου, 617d6–7.
619	—	1	
620	—	5	
621	—	2	
	(14)	(46)	
Total	427	225	

TABLE 2. Review of explicit utterances saying that *polis* illustrates man

1	2
Location, Steph.pag. Modes of the motif	Text and brief indication of context. Nrs.

Bk I.
338d7–339a4.
Preparatory view:
there are the cities and their
different forms of government
to observe.

(1) ἐν ἁπάσαις ταῖς πόλεσιν ταὐτὸν εἶναι δίκαιον, τὸ τῆς καθεστηκυίας ἀρχῆς συμφέρον·—The passage answers to the demand: ἀλλὰ σαφέστερον εἰπὲ τί λέγεις, 338d5–6.

344a3–b1.
Preparatory view:
look for instance at tyranny,
the extreme form of *adikia.*

(2) πάντων δὲ ῥᾷστα μαθήσῃ, ἐὰν ἐπὶ τὴν τελεωτάτην ἀδικίαν ἔλθῃς, ... ἔστιν δὲ τοῦτο τυραννίς, κτλ.—Thrasymachus refers to tyranny as a good example of complete *adikia.*

351d4–6.
Preparatory view
adikia creates divisions, *dikaio-*
syne unifies men and makes
them friendly.

(3) Στάσεις γάρ που, ὦ Θρασύμαχε, ἥ γε ἀδικία καὶ μίση καὶ μάχας ἐν ἀλλήλοις παρέχει, ἡ δὲ δικαιοσύνη ὁμόνοιαν καὶ φιλίαν· This is a cardinal proposition in the *Republic.*

351e9–352a8.
Preparatory view:
disfunctional effect of *adikia*
in all social and individual
agents.

(4) Οὐκοῦν τοιάνδε τινὰ φαίνεται ἔχουσα τὴν δύναμιν, οἵαν, ᾧ ἂν ἐγγένηται, εἴτε πόλει τινὶ εἴτε γένει εἴτε στρατοπέδῳ εἴτε ἄλλῳ ὁτῳοῦν, πρῶτον μὲν ἀδύνατον αὐτὸ ποιεῖν πράττειν μεθ' αὑτοῦ διὰ τὸ στασιάζειν καὶ διαφέρεσθαι, ἔτι δ' ἐχθρὸν εἶναι ἑαυτῷ τε καὶ τῷ ἐναντίῳ παντὶ καὶ τῷ δικαίῳ; οὐχ οὕτως;—Πάνυ γε.—Καὶ ἐν ἑνὶ δὴ οἶμαι ἐνοῦσα ταὐτὰ ταῦτα ποιήσει ἅπερ πέφυκεν ἐργάζεσθαι· πρῶτον μὲν ἀδύνατον αὐτὸν πράττειν ποιήσει στασιάζοντα καὶ οὐχ ὁμονοοῦντα αὐτὸν ἑαυτῷ, ἔπειτα ἐχθρὸν καὶ ἑαυτῷ καὶ τοῖς δικαίοις· ἦ γάρ;—Conclusively Socrates says that *adikia* generates conflict both in *polis* and in the individual person. Cf. 352c1–d2.

Bk II.
364e3–365a3.
366a6–b2.
Preparatory view.

(5), (6). Not only individuals, but also whole cities tamper with justice and find comfortable ways to use *adikia,* says Adeimantus.

TABLE 2. Review of explicit utterances saying that *polis* illustrates man

I	2
Location, Steph.pag. Modes of the motif	Text and brief indication of context. Nrs.

368e2–369a3.
The fundamental proposition about the method to use polis in order to illustrate man.

(7) δικαιοσύνη, φαμέν, ἔστι μὲν ἀνδρὸς ἑνός, ἔστι δέ που καὶ ὅλης πόλεως;—Πάνυ γε, ἦ δ' ὅς.—Οὐκοῦν μεῖζον πόλις ἑνὸς ἀνδρός;—Μεῖζον, ἔφη.—Ἴσως τοίνυν πλείων ἂν δικαιοσύνη ἐν τῷ μείζονι ἐνείη καὶ ῥᾴων καταμαθεῖν. εἰ οὖν βούλεσθε, πρῶτον ἐν ταῖς πόλεσι ζητήσωμεν ποῖόν τί ἐστιν· ἔπειτα οὕτως ἐπισκεψώμεθα καὶ ἐν ἑνὶ ἑκάστῳ, τὴν τοῦ μείζονος ὁμοιότητα ἐν τῇ τοῦ ἐλάττονος ἰδέᾳ ἐπισκοποῦντες.—This methodological analogy is preceded by another analogy, i.e. *that of the two texts,* 368c7–d7.
(For important keywords and stages in the development of the model *polis* see *TABLE 1,* 369a5, 369c3–4, 369c9, 369d11, 372d4, 372e3, 372e8, 372e6–7, 374a5.)

371e9–12.
Directive mode of the polis–psyche motif.

(8) ... ἤδη ἡμῖν ηὔξηται ἡ πόλις, ὥστ' εἶναι τελέα; ... Ποῦ οὖν ἄν ποτε ἐν αὐτῇ εἴη ἥ τε δικαιοσύνη καὶ ἡ ἀδικία.

Bk IV.
427c6–d7.
Directive mode of the polis psyche motif.

(9) Ὠικισμένη ... ἡ πόλις· τὸ δὲ δὴ μετὰ τοῦτο σκόπει ἐν αὐτῇ, φῶς ποθὲν πορισάμενος ἱκανόν, ... ἐάν πως ἴδωμεν ποῦ ποτ' ἂν εἴη ἡ δικαιοσύνη καὶ ποῦ ἡ ἀδικία, καὶ τί ἀλλήλοιν διαφέρετον, κτλ.—The model *polis* is now established—have a try at it!

431b4–7.
Directive mode of the polis psyche motif.

(10) Ἀπόβλεπε τοίνυν ... πρὸς τὴν νέαν ἡμῖν πόλιν, καὶ εὑρήσεις ἐν αὐτῇ τὸ ἕτερον τούτων ἐνόν·

434d6–e4.
The fundamental method of using polis to illustrate man's ethical standard is again mentioned, cf. nr. (7) above.

A methodological comple-ment is mentioned.

(11) νῦν δ' ἐκτελέσωμεν τὴν σκέψιν ἣν ᾠήθημεν, εἰ ἐν μείζονί τινι τῶν ἐχόντων δικαιοσύνην πρότερον ⟨ἢ⟩ ἐκεῖ ἐπιχειρήσαιμεν θεάσασθαι, ῥᾷον ἂν ἐν ἑνὶ ἀνθρώπῳ κατιδεῖν οἷόν ἐστιν. καὶ ἔδοξε δὴ ἡμῖν τοῦτο εἶναι πόλις, καὶ οὕτω ᾠκίζομεν ὡς ἐδυνάμεθα ἀρίστην, εὖ εἰδότες ὅτι ἔν γε τῇ ἀγαθῇ ἂν εἴη. ὃ οὖν ἡμῖν ἐκεῖ ἐφάνη, ἐπαναφέρωμεν εἰς τὸν ἕνα, κἂν μὲν ὁμολογῆται, καλῶς ἕξει· — This reminder of the analogical method is followed by an important complement: ἐὰν δέ τι ἄλλο ἐν τῷ ἑνὶ ἐμφαίνηται, πάλιν ἐπανιόντες

246

TABLE 2. Review of explicit utterances saying that *polis* illustrates man

1	2
Location, Steph.pag. Modes of the motif	Text and brief indication of context. Nrs.

	ἐπὶ τὴν πόλιν βασανιοῦμεν, καὶ τάχ' ἂν παρ' ἄλληλα σκοποῦντες καὶ τρίβοντες, ὥσπερ ἐκ πυρείων ἐκλάμψαι ποιήσαιμεν τὴν δικαιοσύνην· καὶ φανερὰν γενομένην βεβαιωσόμεθα αὐτὴν παρ' ἡμῖν αὐτοῖς, 434e4–435a3. The *methodological complement* says that what is discovered in *polis* must by confrontation be confirmed in man, cf. 435b1–2.
435b9–c2. *Executive mode of the polis-psyche motif.* *An argument for expecting polis to have illustrative capacity is given.*	(12) The socio-cultural pattern has been discovered in *polis*. Proceed now to *psyche:* Καὶ τὸν ἕνα ἄρα, ὦ φίλε, οὕτως ἀξιώσομεν, τὰ αὐτὰ ταῦτα εἴδη ἐν τῇ αὑτοῦ ψυχῇ ἔχοντα, διὰ τὰ αὐτὰ πάθη ἐκείνοις τῶν αὐτῶν ὀνομάτων ὀρθῶς ἀξιοῦσθαι τῇ πόλει.——It is not easy to decide whether *psyche* really also is tripartite. For a wholly reliable answer there is a longer way (μακροτέρα καὶ πλείων ὁδός, 435d3). The analogical method will, however, do for the present purpose, 435d4–d8. Next, 435e1–436a3, an argument for expecting *polis* to be illustratively useful: what capacities you find in *polis* (the social body) comes from the individuals who compose it.
440e10–441a3. *Executive mode of the polis psyche motif.*	(13) It has been found out by independent arguments that there are a rational part and an appetitive part in man, 436a8–439e5. Certain arguments indicate that there is also a third part, 439e6–440e6. This question must now be settled. ἢ καθάπερ ἐν τῇ πόλει συνεῖχεν αὐτὴν τρία ὄντα γένη, χρηματιστικόν, ἐπικουρητικόν, βουλευτικόν, οὕτως καὶ ἐν ψυχῇ τρίτον τοῦτό ἐστι τὸ θυμοειδές, ἐπίκουρον ὂν τῷ λογιστικῷ φύσει, ἐὰν μὴ ὑπὸ κακῆς τροφῆς διαφθαρῇ;
441c4–c7. *Conclusive mode of the polis psyche motif.*	(14) Ταῦτα μὲν ἄρα, ἦν δ' ἐγώ, μόγις διανενεύκαμεν, καὶ ἡμῖν ἐπιεικῶς ὡμολόγηται τὰ αὐτὰ μὲν ἐν πόλει, τὰ αὐτὰ δ' ἐν ἑνὸς ἑκάστου τῇ ψυχῇ γένη ἐνεῖναι καὶ ἴσα τὸν ἀριθμόν.—From this conclusion about the tripartite structure of *polis* and *psyche*, Socrates next proceeds to the matter of the cardinal virtues in man.

TABLE 2. Review of explicit utterances saying that *polis* illustrates man

1	2
Location, Steph.pag. Modes of the motif	Text and brief indication of context. Nrs.

Bk IV (continued) 441c9–d6. *Conclusive modes* (a) *concerning sophia;* (b) *concerning andreia and* *other virtues;* (c) *concerning dikaion.*	(15) Οὐκοῦν ἐκεῖνό γε ἤδη ἀναγκαῖον, ὡς πόλις ἦν σοφὴ καὶ ᾧ, οὕτω καὶ τὸν ἰδιώτην καὶ τούτῳ σοφὸν εἶναι; (16) Καὶ ᾧ δὴ ἀνδρεῖος ἰδιώτης καὶ ὥς, τούτῳ καὶ πόλιν ἀνδρείαν καὶ οὕτως, καὶ τἆλλα πάντα πρὸς ἀρετὴν ὡσαύτως ἀμφότερα ἔχειν; (17) Καὶ δίκαιον δή, ὦ Γλαύκων, οἶμαι φήσομεν ἄνδρα εἶναι τῷ αὐτῷ τρόπῳ ᾧπερ καὶ πόλις ἦν δικαία.
441d8–e2. *Conclusive mode explicating* *dikaion.*	(18) τὸ τὰ αὑτοῦ πράττειν, this is righteousness in both *polis* and *psyche.*
442d2–d3. *Conclusive mode concerning* *sophrosyne.*	(19) Aided by the analysis of the cardinal virtues in *polis* Socrates has (441e4–442d1) summed up what *sophia, andreai* and *sophrosyne* are in the soul. *Sophrosyne* means friendship and harmony between the three fundamental parts; there is agreement on the ruling principle. Glaucon confirms: Σωφροσύνη γοῦν, ἦ δ' ὅς, οὐκ ἄλλο τί ἐστιν ἢ τοῦτο, πόλεώς τε καὶ ἰδιώτου.
442d7–d9. *Conclusive mode concerning* *dikaiosyne.*	(20) μή πῃ ἡμῖν ἀπαμβλύνεται ἄλλο τι δικαιοσύνη δοκεῖν εἶναι ἢ ὅπερ ἐν τῇ πόλει ἐφάνη;—Οὐκ ἔμοιγε, ἔφη, δοκεῖ.
442e4–443a1. *Explicit reference to the* *ethical standard of the model* *polis and the corresponding man.*	(21) ... περί τε ἐκείνης τῆς πόλεως καὶ τοῦ ἐκείνῃ ὁμοίως πεφυκότος τε καὶ τεθραμμένου ἀνδρός, κτλ.
443b7–c2. *Conclusion concerning the* *fruitfulness of the polis-psyche* *method.*	(22) Τέλεον ἄρα ἡμῖν τὸ ἐνύπνιον ἀποτετέλεσται, ὃ ἔφαμεν ὑποπτεῦσαι ὡς εὐθὺς ἀρχόμενοι τῆς πόλεως οἰκίζειν κατὰ θεόν τινα εἰς ἀρχήν τε καὶ τύπον τινὰ τῆς δικαιοσύνης κινδυνεύομεν ἐμβεβηκέναι.
444a4–a6. *Final conclusive mode of the* *polis-psyche motif.*	(23) τὸν μὲν δίκαιον καὶ ἄνδρα καὶ πόλιν καὶ δικαιοσύνην, ὃ τυγχάνει ἐν αὐτοῖς ὄν, εἰ φαῖμεν ηὑρηκέναι, οὐκ ἂν πάνυ τι οἶμαι δόξαιμεν ψεύδεσθαι.

TABLE 2. Review of explicit utterances saying that *polis* illustrates man

1	2
Location, Steph.pag. Modes of the motif	Text and brief indication of context. Nrs.

444b1–b8.
A criterion for the analysis of adikia in polis and psyche (cf. preparatory view, nr 4 above)

(24) Οὐκοῦν στάσιν τινὰ κτλ.
τοιαῦτ' ἄττα οἶμαι φήσομεν καὶ τὴν τούτων ταραχὴν καὶ πλάνην εἶναι τήν τε ἀδικίαν καὶ ἀκολασίαν καὶ δειλίαν καὶ ἀμαθίαν καὶ συλλήβδην πᾶσαν κακίαν.

445c9–d1
Preparatory view for the analysis of adikia in polis and psyche.

(25) Ὅσοι, ἦν δ' ἐγώ, πολιτειῶν τρόποι εἰσὶν εἴδη ἔχοντες, τοσοῦτοι κινδυνεύουσι καὶ ψυχῆς τρόποι εἶναι.— Πόσοι δή;—Πέντε μέν, ἦν δ' ἐγώ, πολιτειῶν, πέντε δὲ ψυχῆς.

Bk V.
449a1–a5.
Preparatory statement about the one good pattern and the four bad.

(26) Ἀγαθὴν μὲν τοίνυν τὴν τοιαύτην πόλιν τε καὶ πολιτείαν καὶ ὀρθὴν καλῶ, καὶ ἄνδρα τὸν τοιοῦτον· κακὰς δὲ τὰς ἄλλας καὶ ἡμαρτημένας, εἴπερ αὕτη ὀρθή, περί τε πόλεων διοικήσεις καὶ περὶ ἰδιωτῶν ψυχῆς τρόπου κατασκευήν, ἐν τέτταρσι πονηρίας εἴδεσιν οὔσας.

472c4–d2.
Retrospective view of the double text method, cf. 471c4–e5

(27) Παραδείγματος ἄρα ἕνεκα, . . ., ἐζητοῦμεν αὐτό τε δικαιοσύνην οἶόν ἐστι, καὶ ἄνδρα τὸν τελέως δίκαιον εἰ γένοιτο, καὶ οἷος ἂν εἴη γενόμενος, καὶ ἀδικίαν αὖ καὶ τὸν ἀδικώτατον, κτλ.

Bk VI.
497c7–d2.
Further aspects on the polis-psyche relation.

(28) The motif *polis illustrates psyche* is abandoned for two other *polis-psyche* relations: *polis forms man*, cf 492e2–493a2, and *man forms polis;* the special version of the latter proposition is *to allow the philosopher-kings to form the polis*, cf 497c8–d2: ὅτι δεήσοι τι ἀεὶ ἐνεῖναι ἐν τῇ πόλει λόγον ἔχον τῆς πολιτείας τὸν αὐτὸν ὅνπερ καὶ σὺ ὁ νομοθέτης ἔχων τοὺς νόμους ἐτίθεις.—This is an important contribution. It says that in this good *polis* there must always be present a mind possessing a reasoned theory of the constitution so that what is achieved can be preserved, cf. 498e3–499a2.

TABLE 2. Review of explicit utterances saying that *polis* illustrates man

I	2
Location, Steph.pag. Modes of the motif	Text and brief indication of context. Nrs.

Bk VII.	(The task of creating capable rulers having a reliable standard for ordering individual and public life is undertaken; the élite is instrumental to the common good and the unity of the whole *polis*, cf. 519b7–521b10.)
541b2–b3. *Conclusion about the good polis and its representative person.*	(29) Οὐκοῦν ἄδην ἤδη, εἶπον ἐγώ, ἔχουσιν ἡμῖν οἱ λόγοι περί τε τῆς πόλεως ταύτης καὶ τοῦ ὁμοίου ταύτῃ ἀνδρός;
Bk VIII. 543c8–d1. *Retrospective view of the fundamental method.*	(30) λέγων ὡς ἀγαθὴν μὲν τὴν τοιαύτην, οἵαν τότε διῆλθες, τιθείης πόλιν, καὶ ἄνδρα τὸν ἐκείνῃ ὅμοιον, κτλ.
544a2–8. *Preparatory view repeated.*	(31) τῶν δὲ λοιπῶν πολιτειῶν ἔφησθα, . . ., τέτταρα εἴδη εἶναι, κτλ. cf. 449a1–5.
544d6–e2. *Argument for believing in the illustrative power of the polis, fundamental view.*	(32) . . . ὅτι καὶ ἀνθρώπων εἴδη τοσαῦτα ἀνάγκη τρόπων εἶναι, ὅσαπερ καὶ πολιτειῶν; ἢ οἴει ἐκ δρυός ποθεν ἢ ἐκ πέτρας τὰς πολιτείας γίγνεσθαι, ἀλλ' οὐχὶ ἐκ τῶν ἠθῶν τῶν ἐν ταῖς πόλεσιν, ἃ ἂν ὥσπερ ῥέψαντα τἆλλα ἐφελκύσηται;
544e4–5. *Fundamental view repeated.*	(33) Οὐκοῦν εἰ τὰ τῶν πόλεων πέντε, καὶ αἱ τῶν ἰδιωτῶν κατασκευαὶ τῆς ψυχῆς πέντε ἂν εἶεν.
545b3–6. *The method of using polis illustratively now to be employed. Directive mode.* cf. 545c8–9.	(34) Ἆρ' οὖν, ὥσπερ ἠρξάμεθα ἐν ταῖς πολιτείαις πρότερον σκοπεῖν τὰ ἤθη ἢ ἐν τοῖς ἰδιώταις, ὡς ἐναργέστερον ὄν, καὶ νῦν οὕτω πρῶτον μὲν τὴν φιλότιμον σκεπτέον πολιτείαν κτλ. Having compared timocracy-timocratic man, next oligarchy-oligarchic man should be studied, and then democracy-democratic man, and tyranny-tyrannic man, cf. 545b6–c5.
548d6 *Executive mode of the polis-psyche motif.*	(35) The timocratic *polis* is described. Τίς οὖν ὁ κατὰ ταύτην τὴν πολιτείαν ἀνήρ;

TABLE 2. Review of explicit utterances saying that *polis* illustrates man

1	2
Location, Steph.pag. Modes of the motif	Text and brief indication of context. Nrs.

549b9–10.
Conclusive mode of the polis-psyche motif.

36) Καὶ ἔστι μέν γ', ἦν δ' ἐγώ, τοιοῦτος ὁ τιμοκρατικὸς νεανίας, τῇ τοιαύτῃ πόλει ἐοικώς.

550c1–2.
Directive mode of the polis-psyche motif and systematic step to oligarchy.

(37) Ἔχομεν ἄρα, ..., τήν τε δευτέραν πολιτείαν καὶ τὸν δεύτερον ἄνδρα.

553a1–4.
Executive mode of the polis-psyche motif.

(38) The oligarchic *polis* is described.
Ἀπειργάσθω δὴ ἡμῖν καὶ αὕτη, ..., ἡ πολιτεία, ἣν ὀλιγαρχίαν καλοῦσιν, ... τὸν δὲ ταύτῃ ὅμοιον μετὰ ταῦτα σκοπῶμεν, κτλ.

553e2–3.
Conclusive mode.

(39) Ἡ γοῦν μεταβολὴ αὐτοῦ ἐξ ὁμοίου ἀνδρός ἐστι τῇ πολιτείᾳ, ἐξ ἧς ἡ ὀλιγαρχία μετέστη.

554a2–8.
Conclusive mode.

(40) Οὐκοῦν πρῶτον μὲν τῷ χρήματα περὶ πλείστου ποιεῖσθαι ὅμοιος ἂν εἴη; ... Καὶ μὴν κτλ.

554a10–b1.
Conclusive mode.

(41) Αὐχμηρός γέ τις, ...—ἢ οὐχ οὗτος ἂν εἴη ὁ τῇ τοιαύτῃ πολιτείᾳ ὅμοιος;

554b2–3.
Conclusive mode.

(42) (... ἢ οὐχ οὗτος ἂν εἴη ὁ τῇ τοιαύτῃ πολιτείᾳ ὅμοιος;) — χρήματα γοῦν μάλιστα ἔντιμα τῇ τε πόλει καὶ παρὰ τῷ τοιούτῳ.

555a8–b2.
Conclusive mode of the polis-psyche motif summing up oligarchy.

(43) Ἔτι οὖν ... ἀπιστοῦμεν μὴ κατὰ τὴν ὀλιγαρχουμένην πόλιν ὁμοιότητι τὸν φειδωλόν τε καὶ χρηματιστὴν τετάχθαι;

555b3–6.
Directive mode of the polis-psyche motif and systematic step to democracy.

(44) Δημοκρατίαν δή, ὡς ἔοικε, μετὰ τοῦτο σκεπτέον, τίνα τε γίγνεται τρόπον, γενομένη τε ποῖόν τινα ἔχει, ἵν' αὖ τὸν τοῦ τοιούτου ἀνδρὸς τρόπον γνόντες παραστησώμεθ' αὐτὸν εἰς κρίσιν.

557a9–b2.
Executive mode.

(45) Τίνα δὴ οὖν ... οὗτοι τρόπον οἰκοῦσι; καὶ ποία τις ἡ τοιαύτη αὖ πολιτεία; δῆλον γὰρ ὅτι ὁ τοιοῦτος ἀνὴρ δημοκρατικός τις ἀναφανήσεται.

TABLE 2. Review of explicit utterances saying that *polis* illustrates man

1	2
Location, Steph.pag. Modes of the Motif	Text and brief indication of context. Nrs.
558c8–9. Executive mode.	(46) *Ἄθρει δή ... τίς ὁ τοιοῦτος ἰδίᾳ. ἢ πρῶτον σκεπτέον, ὥσπερ τὴν πολιτείαν ἐσκεψάμεθα, τίνα τρόπον γίγνεται;*
559e4–7. Conclusive mode	(47) *... ὥσπερ ἡ πόλις μετέβαλλε ... οὕτω καὶ ὁ νεανίας μεταβάλλει κτλ.*
561e3–7. Conclusive mode.	(48) *... ποικίλον, ὥσπερ ἐκείνην τὴν πόλιν, τοῦτον τὸν ἄνδρα εἶναι.*
562a1–2. Conclusive mode summing up democracy.	(49) *τετάχθω ἡμῖν κατὰ δημοκρατίαν ὁ τοιοῦτος ἀνήρ, ὡς δημοκρατικὸς ὀρθῶς ἂν προσαγορευόμενος;*
562a4–5. Directive mode, of the polis-psyche motif and systematic step to tyranny.	(50) *Ἡ καλλίστη δή ... πολιτεία τε καὶ ὁ κάλλιστος ἀνὴρ λοιπὰ ἂν ἡμῖν εἴη διελθεῖν, τυραννίς τε καὶ τύραννος.* cf. 564a3–4.
566d5–6. Directive mode.	(51) *Διέλθωμεν δὴ τὴν εὐδαιμονίαν ... τοῦ τε ἀνδρὸς καὶ τῆς πόλεως, ἐν ᾗ ἂν ὁ τοιοῦτος βροτὸς ἐγγένηται;*
Bk IX. 571a1–3. Executive mode.	(52) The tyrannic *polis* is described. *Αὐτὸς δὴ λοιπός ... ὁ τυραννικὸς ἀνὴρ σκέψασθαι κτλ.*
575a1–3. Conclusive mode.	(53) *... ἀλλὰ τυραννικῶς ἐν αὐτῷ ὁ Ἔρως ἐν πάσῃ ἀναρχίᾳ καὶ ἀνομίᾳ ζῶν, ἅτε αὐτὸς ὢν μόναρχος, τὸν ἔχοντά τε αὐτὸν ὥσπερ πόλιν ἄξει ἐπὶ πᾶσαν τόλμαν, κτλ.*
576c6–8 Conclusive mode of the polis-psyche motif.	(54) *Ἄλλο τι οὖν ... ὅ γε τυραννικὸς κατὰ τὴν τυραννουμένην πόλιν ἂν εἴη ὁμοιότητι, δημοτικὸς δὲ κατὰ δημοκρατουμένην, καὶ οἱ ἄλλοι οὕτω;*
576c10–11. Conclusive mode.	(55) *Οὐκοῦν, ὅτι πόλις πρὸς πόλιν ἀρετῇ καὶ εὐδαιμονίᾳ, τοῦτο καὶ ἀνὴρ πρὸς ἄνδρα;*
Methodological observation for further comparisons.	(The model *polis* and the tyrannical *polis* are opposite extremes, 576d2–5; the whole of the latter *polis* must be carefully examined, 576d8–e2; then a judgement can be passed by a qualified arbiter, 576e6–577b4). Cf. 434e4–435a3.

TABLE 2. Review of explicit utterances saying that *polis* illustrates man

1	2
Location, Steph.pag. Modes of the motif	Text and brief indication of context. Nrs.

577c1–3. *Fundamental method.*	(56) τὴν ἀμοιότητα ἀναμιμνησκόμενος τῆς τε πόλεως καὶ τοῦ ἀνδρός, οὕτω καθ' ἕκαστον ἐν μέρει ἀθρῶν, κτλ
577c5 *Directive mode.*	(57) Πρῶτον μέν ... ὡς πόλιν εἰπεῖν ...
577d1–5. *Conclusive mode*	(58) Εἰ οὖν, εἶπον, ὅμοιος ἀνὴρ τῇ πόλει, οὐ καὶ ἐν ἐκείνῳ ἀνάγκη τὴν αὐτὴν τάξιν ἐνεῖναι, κτλ.
577d10–e3. *Conclusive mode.*	(59) ... καὶ τυραννουμένη πόλις ἥκιστα ... Καὶ ἡ τυραννουμένη ἄρα ψυχὴ ἥκιστα ...
577e5–578a2. *Conclusive mode.*	(60) Πλουσίαν δὲ ἢ πενομένην ἀνάγκη τὴν τυραννουμένην πόλιν εἶναι; ... Καὶ ψυχὴν ἄρα τυραννικὴν πενιχρὰν καὶ ἄπληστον ἀνάγκη ἀεὶ εἶναι.
578a4–5. *Conclusive mode.*	(61) φόβου γέμειν ἆρ' οὐκ ἀνάγκη τήν τε τοιαύτην πόλιν τόν τε τοιοῦτον ἄνδρα;
578b1–5. *Executive mode.*	(62) Εἰς πάντα δὴ οἶμαι ταῦτά τε καὶ ἄλλα τοιαῦτα ἀποβλέψας τήν τε πόλιν τῶν πόλεων ἀθλιωτάτην ἔκρινας —... ἀλλὰ περὶ τοῦ ἀνδρὸς κτλ.
579e2–6. *Conclusive mode.*	(63) ... εἴπερ τῇ τῆς πόλεως διαθέσει ἧς ἄρχει ἔοικεν ἔοικεν δέ· ἢ γάρ;
580d3–5. *Directive mode.*	(64) Ἐπειδή, ὥσπερ πόλις ... διῄρηται κατὰ τρία εἴδη, οὕτω καὶ ψυχὴ ἑνὸς ἑκάστου τριχῇ, κτλ.
590e1–591a3. *Conclusive mode.*	(65) ... ἕως ἂν ἐν αὐτοῖς ὥσπερ ἐν πόλει πολιτείαν καταστήσωμεν, κτλ.
Bk X 605b5–c4. *Conclusive mode of the polis-psyche motif.*	(66) ... ὥσπερ ἐν πόλει ὅταν τις μοχθηροὺς ἐγκρατεῖς ποιῶν παραδιδῷ τὴν πόλιν, τοὺς δὲ χαριεστέρους φθείρῃ· ταὐτὸν καὶ τὸν μιμητικὸν ποιητὴν φήσομεν κακὴν πολιτείαν ἰδίᾳ ἑκάστου τῇ ψυχῇ ἐμποιεῖν, κτλ.

BIBLIOGRAPHY

I. EDITIONS, COMMENTARIES AND TRANSLATIONS

ADAM, J. *The Republic of Plato, edited with critical notes, commentary and appendices.* 2 vols., (1902). 2nd ed. with an introduction by D. A. Rees. Cambridge, 1963.

BURNET, J. *ΠΟΛΙΤΕΙΑ. Platonis Opera,* IV, Scriptorum Classicorum Bibliotheca Oxoniensis, Oxford (1902) Reprinted 1952 and later.

CHAMBRY, E. *Platon. Oeuvres Complètes, VI La République,* with an introduction by A. Diès, Paris 1947.

JOWETT, B. and CAMPBELL, L. *Plato's Republic, the Greek Text, edited, with notes and essays.* 3 vols., Oxford 1894.

SHOREY, P. *Plato. The Republic with an English translation.* 2 vols., London and Cambridge, Mass. (1930–1935) 1953. The Loeb Classical Library.

STEPHANUS, H. *De Republica, Platonis opera quae extant omnia* etc. 3 vols. Paris 1578.

APELT, O. *Platons Staat* (Der Philosophischen Bibliothek, Bd 80), Leipzig, 1916 (and later reprints).

CORNFORD, F. M. *The Republic of Plato, translated with introduction and notes,* Oxford, (1941) 1955.

DALSJÖ, M. *Staten. Valda Skrifter.* Stockholm, 1872.

JOWETT, B. *Republic. vol. II. The Dialogues of Plato, translated into English with analyses and introductions,* 4 vols. 4th ed. revised by order of the Jowett Copyright Trustees. Oxford, 1953.

LEE, H. D. P. *Plato. The Republic, translated with an introduction.* 1955 (and later reprints), Penguin books.

LINDSAY, A. D. *Plato's Republic, translated with an introduction.* London, (1935) reprinted 1969. Everyman's Library.

LINDSKOG, C. *Staten, Platons Skrifter,* tredje delen, Stockholm 1922.

TABACHOVITZ, D. *Platon, Staten.* (en revidering av Dalsjös översättning), Stockholm, 1969.

II. OTHER WORKS

ADKINS, A. W. H. *Merit and Responsibility. A Study in Greek Values.* Oxford, 1960.

ALLPORT, G. W. *Handbook of Social Psychology.* ed. by G. Lindzey. 2 vols. Cambridge, Mass. 1954.

254

ALMBERG, N. *Till Platons Differentiella Psykologi. Tillika ett bidrag till den platonska pedagogiken och politiken.* Lunds Universitets Årsskrift N. F. Avd. 1, Bd 43, Nr 1. Lund, 1946.

ARISTOTLE, *Politica,* ed. W. D. Ross. Scriptorum Classicorum Bibliotheca Oxoniensis. Oxford, 1957.

ARISTOTLE, *Politica,* translated by B. Jowett, vol. X. *The Works of Aristotle translated into English under the editorship of W. D. Ross,* Oxford, rev. ed. 1966.

ASTIUS, D. F. *Lexicon Platonicum sive Vocum Platonicarum,* 3 vols. Leipzig 1835–1838, reprinted Bonn, 1956.

BAMBROUGH, R. *Plato's Political Analogies.* In *Plato, Popper and Politics. Some Contributions to a Modern Controversy.* Ed. by R. Bambrough. Cambridge (Heffer), 1967.

BAMBROUGH, R. *Plato's Modern Friends and Enemies* (Plato, Popper and Politics).

BARKER, E. *Greek Political Theory. Plato and his Predecessors.* London, (1918) 1951.

BARKER, E. *Greek Political Thought and Theory in the Fourth Century. CAH,* vol. VI, 1953.

BECKER, H. and BARNES, H.E. *Social Thought from Lore to Science.* 3 vols. (1938), 3rd. ed. New York, 1961. Dover publ.

BISCHOF, L. J. *Interpreting Personality Theories.* London and Tokyo, 1964.

BLUCK, R. S. *Plato's 'Ideal' State. CQ.* IX, 1959.

BLUCK, R. S. *Plato's Meno. Edited with introduction and commentary.* Cambridge, 1961.

BOGARDUS, E. S. *The Development of Social Thought.* New York, 1940.

BOSANQUET, B. *A Companion to Plato's Republic for English Readers.* London, 1895.

BRÈS, Y. *La Psychologie de Platon,* Paris, 1968.

BROOM, L. and SELZNICK, P. *Sociology.* New York, 1955.

BRUMBAUGH, R. S. *A New Interpretation of Plato's Republic. JPh.* LXIV 1967.

CASSIRER, E. *An Essay on Man. An Introduction to a Philosophy of Human Culture.* New Haven, 1945. (and later reprints).

CASSIRER, E. *Logos, Dike, Kosmos in der Entwicklung der Griechischen Philosophie.* Göteborgs Högskolas Årsskrift, 1941:6. Göteborg 1941.

CASSIRER, E. *Zur Logik der Kulturwissenschaften. Fünf Studien.* Göteborgs Högskolas Årsskrift 1942:1. Göteborg 1942.

CHERNISS, H. *Plato 1950–1957. Lustrum. Internationale Forschungsberichte aus dem Bereich des Klassischen Altertums.* 1959/4 and 1960/5. Göttingen, 1960–1961.

CLASSEN, C. J. *Sprachliche Deutung als Triebkraft Platonischen und Sokratischen Philosophierens.* Zetemata, Heft 22. München, 1959.

CLASSEN, C. J. *Untersuchung zu Platons Jagdbildern.* Berlin, 1960.

COHEN, M. R. and NAGEL, E. *The Nature of a Logical or Mathematical System.* (Readings in the Philosophy of Science). New York, 1953.

CONGER, G. P. *Theories of Macrocosms and Microcosms in the History of Philosophy.* New York, 1922.

CORNFORD, F. M. *Plato's Commonwealth.* In *The Unwritten Philosophy and Other Essays.* Edited with an introductory memoir by W. K. C. Guthrie. Cambridge, 1950. (and later reprints).

CROMBIE, I. M. *An Examination of Plato's Doctrines.* 2 vols. London, 1962–1963.

CROMBIE, I. M. *Plato. The Midwife's Apprentice.* London, 1964.

CROSS, R. C. and WOOZLEY, A. D. *Plato's Republic, A Philosophical Commentary.* London, 1964.

CURTIUS, E. R. *Europäische Literatur und Lateinisches Mittelalter.* Bern, 1954.

DEMOS, R. *A Note on Σωφροσύνη in Plato's Republic.* Ph & PhenR XVII 1956.

DEMOS, R. *Paradoxes in Plato's Doctrine of the Ideal State.* CQ, VII 1957.

DEMOS, R. *A Note on Plato's Republic.* RM, XII 1958.

DEMOS, R. *A Fallacy in Plato's Republic?* PhR LXXIII 1964.

DICTIONARY *of World Literary Terms,* ed. by J. T. Shipley. London, 1955.

DODDS, E. R. *The Greeks and the Irrational.* Berkeley & Los Angeles, 1951.

EDELSTEIN, L. *The Function of Myth in Plato's Philosophy.* JHI X 1949.

EHRENBERG, V. *The Greek State.* 2nd. ed. London 1969.

EHRENBERG, V. s.v. *Aristocracy, Oligarchy, Tyranny,* OCD. Oxford, 1950. (and later editions).

ENCYCLOPEDIA *of Poetry and Poetics,* ed. by A. Preminger. N. J. 1965.

FERGUSON, J. *Moral Values in the Ancient World.* London, 1958.

FERGUSON, W. S. *The Fall of the Athenian Empire.* CAH, vol. V 1958.

FIELD, G. C. *The Philosophy of Plato.* Home University Library. London, 1949.

FIELD, G. C. *Plato and his Contemporaries.* London (1930) 3rd ed. 1967.

FOSTER, M. B. *The Political Philosophies of Plato and Hegel.* Oxford (1935) 1968.

FOSTER, M. B. *A Mistake of Plato's in the Republic.* Mind XLVI 1937.

FRENZEL, E. *Stoff-, Motiv- und Symbolforschung.* Stuttgart, 1963.

FRIEDLÄNDER, P. *Plato.* Translated by H. Meyerhoff. 3 vols. London, 1958–1969.

FRITZ, K. von, *The Theory of the Mixed Constitution in Antiquity. A Critical Analysis of Polybius' Political Ideas.* New York, 1954.

FRUTIGER, P. *Les Mythes de Platon. Étude Philosophique et Littéraire. Paris, 1930.*

GADAMER, H-G. *Platos dialektische Ethik und andere Studien zur platonischen Philosophie.* Hamburg, 1968.

GAISER, K. *Platons Ungeschriebene Lehre. Studien zur systematischen und geschichtlichen Begründung der Wissenschaften in der Platonischen Schule.* Stuttgart, 1963.

GAUSS, H. *Philosophischer Handkommentar zu den Dialogen Platos,* vol. II/2 Bern, 1958.

GIGON, O. *Psyche. Lexikon der alten Welt.* Zürich und Stuttgart, 1965.

GLOTZ, G. *The Greek City and its Institutions.* Translated by N. Mallinson. London (1929), reprinted 1969.

GLOTZ, G. *Ancient Greece at Work,* London, 1965.

GLOTZ, G. *Le Travail dans la Grèce Ancienne,* Paris, 1920.

GOMPERZ, T. *Griechische Denker. Eine Geschichte der antiken Philosophie,* 3 vols. Leipzig. Vol. 1–2, 3. Aufl. 1911–12, vol 3, 1. und 2. Aufl. 1909.

GOSLING, J. *Republic, Book V: τὰ πολλὰ καλά etc, Phron.,* V 1960.

GOULD, J. *The Development of Plato's Ethics.* Cambridge, 1955.

GOULD, T. *Platonic Love.* London, 1963.

GOULDNER, A. W. *Enter Plato. Classical Greece and the Origins of Social Theory.* London, 1967.

GRAESER, A. *Probleme der platonischen Seelenteilungslehre. Überlegungen zur Frage der Kontinuität im Denken Platons.* (Zetemata, Heft 47) München, 1969.

GREEK-ENGLISH LEXICON, compiled by H. G. Liddell and R. Scott; rev. by H. S. Jones. Oxford, 1953.

GREENLEAF, W. H. *Order, Empiricism and Politics. Two Traditions of English Political Thought 1500–1700.* London, 1964.

GRENET, P. *Les Origines de L'Analogie Philosophique dans les Dialogues de Platon.* Paris, 1948.

GROSSMANN, E. M. *Die Problematik des Dazwischenstehens.* München, 1967.

GROTE, G. *Plato and the Other Companions of Sokrates.* 3 vols. London, 1865.

GRUBE, G. M. A. *Plato's Thought.* London (1935) University Paperback 1970.

GRUBE, G. M. A. *The Greek and Roman Critics.* London (1965) 1968.

GUTHRIE, W. K. C. *A History of Greek Philosophy.*, 3 vols. hitherto published. Cambridge, 1962, 1965, 1969.

GUTHRIE, W. K. C. *In the Beginning. Some Greek views on the origins of life and the early state of man.* London, 1957.

GUTHRIE, W. K. C. *The Greeks and their Gods.* London, 1962.

HALL, C. S. and LINDZEY, G. *Theories of Personality.* New York, 1959.

HALL, R. W. *Justice and the Individual in the Republic. Phron.,* IV 1959.

HALL, R. W. *Plato and the Individual.* The Hague, 1963.

HARRISON, E. L. *A red Herring in Plato's Republic.* Eranos, 60 1962.

HAVELOCK, E. A. *Preface to Plato.* Oxford, 1963.

HAVELOCK, E. A. *The Liberal Temper in Greek Politics.* London, 1957.

HEICHELHEIM, F. M. *Bee-keeping, OCD.*

HIGNETT, C. *A History of the Athenian Constitution to the End of the fifth Century BC.* Oxford, 1958.

HIRZEL, R. *Zu Platons Tugendlehre,* Hermes, Bd 8, 1874.

HOURANI, G. F. *Thrasymachus' Definition of Justice in Plato's Republic. Phron.* VII, 1962.

HOERBER, R. G. *More on Justice in the Republic. Phron.,* V, 1960.

HOERBER, R. G. *Note on the Structure of the Republic. Phron.,* VI, 1961.

HÖISTAD, R. *Cynic Hero and Cynic King. Studies in the Cynic Conception of Man.* Uppsala, 1948.

JAEGER, W. *A New Word in Plato's Republic.* Eranos XLIX, 1946.

JAEGER, W. *Paideia: the Ideals of Greek Culture.* Translated by G. Highet. 3 vols. New York 1943–1945.

JONSSON, I. *Idéer och teorier om ordens konst. Från Platon till strukturalismen.* Lund, 1971,

JOSEPH, H. W. B. *Essays in Ancient and Modern Philosophy.* Oxford, 1935.

KAKRIDIS, J. T. *The Part of Cephalus in Plato's Republic.* Eranos XLVI, 1948.

KATEB, G. s. v. *Utopianism, IESS.*

KAYSER, W. *Das Sprachliche Kunstwerk.* 11. Aufl. Bern und München, 1965.

KERFERD, G. B. *Thrasymachus and Justice: a Reply. Phron.,* IX, 1964.

KING, L. S. *Plato's Concept of Medicine*. *JHM*, IX 1954.

KIRWAN, C. *Glaucon's Challenge*. *Phron.*, X 1965.

KRÄMER, H. J. *Arete bei Platon und Aristoteles. Zum Wesen und zur Geschichte der platonischen Ontologie*, Abhandlungen der Heidelberger Akademie der Wissenschaften. Heidelberg, 1959.

KROGMANN, W. *Reallexikon der Deutschen Literaturgeschichte*. Berlin, 1965.

KROHN, A. *Der Platonische Staat*. Halle, 1876.

LAGERBORG, R. *Den Platoniska Kärleken*. Stockholm 1915.

LALANDE, A. *Vocabulaire Technique et Critique de la Philosophie*. Paris, 1956.

LA PILLONNIÈRE, *La Republique de Platon. Du Juste, et de L'injuste*. Paris. 1726,

LARSON, C. W. R. *The Platonic Synonyms, ΔΙΚΑΙΟΣΥΝΗ and ΣΩΦΡΟΣΥΝΗ. AJPh*, 72, 1951.

LEISEGANG, H. *Plato, RE*.

LESKY, A. *Geschichte der Griechischen Literatur*. Bern 1957–1958.

LEVINSON, R. B. *In Defense of Plato*. Cambridge Mass. 1953.

LINTON, R. *The Study of Man. An Introduction*. New York and London 1936.

LLOYD, G. E. R. *Polarity and Analogy. Two Types of Argumentation in Early Greek Thought*. Cambridge, 1966.

LOUIS, P. *Les Métaphores de Platon*. Rennes, 1945.

LOVEJOY, A. O. and BOAS, G. *Primitivism and Related Ideas in Antiquity*. 2nd. ed. New York, 1965.

LUCCIONI, J. *La Pensée Politique de Platon*. Paris, 1958.

LUTOSLAWSKI, W. *The Origin and Growth of Plato's Logic. With an Account of Plato's Style and of the Chronology of his Writings*. London, 1905.

MABBOTT, J. D. *Is Plato's Republic Utilitarian?* Mind, XLVI, 1937.

MACIVER, R. M. *The Modern State*, (1926) London, Oxford Paperbacks 1964.

MACIVER, R. M. *Community. A Sociological Study*. London, 1936.

MADGE, J. *The Origins of Scientific Sociology*. London, 1963.

MAGUIRE, J. P. *The Individual and the Class in Plato's Republic*. *CJ*, LX 1964/65.

MANNHEIM, K. *Ideology and Utopia. An Introduction to the Sociology of Knowledge*. London, With a preface by L. Wirth. (1936) 1960.

MANNSPERGER, D. *Physis bei Platon*, Berlin, 1969.

MAUS, H. *Geschichte der Soziologie*, in Handbuch der Soziologie, Stuttgart, 1955.

MENZEL, A. *Griechische Soziologie*. Akademie der Wissenschaften in Wien, Sitzungsberichte 216. Wien und Leipzig, 1936.

MERTON, R. K. *Social Theory and Social Structure. Toward the Codification of Theory and Research*. Glencoe Ill. 1951 (and later editions).

MILLS, T. M. *The Sociology of Small Groups*. New Jersey, 1967.

MITTELSTRASS, J. *Die Rettung der Phänomene. Ursprung und Geschichte eines antiken Forschungsprinzips*. Berlin, 1962.

MORRIS, C. R. *Plato's Theory of the Good Man's Motive*. *PAS*, XXXIV, 1933–1934.

MOSSÉ, C. *La Fin de la Démocratie Athénienne*. Paris, 1962.

MULGAN, R. G. *Individual and Collective Virtues in the Republic*. Phron, XIII, 1968.

MURPHY, N. R. *The Interpretation of Plato's Republic*. Oxford, 1951.

NETTLESHIP, R. L. *Lectures on the Republic of Plato.* London, (originally published 1897; reprinted many times), 2nd. ed. 1961.

NILSSON, M. P. *A History of Greek Religion*, Oxford, 1956.

NILSSON, M. P. *Geschichte der Griechischen Religion.* 3. Aufl. München, 1967.

NISBET, R. A. *The Sociological Tradition.* New York, 1966.

NORTH, H. *Sophrosyne. Self-Knowledge and Self-Restraint in Greek Literature.* New York, 1966.

NOTOPOULOS, J. A. *The Symbolism of the Sun and Light in the Republic of Plato. CPh* XXXIX, 1944.

OLLIER, F. *Le Mirage Spartiate.* Paris, 1933.

POHLENZ, M. *Aus Platos Werdezeit.* Berlin, 1913.

POPPER, K. R. *The Open Society and its Enemies*, 2 vols. Vol. I. *The Spell of Plato.* (1945) 2nd. ed. London, 1952.

PRAECHTER, K. *Die Philosophie des Altertums.* In F. Ueberweg, *Grundriss der Geschichte der Philosophie.* Vol. I, Berlin, 1926.

PRICHARD, H. A. *Moral Obligation. Essays and Lectures.* Oxford, 1949.

RANKIN, H. D. *Plato and the Individual.* London, 1969.

RAVEN, J. E. *Plato's Thought in the Making. A Study in the Development of his Metaphysics.* Cambridge, 1965.

REGENBOGEN, O. *Kleine Schriften* (ed. F. Dirlmeier). München, 1961.

REGNÉLL, H. *Ancient Views on the Nature of Life. Three Studies in the Philosophies of the Atomists, Plato and Aristotle.* Library of Theoria 10, Lund, 1967.

RICHARDS, I. A. *Practical Criticism. A Study of Literary Judgement.* Routledge Paperback London, 1964.

RICHARDS, I. A. *Principles of Literary Criticism.* 2nd. ed. London, 1960.

ROBIN, L. *La Pensée Grecque et les Origines de L'Esprit Scientifique.* Ed. P-M. Schuhl. Paris, 1963.

ROBINSON, R. *Plato's Earlier Dialectic.* 2nd. ed. Oxford, 1953.

ROBINSON, T. M. *Soul and Immortality in the Republic X, Phron.* XII, 1967.

ROHDE, E. *Psyche. Seelencult und Unsterblichkeitsglaube der Griechen.* 5. und 6. Aufl., Tübingen, 1910.

ROSS, D. *Plato's Theory of Ideas.* Oxford, 1961.

RUNCIMAN, W. G. *Social Science and Political Theory.* 2nd. ed. Cambridge, 1969.

RYFFEL, H. *ΜΕΤΑΒΟΛΗ ΠΟΛΙΤΕΙΩΝ. Der Wandel der Staatsverfassungen.* Noctes Romanae. Bern, 1949.

RYLE, G. *Plato's Progress.* Cambridge, 1966.

SACHS, D. *A Fallacy in Plato's Republic. PhR* LXXII, 1963.

SARTORI, G. *Democracy, IESS.*

SCHILLER, J. *Just Men and Just Acts in Plato's Republic. JHPh,* VI 1968.

SCHOLIA PLATONICA, ed. by W. C. Greene. Philological Monographs published by the American Philological Association. VIII, 1938.

SCHUHL, P-M. *Etudes sur la Fabulation Platonicienne.* Paris, 1947.

SHOREY, P. *What Plato Said.* Chicago and London, (1933) 1965.

SHORTER OXFORD ENGLISH DICTIONARY, Rev. and ed. by C. T. Onions. Oxford, 1964.

SINCLAIR, T. A. *A History of Greek Political Thought.* London, Routledge Paperback 1961.

SINCLAIR, T. A. *CR.* LXII, 1948.

SKEMP, J. B. *Comment on Communal and Individual Justice in the Republic.* Phronesis V, 1960.

SKEMP, J. B. *Individual and Civic Virtue in the Republic. Phron.*, XIV, 1969.

SMALL, A. W. *Sociology and Plato's Republic. AJS* XXX, 1924/25.

SNELL, B. *Die Entdeckung des Geistes. Studien zur Entstehung des europäischen Denkens bei den Griechen.* Hamburg, 1955. 3:te Aufl.

SÖRBOM, G. *Mimesis and Art. Studies in the Origin and Early Development of an Aesthetic Vocabulary.* Stockholm, 1966.

STARK, W. *The Fundamental Forms of Social Thought.* London, 1962.

STENZEL, J. *Platon der Erzieher.* Mit einer Einführung von K. Gaiser. Hamburg (1928), 1961.

STENZEL, J. *Wissenschaft und Staatsgesinnung bei Platon.* (Reprinted in *Das Platonbild,* ed. K. Gaiser). Hildesheim, 1969.

STEVENSON, C. L. *Ethics and Language,* New Haven, 1953 (and later editions).

TAYLOR, A. E. *Plato. The Man and his Work.* New York, 1957. Meridian Books.

THOMSON, G. *Aeschylus and Athens. A Study in the Social Origins of Drama.* 2nd. ed. London, 1946.

THUCYDIDES, *History of the Peloponnesian War,* trans. by C. F. Smith. 4 vols. Loeb ed. 1930–1935.

TIGERSTEDT, E. N. *The Legend of Sparta in Classical Antiquity.* Vol. 1. Acta Universitatis Stockholmiensis 9. Stockholm, 1965.

TIRYAKIAN, E. A. *Typologies, IESS.*

TÖNNIES, F. *Gemeinschaft und Gesellschaft. Grundbegriffe der reinen Soziologie.* 6. und 7. Aufl. Berlin, 1926.

TOPITSCH, E. *Vom Ursprung und Ende der Metaphysik. Eine Studie zur Weltanschauungskritik.* Wien, 1958.

TOPITSCH, E. *Sozialphilosophie zwischen Ideologie und Wissenschaft.* Neuwied, 1961.

TIMASHEFF, N. S. *Sociological Theory.* New York, 1955.

UTERMÖHLEN, O. *Die Bedeutung der Ideenlehre für die platonische Politeia.* Heidelberg, 1967.

VERDROSS-DROSSBERG, A. *Grundlinien der antiken Rechts- und Staatsphilosophie.* Wien, 1946.

VISCHER, R. *Das Einfache Leben. Wort- und motivgeschichtliche Untersuchungen zu einem Wertbegriff der antiken Literatur.* Göttingen, 1965.

VOEGELIN, E. *Order and History.* Vol. III, *Plato and Aristotle,* Lousiana State University Press, 1957.

VRETSKA, K. *Typische und Polare Darstellung bei Platon. SO* XXX, 1953.

WEDBERG, A. *Plato's Philosophy of Mathematics.* Stockholm, 1955.

WELLEK, R. and WARREN, A. *Theory of Literature.* London, 1955.

WILAMOWITZ-MOELLENDORFF, U. von, *Platon,* 2 vols. Berlin, 1919.

WILD, J. *Plato's Theory of Man. An Introduction to the Realistic Philosophy of Culture.* Cambridge, Mass. 1946.

WILFORD, F. A. *The Status of Reason in Plato's Psychology, Phron.*, IV, 1959.

WINSPEAR, A. D. *The Genesis of Plato's Thought.* 2nd. ed. New York, 1956.

YOUNG, K. *Social Psychology*, in *Encyclopaedia Britannica*.

ZELLER, E. *Die Philosophie der Griechen in ihrer Geschichtlichen Entwicklung.* Zweiter
  Teil, Erste Abt. Im Anhang der Gegenwärtigen Stand der Platonforschung
  von E. Hoffmann. Hildesheim, 1963.

ZWICKER, J. s.v. *Plutus, RE.*

The bibliography contains only works which I have consulted myself, not books mentioned by other authors.

INDEX OF AUTHORS